To Bobbie,

back [...] [...]
Cou[...] [...]
of my experie[nce] [of]
Wendy's strength of
character + a bit of
serious intimidation

All the best
Randall Baker
July 4/05

ADOPTING ELDAR: JOY, TRAGEDY AND RED TAPE

A UNIQUE INTERNATIONAL ADOPTION

by

RANDALL BAKER

authorHOUSE™

1663 Liberty Drive, Suite 200
Bloomington, Indiana 47403
(800) 839-8640
www.AuthorHouse.com

© 2005 RANDALL BAKER. All Rights Reserved.

No part of this book may be reproduced, stored in a retrieval system, or transmitted by any means without the written permission of the author.

First published by AuthorHouse 04/26/05

ISBN: 1-4208-2970-X (e)
ISBN: 1-4208-2969-6 (sc)
ISBN: 1-4208-5176-4(dj)

Printed in the United States of America
Bloomington, Indiana

This book is printed on acid-free paper.

CONTENTS

Prologue vii

Chapter 1:	The Fax	1
Chapter 2:	The Pizza	7
Chapter 3:	The Meeting in the Caucasus	12
Chapter 4:	Making Contact	32
Chapter 5:	The Hand of Fate	39
Chapter 6:	Corridors of Power	45
Chapter 7:	Crisis in Vienna	51
Chapter 8:	August 24, 1992	58
Chapter 9:	Settling In	71
Chapter 10:	Defining the Options	83
Chapter 11:	Where Next?	90
Chapter 12:	Indecision and Confusion	98
Chapter 13:	The Hand of Fate…Again?	107
Chapter 14:	Love's Young Dream	130
Chapter 15:	The Anniversary	137
Chapter 16:	Our Son	143
Chapter 17	The Cold Hand of Fear	161
Chapter 18:	The Way Back	177
Chapter 19:	Life Begins Again	193
Chapter 20:	Shortening Odds	205

Epilogue 221

Acknowledgements

I have no idea where to begin, so many people have had a hand in the unfolding of this most unusual tale. It has taken a long time until we felt that the time was right to publish this book, and my special thanks must be reserved for my editor, Wendy Read Wertz who must feel like she has lived through this story ten times or more.

Prologue
Eldar Nurisovich Urumbaev, age 15.

My name is Eldar—it means Leader of Men. My middle name is Nurisovich, and that comes from my father's name Nuris. My last name is Urumbaev, which is a typical name from Kazakhstan in Central Asia. Now you know who I am, let me tell you a little more about my early life.

Before I was born, my parents and my brothers really wanted a girl, because they already had two boys.

My brothers said, "Mom, can you buy a sister instead of a brother, because we could help daddy and she could help you."

When I was born, on the 27th of September, 1978, my brothers asked my parents who I was and they said that I was a boy. When they asked why, my mom said: "Well, you know girls are very expensive now."

I was born in the tiny town of Terskol, which is in the Caucasus, a vast alpine region of southern Russia, not that far from the troubled region of Chechnya. This village of Terskol is at the foot of Mount Elbrus, the tallest mountain in Europe. Most people don't know that Elbrus is the highest mountain in Europe; they usually think of Mount Blanc, in France. Elbrus is a huge, old volcano with two peaks and is always covered in snow.

This area is called the Kabardino-Balkarian Autonomous Republic; it's next to Georgia. Terskol, itself, has a population of 500-600 people in ten apartment buildings and about 20-30 houses. There is only one road, which goes

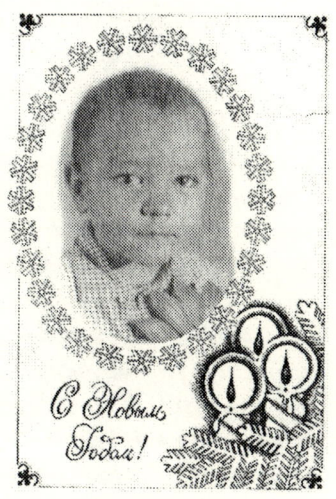

The baby Eldar

from the city of Nalchik, the capital of Kabardino-Balkaria, to Mount Elbrus where it ends. Terskol was a tourist area popular with alpinists, until the troubles began after the fall of the USSR. There were seven hotels for tourists. Elbrus was a great place for skiing, mountain climbing, and other alpine activities.

I have two older brothers. My oldest brother, Roman, is ten years older than I. Timur, my middle brother, is six years older. It's great to have older brothers because they know more than you, and you always want to be around older people, but at the same time you get beat up a lot. I always made fun of Timur or irritated him in front of his friends and especially his girlfriends. Once, at night, when we were going from another town to Terskol, my brothers said, "Let's go through the forest." I said that it was too scary there at night. So they went into the trees while I stayed on the road. After five minutes I started hearing these weird noises from the forest and saw lights flashing. When we were walking on the road, before we separated, they told me a story about cannibals. They said that long ago there were these prisoners who escaped from the prison and went into the forest. Since they didn't have any weapons to kill animals, they started eating people who walked on this road at night. So I kept hearing these quiet whispers coming from the forest. Then two people ran out of the forest with glowing faces and started chasing me down the road. I started crying and pleading with them not to eat me. I was so scared that my brothers finally told me that was just them holding their flashlights under their chins, and that they were only playing.

A young Eldar

My father, Nuris, was from Kazakhstan, and though he was a Kazakh, his family lived in Uzbekistan in Central Asia; he had two brothers and one sister. He was the only one in his family to go to university, and nobody had even dreamed of doing that because they lived in such a small town and people there were not really educated. When he went to university he became a specialist in snow, ice, and avalanches. He worked in the mountains and of course he learned how to ski. He then put the whole family on skis. My older brothers started skiing when they were about three years old and could still barely walk. I started skiing when I was four because we lived in Moscow at that time and my parents were very busy. Still, skiing became my favorite sport. My father was a really respected person in Terskol, because he saved so many people from avalanches by correctly predicting when they were likely to happen. So everybody who worked on the lifts on the mountain were either children of people who knew my father or his *friends, and because of that I never had to pay for skiing. I lived right next to the mountain and I went skiing all the time. My father took me skiing to one of the hardest and most beautiful places on Elbrus, and he also took me helicopter skiing. Helicopter skiing is when the helicopter takes you high up into remote places, drops you off and picks you up at the bottom.*

My mom, Ludmila, was born in Siberia, and went to university in Leningrad. She has a brother and a sister and all her siblings live in Leningrad (now St. Petersburg). My mother and father met in Terskol. My dad was working as an instructor of mountain climbing on Elbrus and my mom was a student alpinist in a camp. My dad was going to go to the university, so they didn't get married till he graduated. My mom was the one I would always ask for things, because she was less strict than my father.

In 1980 we moved to Moscow, because my father got a job there and my middle brother had to go to school. Still, on every school break, we went back to Terskol. When I was four we went to Terskol for the summer. We decided to go through the mountain pass from Elbrus to the Black Sea. It took us about 24 hours to walk across the towering Caucasus Range to Georgia. It was a long, tiring, but wonderful walk. We spent the night on the other side of the pass, and early in the morning we got on a bus and went to the Black Sea. We arrived at a city called Suhumy in Abhazia (now a breakaway part of Georgia), where we spent a week swimming, going to the zoo, and doing all sorts of things. Then we had to go back the same way we came. It was a great experience, because I had never seen the sea before.

I don't remember much of kindergarten, but I was eager to go to school, although once I was there I never got good grades and I hated it. I began in first grade in Moscow. When I was eight years old, my parents went to Afghanistan with the military, and I went to Uzbekistan, to stay with my dad's relatives not too far from Tashkent on the old Silk Road to China. There I started third grade. I lived with my dad's middle brother, Saigit, who has three kids. His kids also skied, so almost every weekend or break we went skiing. I made a lot of friends there. My uncle also liked fishing, so on the weekends we went fishing at the lake. We would catch fish, bring them home, and make a wonderful fish soup or just fry them. We went swimming in the river and jumped into the cold water from a tall bridge. In Uzbekistan, there were a lot of fruits, like huge watermelons, melons, grapefruit, strawberries, and others. People there like to eat, but they were not as fat as they are in Indiana. When I came to Uzbekistan I was so skinny that you could see my bones, and when I left, I was about twenty pounds heavier. I loved Uzbekistan, because it never got too cold, and because there were always kids around me. I had so many relatives there that I can't even count them all.

After two years in Uzbekistan I came back to Moscow and went to a different school, not the one I started the first grade in. Now I was in fifth grade, and as usual, I never did well at school, because I never liked it. The first half of this book is my story. I think you will find that it is very unusual, maybe unique? Most of the storytelling will be done by Randall, but I give you my perspective on things from time to time—I am the one in Italics.

The Urumbaev Family c1983

Since this is a story of people, and now that you know one of the central characters, it is necessary for the writer to intercede and sketch a word picture of the two people into whose lives Eldar dropped so unexpectedly. I, Randall Baker, who have committed this tale to paper, am an immigrant in the true American tradition, living in the Hoosier state. My origins, half a century ago, lie in more primitive terrain: in Wales, whose timeless hills in that windswept principality support more sheep than there are people. I confess to having an insatiable, and lifelong, wanderlust. Without it this book could not have been written. My journeys, from my teenage years, have taken me, among many other places, to the Spanish Sahara (and the Spanish Foreign Legion), the Uganda of Idi Amin, and on a jeep journey through every village and oasis of western Arabia.

My studies had been, initially, in the now much-neglected field of geography, and my profession is, and always has been, that of an academic. This has provided me the flexibility to indulge my passion for globe-trotting, especially as I am the director of international programs for my school at

Portrait of the Author as a Youngish Man

Bloomington. Before I came to Indiana University, where I hold a chair in Public and Environmental Affairs—a curious late twentieth century fashionable concoction of disciplines, my work had indulged me with an opportunity to spend a lotus-eating three years in the Fiji Islands. It was in that most unlikely and serene of places that I met the other principal American character who inhabits these pages: Susan. She was, by some happy act of chance, my neighbor in the South Pacific, and I admit that I was hopelessly smitten with her from the outset, and the love was mutual, overcoming the 17-year difference in our ages.

How to describe Susan? Let's put it this way. If she had been in charge of organization for Rommel, Libyans would be speaking German today. It happened that I was on my balcony, with its breathtaking vista of the Pacific when, amid the shrubbery of my neighbor's garden I caught sight of a slight figure talking with great animation. I confess what I noticed first were the attenuated blue shorts she was wearing, and that she was intriguingly, a little bit androgynous with her close-cropped dark hair and boyish figure. Even from this distance, I could not fail to notice the deep, flashing and alert eyes. I recognized one of the people with her as a Peace Corps volunteer whom I had previously met, and so I fancied I could use one to meet the other. I had not seen that much energy in one person in a long time. As I watched her she seemed like a greyhound in a trap, and at one point she actually jumped up and down as she spoke as though words alone were not enough to channel her thoughts.

So it was that we met, fell immediately in love in the most unashamedly adolescent way, and began a real friendship. I was surprised to learn that she was actually my neighbor, and was in the Peace Corps engaged in writing a dictionary of Fijian Hindi. Her unrestricted zest for life, physical and mental, seemed to me to be more than any one person could contain. Life was an adventure for her, no question about that. There was a seventeen-year difference in our ages, but we were never aware of it, except when running together for a bus.

Susan

Her ancestry, as she related it to me, was remarkable. It had been traced back to one of the Saxon kings of ninth-century England. I had no trouble believing that. Later, it proceeded across the Atlantic in the person of Virginia's first governor, Sir George Yeardley, who was shipwrecked in the Sea Venture on the island of Bermuda en route to take up his post. The story of the Sea Venture is nothing short of miraculous (see box). Of Yeardley, it was commented by one of his descendents: "George Yeardley set up the first Legislative Assembly in the infant colony of Virginia and it was intended to be rather like devolved government I suspect. However after three years James 1st ended it. Not really surprising given his philosophy on kingship. Nevertheless, it means that our ancestor gave 'independence' to America long before George Washington was born."[1]

> The "Sea Venture" (also called the Seaventure or Sea Adventure) sailed as part of a flotilla of nine ships commanded by Admiral Sir George Somers. Intended destination was Jamestown, Virginia. On 2 June 1609, "Sea Venture", flagship of the "Third Supply" (six ships and two pinnaces), departed London. On 23 July, a hurricane at sea separated the Sea Venture from the other vessels. After four days, she began taking on water. Land was sighted and she wrecked between two reefs off the shores of Bermuda on 28 July 1609. All of approximately 150 passengers safely made land. Two pinnaces were built during the following nine months; the "Deliverance" and the "Patience". These vessels sailed on to Virginia 10 May 1610, leaving two men behind. 19 June 1610 Sir George Yeardley volunteered to return to Bermuda aboard the "Patience" with supplies for the struggling colony of Virginia. He arrived in Bermuda, dying there in November of 1610. Captain Matthew Somers returned to England aboard the "Patience" with his uncle's body. Three men were left on the islands to hold the claim.
> http://www.rootsweb.com/~bmuwgw/seaventure.htm

It is beginning to be clear where Susan's steely character came from. That, however, was only the beginning of the Susan DNA process. There then followed the next ancestor, the ultimate American polymath, *Francis Hopkinson*. He signed the Declaration for the Colony of New Jersey, was a distinguished musician, a friend of Jefferson, the inheritor of Ben Franklin's library. Not only was he partly responsible for paying off the debt to France, but he gave us the American Flag—his was the successful design submitted to Congress, for which, incidentally, he was never paid. Susan had Hopkinson written all over her: slight, intense, with a brain that raced around relentlessly through the disciplines. She was also musical (though flute, not harpsichord). And she had those quintessentially Bostonian roots and a habit of worrying at a problem like a dog with a rag. The lineage

---

[1] Posted By: Robert F Eardley <robtim@globalnet.co.uk> Date: Wednesday, 27 September 2000, at 11:11 a.m.

then continued through Irwin Smith, the great illustrator, who wrote a book on Shakespeare's *Globe Theater*, and whose meticulous black-and-white drawings illustrated the *Reader's Digest* in the immediate post-war years. Her grandmother Mitzi, a figure that defined the word matriarch, had been the secret love of E. B. White.[2]

Francis Hopkinson

So far I have concentrated on Susan's maternal line, but on the paternal side, it was no less intimidating, going back, this time, through the Wheelwrights, one of whose "imagined" scions became the narrator of John Irving's book, *A Prayer for Owen Meany*. I happened to read this book on vacation, and I noticed at once the similarity of names between the narrator and my father-in-law. As I read on, I had a creepy feeling that this was going beyond a joke, since they both lacked the top of one middle finger, both had moved to Toronto, and so on. I eventually mentioned these coincidences to Susan who made them her campaign of the day.

She wrote to her father asking if, by any chance, he had ever encountered John Irving. "Went to school with him," he responded, for they had both attended New Hampshire's Phillips-Exeter Academy, (founded by another of her father-in-law's ancestors, as was New Hampshire itself). A detailed correspondence followed between Irving and father-in-law Peter Wheelwright Hobbs. One ancestor of Peter had gone back to the "Old Country" to fight for Cromwell, and another had founded the state of New Hampshire. And so it went on. I assembled Susan's family tree attempting to use one of those proprietary programs that will build it for you, but I had the overload response so many times, I almost gave up.

The Hobbs Family with Ancestral flag

So, despite her sparse frame, kept in shape by a rigorous regime of exercise and healthy eating, was she intimidating? Yes, but wrapped up in such a

---

[2] E. B. White is best known for the children's classics *Charlotte's Web* and *Stuart Little*.

wonderful package that I believe no two people could have been happier or better matched.

She left the Fiji Islands one year after I did following me to Bloomington, where we were married in August 1990, immediately after my first meeting with Eldar. It was his good fortune to be brought within the orbit of one of the world's most organized people who, at one point, I discovered compiling a list of her lists. My mother-in-law once told me that there had been a quite noticeable transition during Susan's childhood, when she ceased to be a child and basically took over her parents. "How old was she then?" I asked. "I would say, about six," she replied. I believe it. Nonetheless, lurking away inside, there was another—I won't say *real*—Susan. This doppelganger emerged only at Sting concerts when she morphed into a more primitive form; but we had better draw a veil over that.

Fate was wonderfully generous to match us up. But, as this story demonstrates only too eloquently, Fate also can be a capricious friend.

There remains, by way of introduction, only *Dolli*, the calico cat, who was around long before Susan ever appeared in the state of Indiana. And, I have to report, eighteen years later, is *still* around having gone through no visible physical ageing process. This was demonstrated recently in 2003 when she had her annual check-up. The veterinarian, a recent addition to the practice, picked up this sleek, spry, bright-eyed cat and then, looking down at the ratty, dog-eared file she had laid on the counter and remarked: "I see you call *all* your cats Dolli." I told her that she was looking at the one and only. I have come to believe there is some feline Faustian pact at work here. Dolli was there, a part of my life, long before this story begins; she is here (waiting to be let in) as it concludes.[3]

Dolli

---

[3] Dolli eventually passed away in August, 2004.

xiv

Chapter 1
The Fax

There were no omens, no manifestations; nothing indeed to suggest, on this March day that it was anything other than a routine teaching day at the university. When I was not teaching I was usually engaged in trying to find the materials for the next class. So it was on the morning of March 20, 1992. While my secretary, Kathleen—a no-nonsense Minnesota farm woman—was mining the filing cabinets for overhead transparencies for my next class, I sat at the small round table that was the central feature of the school's international programs area, my other responsibility. The table groaned under old and neglected files housing long-dead thoughts and inspirations.

Below this scene of predictable confusion sat the mail and print room. It was parked in the space that was left after the builders constructed the elevator shaft, put in the heating unit to keep us in a steady state of tropical lassitude, and built the wire-mesh cage that houses the unfathomable things that environmentalists take into the field. Also in the mail room, far beyond the copiers and collators that fed the unquenchable appetites of academics, sat the school fax machine. It is still a miracle to me that someone, anywhere, could push a button and cause a printed page magically to appear somewhere else in the world.

Heralded by that strange assembly of shrieks and buzzes by which fax machines greet each other, a roll of curled paper unwound into the waiting tray. As it unfolded, Tom, the philosopher king of the print and mail room, looked at it quizzically. It appeared that the machine was having a brainstorm, or was, perhaps, printing backwards. It was Tom's unbroken rule that anything weird, unintelligible, or incomprehensible must be the property of the international programs office. Briefly he left his kingdom and came up through the atrium. Meanwhile, Kathleen and I, having triumphed in our search for long-lost teaching aids, were starting into the first coffee of the day. Around us the posters of exotic and usually warm places challenged the reality of the monochromatic world that confronted us that overcast day through the huge picture windows that formed two sides of our reception area. Outside, slowly and endlessly, a trainload of coal swayed along the elevated railroad track that determined our horizon as it headed for Indianapolis. It was too early for talk, so we contemplated the grayness and consumed the Stygian brew Kathleen so favored.

Tom let the fax flutter onto the desk with the aside, "Here's another live one for you. Good luck."

Kathleen looked at it, inverted it, and held it up to the light.

"Do you have any idea what this is?" she asked me, holding it at a distance as though its alien appearance carried some unspeakable threat.

"Yes," I replied, "It's Russian."

I was able to make out the word *Mockba* (Moscow). At the bottom of the fax was a name, in Latin letters, which I knew. Urumbaev was the family name of a scientist who was an expert on avalanches and glaciers, and who had been my genial and tireless host when I was on an exchange program in the Russian Caucasus two years earlier. I remembered that overwhelmingly beautiful country where the Alps soared through the borderlands between Russia and Georgia, and I recalled that toward the end of my stay, over coffee in his office, I had suggested to Professor Urumbaev that he should send his young son, Eldar, to visit us in the United States where he could learn English. Eleven-year-old Eldar had trekked with us up Mt. Elbrus—Europe's highest peak—hiked over glaciers, and languished with us in the hot springs. Since Eldar had some interest in becoming a scientist and since English is the language of science, a stay in the USA had seemed like a sensible idea. It would also help me repay the marvelous hospitality of his father, Nuris.

Now, I suspected, my number had been called on that offer. Though I could not read the message, I had a pretty good idea of what it must contain.

"What is it about? Can you tell?" Kathleen asked.

"Yes, I think I am about to change my summer plans to accommodate a small Russian."

She smiled the smile of a knowing parent, and replied, "Well, now you can finally find out what it's like for yourself."

My wife, Susan, and I had never had, nor planned to have, children, and my constant pronouncements on the benefits of unencumbered freedom had begun to grate on the married-with-children community on the second floor, where I worked.

"I do believe it is justice at last," Kathleen laughed waving the fax around. "But seriously, you will have to find out what this thing says. What if he is arriving Thursday, or was to arrive yesterday? Is he coming alone? How long does he intend to stay?"

The questions that had never occurred to me flowed forth. I remembered that one of my graduate students, who had helped me greatly with a joint American-Soviet conference I had co-hosted in 1990, was fluent in Russian.

"Where is Doreen?" I asked.

"Oh, she's no longer in the building," Kathleen informed me. "She told me she had a temporary job over in the Computing Center. She may be there now"

I called the Computing Center and found Doreen right away.

"Doreen, I need your help."

"Not more of those crazy scientists, I hope?" she asked anxiously, remembering the conference and the scientists' obsession with shopping.

"No, I have a fax that just arrived from Russia. I am pretty certain I know what it is, but I need a translation, and perhaps you would help me with that. I'm sure it's not urgent, but I should know what it says—it may need a reply."

"OK," Doreen responded, "why not fax it over to me and I'll look it over. It's pretty quiet right now."

So, for the second time that day the fax encoded itself and made its way electronically, not across continents this time, but across campus to the geek center. Almost immediately the phone rang.

"It's Doreen for you," said Kathleen.

"Heck, that was fast." I whispered to Kathleen.

"Hi Doreen, didn't it print?"

"Are you sure you know what this is?" was the response.

"Yes, I think so."

"Hmm, I don't think you do. But rather than read it to you, I think it would be better if I were to send you the translation on e-mail. It's pretty amazing. You'd better be ready for this."

"What are you trying to say Doreen? Is he here? What's the panic?"

"You'll see," she said, and hung up the phone.

Kathleen sensed the excitement and inquired, "What's happening? What was all that about?"

In order to find out, I had to go back to my office, which was adjacent to the main program area, fire up my computer, and log on to the network. Eventually the ghostly green screen glowed: "You have one new mail message."

I pressed the enter key, and before me, now translated into English, shone the following message. I think I know it by heart now. It began:

From: PRISM: CORNWELL
To: BAKERR
Subject: The fax from *Eldar*

I was astonished even before I read the message. The fax was not from Nuris, whom I'd suspected would be writing about his son. It was from the now 13-year-old Eldar *himself,* and it was about his father. This seemed unbelievable, for how could a child send a fax from Moscow? It was an achievement for my colleagues at Moscow State University to get a fax through to me at that time, and here was one from a barely adolescent boy. Now completely puzzled I read on:

Hello, Dear Randal

How are you doing? It's very difficult for me to tell you about our misfortune. On 1/28/92, my father Nuris Urumbaev died in the Caucasus. He was killed in an avalanche, which is especially hard because all his life he worshiped mountains and avalanches, and then he died in them. I still can't believe all this and cannot forget the walks we took with you. My father really loved the mountains, and he has stayed there, only not with us. They buried him in his homeland in Uzbekistan. I can't even imagine life without him. He was a happy person, though one pays for everything with one's life or with something else. That is, this is fate, and there's no way to change it. Probably God needed him, but he still hadn't finished everything on earth, and we needed him too. He was 50 years old.

I was completely stunned, and totally unprepared for what I was reading. My thoughts focused on this awful tragedy that had killed my friend in such a cruel way. I remembered so well how Eldar had been in awe of his father and would listen to every word as Nuris explained the geography of this glacier or the source of that mountain stream. I felt a terrible sense of loss not just for myself but for Eldar too, who was expressing his emotions so beautifully and innocently. The fax contained just two more sentences, and these were to become the two most important sentences in my life and in that of my wife, though, at the time, this was not immediately obvious.

Do you remember our joint plans and propositions? Is it still possible to carry them out, even if only partially? Do svidaniia: all the best to you

Eldar Urumbaev

What did this mean? Our "plans and propositions" I understood to refer to the summer visit, learning English, and so forth. At the top of the message was the number of the fax used to send the letter, and at the bottom Eldar's Moscow address and telephone number.

"What's it all about?" asked Kathleen, fluttering around my door, still intrigued by the tone of Doreen's call.

"I'm not entirely sure," I replied. "It seems his father was killed in an avalanche about two months ago."

"Whose father?" she asked.

"Oh, I'm sorry. The fax was from the boy, telling me his father was killed at the end of January in an avalanche."

"Oh my God, that's terrible! What will happen to the boy now? Does he have a mother?"

At that point I realized that, remarkably, I had no idea whatsoever of the answer to that question. During the entire time that I had known Nuris and Eldar, they had been at the research station in Caucasia, and I had neither seen nor heard of a mother.

"Don't you think it's strange that his mother didn't send you this fax? I mean, why would a 13-year-old be sending it? Do you think it was really *he* who sent it, or did someone else write it for him? What's going on here?"

I had to confess that the style of the letter seemed more mature than what I would have expected from a young teen. But that might have resulted from Doreen's expert translation, combined with a certain degree of stylistic license. I called Doreen.

"No, I tried very hard to convey the exact meaning, and if you ask me this is a child, one who writes like a poet. But it also seemed to me unlikely that someone that age could type up this message on a computer, then get access to a fax with an international line. I mean, I've lived there, I know how impossible these things are."

"You really honestly think he wrote it?" I remarked.

"Yes, I do. But what is he asking you in the last two sentences? I didn't know what that refers to."

Her question echoed exactly what was going through my mind at that time. What did it mean? Who was looking after the boy now? Thirteen-year-olds from Russia couldn't just pack up and head off for the States without help from someone. If he had a mother, why didn't she write the fax? The answer to that question would emerge only much later, and was just as surprising as the fax itself.

"What are you going to do?" Kathleen asked as I read and reread the printout of the e-mail translation.

"First, I think I had better try to find out a few basic details, such as does he have parents or guardians? What exactly was he asking of me in that last part? Those would do for starters."

"I think Susan would like to know about this," said Kathleen with a loud laugh. "Don't forget to mention it before the boy arrives. Oh my God, you never know what's around the corner."

Chapter 2
The Pizza

Throughout the rest of that day I thought about breaking the news to Susan. The problem was that I really didn't know the full implication of Eldar's message. Perhaps, if Eldar did not have a mother, or other close relatives, he was suggesting something more than a summer, a semester, or a year. Such an open-ended commitment could well have consequences way beyond those accompanying the offer I had proposed to Nuris in his office two years before.

Our original decision not to have children had many roots, though it did not mean that either of us disliked children in theory or in practice. To start with I was a good deal older than Susan, and could easily leave her with the burden of raising a child alone when he or she reached college years. Next, we did not really respond well to the idea of infants, and I suppose that we could be accused of the worst of yuppiness and selfishness right there. Lastly, my job at the university, apart from teaching, involved a great deal of travel, much of it international, and that would leave an unfair burden on Susan to look after any small child during those periods. And besides, she had a full-time job as a writer-editor, which she loved. Anyway, our decision not to have children was relatively easy to rationalize at that point.

Of course, a 13-year-old was a different matter. Some would say that this age is the worst, but it could resolve a lot of the problems that we had discussed regarding bringing up a family from infancy at this point in our lives. Also, I knew this boy and had been really taken with him when he had accompanied Nuris and me on our walks through the magic of southern Russia's mountains and glaciers. Still, I had no idea how Susan would react. She was extraordinarily organized and businesslike, and these were hardly the characteristics of an adolescent boy. I was already aware that my instinctive response to the faxed request had been strongly positive. I supposed that my reaction derived in part from a sense of compassion for Eldar's situation, as well as from a desire to respond to a terrible tragedy in the family of a friend. But it also went beyond duty and responsibility, though I had no idea why. I could not say that the feeling came from "a longing to be a parent" or anything as mystical as that. It was simply an immediate response that I did not rationalize or explain in any way, and never have since. From the first moment I thought about it, I wanted Eldar to come and live with us.

It was our habit each Friday to mark the end of the week by dining out. Susan was a talented cook, and she worked all week to keep a supply of imaginative and healthy food on the table. This counteracted my natural tendency to eat everything in sight that is bad for me. On Friday the rules were relaxed.

That evening we craved pizza and soon found ourselves in a booth at a local pizzeria, slouched over sangria and waiting the 20 or so minutes that the pizza preparation requires. This was the moment.

"Every so often," I started smugly, "something comes along that has the potential to change your life totally. I think that this document may be just such a 'something.'"

So saying, I slid the fax in the original Russian across the table, just to extract the full melodrama from the situation. Seeing the Cyrillic script and the name Urumbaev, Susan suspected right away the contents of this document.

"Does this mean that Eldar is coming?" she asked, remembering that we had discussed this possibility when I first came back from Russia, although nothing much had been said about it for the last two years.

Saying nothing, I passed over the English translation of the letter, and watched as Susan began to take in the implications of what was written there.

"Oh, this is awful," she said, as she read the opening statement about Nuris' death. This was swiftly followed with "But what does it mean? Does he have a family? What is he proposing? Where would he sleep?" That rapidly moved into "We could always turn your study into a bedroom and move him in there, and you could put your desk in the music room. . . ."

For Susan too, the first reaction was instinctive and positive. There was no mention of our decision regarding children, the "inconvenience," nor the fact that Eldar—to the best of our knowledge—spoke no English.

"How long do you think this will be for?" Susan asked, raising the key question in my mind.

"I have no idea, though the original plan was for a summer, or maybe a year."

"There are many things we are going to have to find out and soon," she went on, and reached in her bag for the ever-present spiral-bound notebook into which our destinies were regularly interred in the form of endless lists. In short order she wrote, "Does he have a family? How long??? When?? Draft response right away!!"

We devoted the rest of the evening to composing a response to the fax, and we decided that it would have to be written in good, sympathetic Russian. For that we would call upon the services of a Bulgarian friend and graduate student whose husband, Voiko, had spent many years in Russia as the correspondent for a Bulgarian newspaper. His Russian was excellent, and he had an understanding nature. Already we had come to accept the Eldar situation as reality. We were even now planning for it, whereas 30 minutes ago Susan was unaware that the possibility existed. More than that, we were excited. Pizza never tasted so good. Our heads buzzed with frenzied thoughts as we made our way home to bed. The next few months were going to be busy, and quite different from what we had expected.

The Response

Our highly charged state carried through Saturday as we tried to sketch out all the elements that we would put into a fax in response to Eldar's last question. By coincidence we had been invited to dinner at the home of Voiko and his wife, Ekaterina, in one of the student apartments on campus. I had visited Bulgaria the previous year to help develop a program between a new university there and my own school. Bulgarians were few and far between in Bloomington, Indiana, where we lived and worked. Voiko and his wife were also intrigued that I had been to their country, and they had offered to help me relive my experience with some Balkan cuisine. Over a wonderful dinner and heady *Rakia* (Bulgarian brandy), Susan and I recounted the "Eldar story" for the first of hundreds of times. Voiko and Ekaterina studied the fax in the original Russian and declared Doreen's translation to be very accurate.

"It is like something from a novel," said Voiko, still sporting his beard that had been the hallmark of the Bulgarian democrats during the times of protest. "But are you sure that this is from him? It seems awfully mature for such a young child. And yet, there is an innocence about it that would be hard to achieve for an adult drafting a letter for a child. What are you going to do?"

At that point we handed Voiko the English draft of our response.

> "We really want to keep the tone of what we have written in English," said Susan. "We want him to understand that we are sympathetic and that we want to encourage him, not put him off. But we need to find out a lot of things from him."

Voiko agreed to prepare a Russian translation and type it up on an old manual Cyrillic typewriter that was a veteran of his coverage of the USSR's collapse. We all felt that this was a most unusual letter, and we had to get it right. Together, over the remains of dinner, we worked on the English draft, and came up with something that sounded compassionate and practical. Part of it read as follows:

Voiko Tanev, The Bulgarian Intermediary

> *Dear Eldar,*
>
> *First, and most important, I have to tell you that I was very, very sad when I read your letter. I can't believe that Nuris is dead—it seems like only yesterday that we were walking up the glaciers, climbing Elbrus, and riding around in the helicopter. I remember so well the sad time when I got on the bus and left for the airport. I felt I was leaving one of my best friends behind, even though I did not know that I would never see him again. Your letter was so beautifully written that I can see how much you loved him and must miss him. He was a great and good man, a scholar, a friend, and someone who loved the nature he studied. You are right when you say his work on Earth was not finished. You must be proud to be his son. God bless him. I promised your father when he was alive that I would look after you if he sent you to the United States, and my wife and I are happy to honor that promise. The most important thing is that you must tell us exactly what you want. Don't try to be polite, just say it as you mean it. We will try to help make your wishes come true. Tell us what is in your mind and your heart. Don't worry about us. Life is always simplest when we speak clearly, directly, and precisely. Are you thinking about coming to the USA for a short visit,*

*a year, or forever? Or maybe a year to see how it is, and then decide about other plans when you are here. You are welcome to choose any of these options. Even if you wish to live with us forever, that is possible. Everything is possible. Tell us what **you** want. . . . Life would be much easier here if you can speak some English. Once you are here you will learn very quickly, don't worry—other people have done it before! You would have your own room in our house for as long as you like, and we shall look after you like our own son (we don't have any children though your father was always telling me to have some!). We will pay all your expenses.*

The text continued with the names and addresses of some friends and colleagues in Moscow who could help Eldar, because we still had no idea whether he had a family to which he could turn. Already a considerable network of people was beginning to form, each of whom would play a key role.

As we drove home we remembered that in the excitement of the day we had forgotten to pick up the mail from the box at the end of the drive. Typically on Saturdays there was little of interest, and at first glance it seemed to be a small pile of boring metered envelopes and circulars. We had opened almost all of these (and tossed most of them) when we came to a long, gray envelope containing a letter on stiff, gray paper. "Congratulations," it said, "Your application for a Fulbright Award has been successful and we are making arrangements for the immediate transfer of the funds necessary to cover the expenses."

"Oh my God." I exclaimed.

Susan immediately suspected that we had received news of some terrible tragedy. No Fulbright was ever received with such a perverse response.

"We forgot in all this," I muttered, "that I had applied for a Fulbright grant for us to spend the entire summer in Bulgaria. Well I got it! How on earth are we going to deal with the nightmare of getting a Russian teen out of Moscow and into the United States when we will be living in Bulgaria?"

Chapter 3
The Meeting in the Caucasus

My visit to Russia in 1990 had been totally unexpected. I was not in any way a specialist on that part of the world. In fact my special area is the tropics, and nothing could be further from that than Moscow. As far as I knew, my summer travel plans consisted solely of a trip to Paris in late May to coordinate one of the overseas programs for which I was responsible.

Indiana University had many overseas interests, and one of these was a long-standing link with Moscow State University (MSU), the premier institution of higher learning in the then-USSR. This exchange link provided a useful base for linguists, literature specialists, historians, and others. However, in 1990 it seems there was some problem finding anyone to fill the American end of the exchange. I had hosted, on behalf of my employer—the School of Public and Environmental Affairs—three very bright Russian women students in earlier years, and so there was some tenuous link in the institutional memory of the university between Russia and me. I was also planning to co-host a major international conference that summer on environmental destruction in Soviet Central Asia.

One afternoon that spring I received a call from the university's office of international programs.

The dean came right to the point and said, "How about Moscow this summer?"

"Can't be done I'm afraid, I have to go to Paris."

"Well, once you're in Paris, you're halfway there."

"True, but I am getting married on August 4, and I would probably be ill-advised to miss that."

"Oh, we can get you back in plenty of time for the wedding. So, it's on then. Thanks. I really thought we might fail to hold up our end this year."

So with that I was corralled into a three-week period of lectures at MSU's Department of Geography, where I already knew some faculty members. I must admit that the major attraction for me was the extraordinary political situation in Central and Eastern Europe. It seemed that almost everyone I knew was sending me photographs or sizable chunks of the Berlin Wall, or was getting involved by attempting to burn down the Communist Party headquarters in Sofia, Bulgaria. I felt that I was missing out on sweeping historical dramas as well as an ongoing social megaevent. I would, after all, have the whole of July to get ready for my wedding in Bloomington.

My business completed, and my camera already stolen, I left Paris on the Air France flight to Moscow. For most of the journey I slept, but I awoke in time to watch us descend from a low, total cloud cover and emerge over miles of dark birch forest being swept by driving rain. This did little to lift my spirits, since all the way I had been wondering what on earth I was going to do in Moscow for three weeks, and now it was raining cats and dogs. My spirits did lift to see my old friends and colleagues from the university at the airport. Battling the weather, they drove me to my accommodations in the Stalinesque tower block of Moscow State University, which dominates the capital from its perch on the Lenin Hills. Here, in the total absence of hot water, I prepared my lectures, met my former students, and held soirees. Furtively, while I was out, my faculty colleagues would come into my room and restock my refrigerator, for at this time only people with Moscow residence cards were able to buy food in the city. Most of the stores I saw were empty, and most of my colleagues left work early to begin the process of searching and bartering.

Moscow State University

Fascinating though it was, my period of teaching in Moscow has little bearing on this story. However, one day, my friend Alex Gennadiyev, vice dean of the geography department, asked me a propos of nothing,

"How is your health?"

I took this to be a general politeness, and with a laugh answered him with his own favorite phrase, "More or less ok."

"No, seriously, how are you? Can you stand something strenuous?"

I was not given to vigorous exercise, and admit to having been somewhat alarmed as to the underlying purpose of this question.

"I think I'm fine. Why?"

Professor Alex Gennadiyev

Alex then went on to explain that they thought that the university had been working me somewhat relentlessly over the previous two weeks, plus there was no hot water anywhere in this part of Moscow. So, the dean and he had agreed that they should send me for some rest and recreation at one of Moscow University's field research stations. I had visions of the frozen wastes of Siberia, but he told a different story.

"We have a station down in Caucasia, in the Elbrus area, and I think you would really like it there."

I raced my brain trying to recall which area we were talking about. Then I remembered that most Europeans think that Mont Blanc (15,771 feet) is the highest peak in Europe, but it is beaten quite considerably by Russia's Mount Elbrus (18,481 feet), which is on the border with Georgia. I really had no mental image of what the region had to offer, but I readily agreed to go to see Europe's premier peak.

Since Alex was not free to accompany me, he had delegated a tall, spare, bearded graduate student called Misha to serve as translator. Misha had worked extensively in Mongolia but had never been to Elbrus, so this was going to be an adventure for both of us.

On June 14, 1990, a gloriously sunny day, Misha arrived at my door in Block B of the MSU tower. He was hot and bothered because his friend's car had had a flat on the way over, so Misha was panicking about missing the plane. As it was, we arrived at the airport with an hour to spare before departure. I told Misha that I still had no clear idea where we were

Mount Elbrus, the highest point in the Caucasus

going, so he informed me that we were flying to the town of Mineral Waters (*Mineralnye Vody*) in the heart of the Sravropolskii *Krai*. Now more confused than ever, I thanked him for the information.

Then, after a moment I said, "Where are we going?"

"Near the border with Georgia and close to the eastern shore of the Black Sea on the southern slopes of Elbrus, eventually," he responded. "However, since we cannot fly there directly, we will fly to a place about four hours away, where someone will meet us and take us to our destination by bus."

This was the sort of detailed answer I would have expected from a geographer (which Misha is). To kill time we ordered coffee, but were kept in line for an eternity by the extraordinary catering system whereby the same lady took the orders, cooked the food, and made change.

We flew down in a cavernous Aeroflot jumbo that looked astonishingly spartan inside. We had to enter from below, up through the luggage bay where we offloaded our cases, and then up a spiral staircase to the main cabin. Despite the three-hour duration of the flight, no food or drink was served. The only attention we received was when something resembling a domestic food cart was wheeled around by people selling tacky toys, white shirts, and plastic shoes. The vibration made by this plane during takeoff was a truly terrifying experience, but we made it to our destination eventually.

Upon landing at Mineral Waters, we found no one on hand to meet us. We were in the middle of open, green country surrounded by low hills. The landscape reminded me a lot of the Welsh borderlands near where I had grown up. But, we did not have too much time to enjoy the glorious sunshine and bucolic surroundings because we were agitated at the fact there was nobody around we could recognize. Our spirits sank, 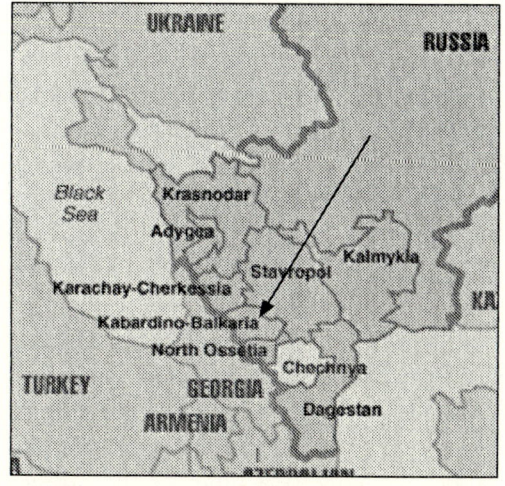 but quickly rose again when Misha recognized the insignia of MSU crudely painted on the side of an ancient, small bus parked in the lot in front of the terminal. After a call had been put out several times over the public-address system, we were approached by a short, jolly, Kazakh man with a beaming smile and a large black mustache.

"This is Nuris," said Misha, introducing me to the man who was already pumping my hand in a fearfully strong grip.

Nuris

"Welcome, welcome," he said, but he had little spoken English beyond that. He grabbed my case and we entered the bus, where there were already several other research students also on their way to the field center.

As we drove along, Nuris kept up a relentless commentary on the landscape, geology, geography, ethnology, and all other aspects of the regions through which we passed, all of which Misha had to translate. We had landed in an area of lush green fields and rolling hills, but as we drove south we rapidly moved out of that environment into ever wilder and more mountainous terrain. We paused along the way at a village, somewhat inappropriately named "Progress," where we found fruit and vegetables in abundance at the roadside stalls. This contrasted starkly with the barrenness of most Moscow foodstores that I had seen in the previous two weeks. Misha bought four pounds of fresh strawberries when he saw my eyes light up upon noticing them. After two hours we entered the world of the Kabardino people immortalized by Leo Tolstoy, and drove through villages where the streets were lined with wooden palisades that enclosed each house. There was a sense of timelessness about everything—so different from the world of workers' apartments and concrete slabs that socialism had produced in all the other parts of Russia I had visited. Into each fence was set a huge gate, and beside each gate was set a bench, upon which members of the family sat each evening and watched the world go languorously by. Each house—and the houses were enormous—had distinctively painted corners: a wonderful and welcome assertion of individualism in this land of uniformity. The whole thing looked like the stage set for a nineteenth century operetta set in Ruritania.

The further we went the more dramatic it became. Vegetation yielded to rocks, and the flanking mountains became taller and steeper with every mile. Soon we were hugging the sides of gorges through which wild rivers crashed. The water was of that strange gray-green color that warns you how awfully cold it is. The light was fading and we were not able to appreciate just how dramatic the landscape would become, for we had to complete the trip in the dark. Eventually we came, quite literally, to the end of the road. It just stopped, and there in front of us was a complex that looked as though it had been transported from Switzerland. At the center was a great chalet, and I was shown into a huge room with several beds, a table, and a television on the chalet's second floor. This was to be my home for the next week.

Nuris invited me to join him, and some of the resident faculty, at dinner. We sat around a long table in his room toasting each other and the world in general and devouring a truly wonderful meal served by a smiling lady named Olga, who seemed to fill the role of general housekeeper at the chalet. The main specialty consisted of a cheese and potato dish of Georgian extraction. The table was covered with side dishes of vegetables and huge hunks of bread. I was, at this time, only dimly conscious of the presence at a small table in the corner of the room, of a small, slender youth with a round face, big eyes, and a crown of thick blue-black hair cut in the inverted-bowl manner of Henry V. I was briefly introduced to him by his father.

"This is Eldar. He is my son." He smiled.

The evening ended in my room with the entire party following, in deepening misery, the progress of the World Cup soccer match (Argentina 2, USSR 0).

The following morning I woke and noticed, before anything else, the remarkable quality of the air I was breathing. It had a live, stimulating essence quite unlike the neutral nature of air with which I was familiar. Taking great drafts of it, I walked over to the window and drew back the curtains. Somehow I was not prepared for what I saw. The most astounding range of snow-capped peaks marched away in the distance. Around us stood tall, dark stands of lofty ancient pines. Through all this thundered the icy Baksan River, and over everything was an azure and totally cloudless sky. I could not move. The beauty of it all stunned the senses. For the next few days I became aware that the only way I could conduct any conversation with anyone was to sit with my back to the window, otherwise it was hopeless. Nothing could compete with what nature wrought across our vision in every direction.

The terrible news that shattered my reverie was that there was no hot water here either. It had previously come from a system based at a hotel across the road, but the attendant forgot to check the furnace and the boiler exploded. Right now it was sitting in the street. The field station had its own backup system connected with its sauna, but that had burned to the ground two days ago, along with the sauna. So we were back to Moscow conditions here, except for the fact that the cold water here was cold in a way I had never experienced in my life. It was not so much cold as frigid.

Somehow, still alive after a freezing wake-up wash, I was ready for Olga's huge breakfast where we devoured our strawberries. Misha and I were to walk up the Baksan valley to the source of the river. We set off through the

Columns of basalt near Azau

pine woods, and very soon I had the distinct impression that I would die. My heart was pounding and every muscle was screaming.

"Oh, just forget it," said Misha. "Keep going and you will not even notice it."

He was right. Soon we were marching up past sheer-sided columns of basalt, jumping only when an eight-foot boulder dropped 200 feet to land about 20 feet from us.

The Baxan river emerges from a glacier

Nuris had said, as we departed, "Watch out for falling rocks." He didn't tell us what we were supposed to do about them. At our feet, bright yellow alpine flowers somehow managed to nestle among the inhospitable gravel; while, to our sides, large stones perched atop earth plinths that they had shadowed, and thus protected, from erosion. It was all encompassed by a great and glorious silence, except for the steady surge of the powerful river. Eventually we traced the river to the point where it emerged from below the Azau glacier, which itself was like a living thing as rocks moved down its face, waterfalls cascaded over it, and the river tumbled out from its throat.

The following day Nuris tested my mettle and said that we should go for a walk. He outfitted me in waterproof gear and stout boots.

"Where are we going, Nuris?" I asked with some trepidation.

"I thought we would go up there," he replied.

My gaze followed his until it stopped in disbelief. First of all the mountain at which he was looking appeared to rise *vertically* for several hundred feet. I could not tell exactly how far because the top of this terrifying phenomenon was hidden somewhere high into the clouds.

Accompanied by Misha, we set off past the exploded boiler and up a rocky slope. This slope, Nuris told me, was composed of a recent rock avalanche, which he called a *sail*, and as he was telling me this the silence of the afternoon was broken by a crashing roar as another rock slide took place somewhere off to our left. Before we could begin the serious ascent, we had to cross to the other side of the steep valley, and that presented us—or more precisely me—with a problem. It was necessary to get across a fast-flowing river of icy water, yet there was no bridge. There were, however, two flexible plastic pipes that afforded the only prospect of getting to the other side. One of these pipes was already partly under the water, and both of them dipped alarmingly in the middle. The diameter of these pipes could not have been more than three inches, and they looked as though they would bend easily! Nuris skipped across with the grace of a ballet dancer. Misha looked doubtful, and I was absolutely convinced that I had come to a defining moment in my life—maybe the end? I could not bring myself to do it.

Nuris skipped back across the pipes with the same effortless ease and fished around in the water. From there he dredged up a 10-foot metal water pipe and motioned to me to use it as a balance bar. Now, poised like Blondin for his attempt to cross Niagara, I gingerly stepped forth. The counterbalance was extraordinarily effective, and with Nuris watching anxiously from the other bank, I fixed my focus on the middle distance and made the crossing: not even wet socks. I was so absurdly proud of this, having believed it totally impossible just minutes ago, that I performed like a gold-medal athlete giving high fives to the entire Caucasus range of mountains.

As we plodded steadily up we saw across the Baksan valley the devastation caused in recent years by some mighty avalanches. Great swathes of trees lay flattened and shattered, while huge mounds of snow lay across the valley bottom where they had come to rest the previous winter. Nuris observed that these avalanches seemed to be getting more frequent, and certainly more damaging. He told me how he had helped dig nine dead people out of the snow right on the edge of the town of Terskol directly below us six months ago. Pausing to take in the view, my Kazakh host started to reminisce about his work and life. He was the protégé of a great alpinist and glaciologist who had been killed some years back in the Pamirs, the highest peaks in the USSR. Nuris had developed a specialty in avalanche warning and detection, and he spent some years with the Russian military as a civilian adviser on this subject in Afghanistan.

His fascinating life story quite masked the hardship of the climb, and soon we were looking down on the research station hundreds of feet below, having ascended, almost without noticing, to the cloud base. Now we were in heavy rain and the going was tough because the ground afforded very poor purchase when it was this wet. We paused on the edge of a dizzying vertical wall, and Nuris pointed to a plaque set into the stone marking the demise of someone who fell from exactly where I was standing now. I hastily backed off. The weather had really closed in, so we started to descend, eventually reaching that same stream and the pipes. This time I was ready for it, grasped the pipe, and strolled over with confidence—or at least the appearance of confidence, I hope. Nuris told me of someone who had fallen in during the winter and had very quickly started to drown, trapped by the skis he was wearing. Nuris plunged in after the hapless skier and pulled him out. In the short time it took to revive the skier, Nuris said he realized that his own clothes had frozen solid.

As we trudged back in the pouring rain, I realized that we had talked all afternoon, even though Nuris spoke little English and I no Russian. Misha, our man-in-the-middle, had allowed two people who shared no common language to begin to construct a true friendship.

A Friendship Grows

That evening, all sources of hot water in the vicinity having become extinct, a group of faculty together with Nuris, Misha, and I, went in search of another sauna that was known to exist somewhere in the nearby village of Terskol. Eventually we came upon a simple, windowless pine structure painted green. Inside we disrobed and entered a small chamber around a central furnace. The dry heat seemed ferocious, and soon the pine benches were too hot for us to sit upon, so we used our towels as cushions. After a short time, the entire party left the searing air to take a shower. That over, wrapped in sheets, we all sat about, eating cookies, and downing tea while tales of avalanches, Afghanistan, and skiing made the rounds of those present. Then back into the furnace. Very soon one's hair became too hot to touch, and Nuris handed me a woolly hat—not to keep warmth in, but to keep it out. Every breath seemed to scorch the inside of the nose, and rivulets of sweat poured onto the floor. At the end of all this, even though I chose to forego the plunge into the icy pool, I felt cleaner than I could ever remember.

The following day, the plans that Nuris had made to take me up Elbrus in the chair lift were scotched by rain and scudding clouds moving in from Georgia. Instead, after Olga had fortified us with porridge and jam, we set off in the minibus. Our destination was the huge Junquat glacier, and to get there we drove over the Baksan River and started a long trek up one of its tributaries. Silent, as always, Nuris' 11-year-old son Eldar, who accompanied us on most of these hikes, strode beside me sporting a pair of knee-length Russian infantry boots that I coveted. From time to time I was aware, as Misha and I discoursed, or as Misha translated for me, that an unwavering pair of eyes was fixed firmly on me from below. As we proceeded, Eldar stopped to gather edible plants, and listened intently as his father offered explanations of the various natural phenomena en route. I kept thinking that Eldar looked like some forest sprite as he disappeared silently off into the trees, or vanished up the steep slopes along the way. I also noticed that when I caught him staring at me he did not avert his gaze. This began to fascinate me.

The going became increasingly more difficult, and the narrow pathway along the riverside was sometimes cut into the sheer rock face, requiring that we hug the cliff and grasp the steel hawser that was looped through rings along the way. At other times, the more open pathway was the domain of grazing cattle that were reluctant to yield the right of way.

Before long we were in mist again. Crossing over an orange-painted bridge of Chinese appearance, we entered a huge, stony flood plain swirling with wisps of ground fog and dotted with dwarf rhododendra. Stunted, wind-blasted pines grew out of impossible homes atop boulders. It all looked quite unreal, and reminded me most of all of the opening scene of *Macbeth*—the "blasted heath." Eldar dropped lengthwise into a push-up position and drank from the icy river rushing by. He fixed me with *that* stare afterward to see what my reaction had been. He seemed more and more to be something that Jean-Jacques Rousseau might have created—a true *Emile*, a child of nature growing up in this impossibly beautiful place.

Eventually, we came to the point where the high gravel plain met the foothills of towering, snow-covered peaks. This was as far as we would go, and the end of the journey was marked by a small hut bearing, in Cyrillic letters on the roof, the inscription *MSU Glaciological Station*. Here we had anticipated we would break open our bottles and eat the lunch that Olga had prepared for us. Instead we found the station was teeming with life. It appeared that a party of 23 alpinists had beaten us to it, along with their venerable guide and tutor. Most of the trainees were young women. The majority was Russian, but there were some flaxen-haired Ukrainians too, with the bluest blue eyes I have seen in a long time. The atmosphere was warm, welcoming, and spontaneously and energetically friendly. Not only were the Russians/Ukrainians always so friendly, but also, for a former Britisher—disturbingly tactile and outgoing. I came, after all, from a race that can share a railroad compartment for many hours with someone on the journey from London to Edinburgh without exchanging a syllable. One has to be introduced, you understand.

Our little party was immediately welcomed and invited to lunch, which was prepared—for 27 of us—over one kerosene stove. The conversation was lively and light-hearted, and after eating we trooped outside for photographs. At some point during the lunch, Nuris had informed the party that I was to be married soon after my return to the USA. At the moment the photograph was being taken, a blond, statuesque Ukrainian woman clutched me in a powerful, and very compromising, embrace and shouted something that reduced the party to laughter. It took some cajoling, but later I got Misha to translate the remark as,

"Let's see how he explains *this* to his new bride."

Eventually we had to leave the alpinists to continue their studies. We all climbed a huge moraine to view an almost perfectly circular lake that it had trapped. But we had a long walk ahead of us. Pausing only to throw small coins in the river—a tradition that existed in Russia as well as elsewhere in the world—to ensure our return, we walked back down the valley.

The walk had taken its toll on my feet, though I was unaware of that during the trek itself. Once we had arrived back at the Institute bus Nuris noticed my somewhat irregular gait, and he removed my boot. We found that my sock was saturated with blood and that the skin had been rubbed away in two areas, though strangely I did not feel any real pain or discomfort.

"The boot is too big," Nuris observed with a laugh.

Back home in the research station, Olga started bandaging the worst parts, and while she was doing so, her tiny daughter Nina wandered in and tried to engage me in conversation. To someone aged three it is incomprehensible why an adult cannot understand your words, since the concept of languages probably does not exist at that age. Failing miserably to get any sensible response from me, Nina skipped over to Misha. (Olga told me that the previous week Nina had been in the yard watching the cat moving its new litter of kittens by picking them up by their necks. After some time Nina decided to help, and the next time Olga saw her, Nina was crossing the yard with a kitten in her mouth too). During a lull in the conversation, Nina looked at Misha, held up a birch twig, and said,

"Hello. Would you like to have a word with my leaf?" Misha, unfazed, remarked that it seemed unusually wet for this time of year. The twig nodded sagely in agreement, and departed with Nina.

June 17 was reserved for the high point of my visit, or so I thought at the time. Nuris had announced that we were going to ascend a substantial part of the ancient volcano at whose foot we were residing. For this Nuris hunted out several pairs of sturdy walking boots, now insistent that I try them out before embarking on this new, and rather daunting challenge. We were also to wear bright orange parkas; in case we plunged down a crevasse I supposed, and could be found by the rescuers—dead or alive!

We proceeded through the pine groves to a cable-car station. The cable car took us up through the forest and above the snow line to the second station at a little over 7,000 feet. From here we proceeded by chair lift in complete silence through the most magnificent alpine landscape. Swaying gently on the chairs we passed over the massive snowfield. The air was extraordinarily pure and a little chilled, the sky was deep blue and totally cloudless, and the glare from the snowfields overpowering. Several times the ground plunged away with terrifying suddenness. At the end of the chair lift was another full day of climbing to the top, but we were not attempting that. Nuris had judged my abilities precisely, and he knew he would be stuck with the problem of getting me down. Anyway, beyond our current destination the climb would have taken us into thinner and thinner air, and the reaction of individuals to that is quite unpredictable. I discovered this ascending Kilimanjaro many years ago. There were two former policemen in the group who quickly vomited, and one passed out. They were nursed back to sufficient strength to turn back by a lady of near 80 years who continued the climb to the top with no apparent difficulty.

Hut Eleven

On now to the last point on our journey: a curious two-story, metal-sheathed structure known, strangely, as Hut (*Prijut*) Eleven. It had no straight edges and looked like an inverted shipwreck. I was reminded of Peggoty's Great Yarmouth home in *David Copperfield:* my all-time favorite book as a child. Hut Eleven, (I never discovered where the other ten were), was situated at around 11,500 feet. Before making the trek to this station we covered ourselves in sunblock, remembering to pay attention to the *under*surfaces, and even the inside of the nose, where reflected glare could cause real damage. As we ascended, skiers swished by with the curiously nautical greeting of *"Ahoy!"* At Hut Eleven we had lunch with the resident director who commanded, quite possibly, the most spectacular view of anyone in the entire world. His window looked *down* on the peaks of the Caucasus under what was now, at this altitude, a truly cobalt sky. After lunch Eldar took off to return on skis to the chalet at an alarming speed, resolving into a tiny, fast-moving dot on the snowfields in seconds before he disappeared totally. He moved with a fluid grace that was extraordinary as he proceeded along this unobstructed 8,000-foot return journey.

Nuris told me, with obvious pride, "He's been on skis since he was four." Eldar clearly did not want us around to slow down his Olympic-style return home.

Our return to the chalet was a little less distinguished, consisting of plunging through soft snow up to our waist, rolling several hundred feet like children on a hillslope, and generally slipping and sliding. Once we were in the cable car, two girls determinedly pestered Misha to get me to part with my US army cap from Panmunjon, in Korea's truce area on the frontier with North Korea. Back home in the chalet I was informed that the grime of the day was to be removed by taking a shower at the R&R facility owned by the (former) Soviet Ministry of Defense.

"Better you don't say anything while you're in there," Nuris advised.

On our way back from the showers, Nuris convinced me to try the local spring water. The spring was located in a small park set back from the road. When we arrived we parked next to a small huddle of men eating and drinking around an improvised table on the trunk of a blue Russian Volga sedan. The central figure in this group rushed forward to greet Nuris like a long-absent brother, and Nuris introduced me to Ilias, the director of the spring (which was the title Nuris gave him, anyway). Ilias was a local Balkarian who, with the rest of his people, was pushed into exile by Stalin for supposedly being too cozy with the invading German forces. They were sent to Kazakhstan, where they received a surprisingly tolerant welcome, in sharp contrast to the reception afforded to other groups such as the Tartars who were sent to Siberia. This was why Ilias felt kindly toward Kazakhs.

The men in Ilias's group were eating cold, fatty mutton and drinking cognac. Neither Misha nor I were capable of handling this combination, so we took off to investigate the spring. The water tasted disgustingly plutonic as if it had come from unexplored depths of the earth. On our way back we watched a young woman, who had been enjoying something considerably stronger than spring water, trying to cross the river by means of a large water pipe. There was a perfectly adequate footbridge next to it, but she eschewed the easy way. She got halfway and then decided to wave to her boyfriend. That was her total undoing. With a horrible slow-motion twist she plunged into the glacial water rushing beneath. Instantly sobered, she waded to the shore, and fell into the arms of her boyfriend, ensuring that he too was soaked.

On Monday, my last full day, Nuris awakened me early, and we set off in the bus with many graduate students, faculty, and Eldar. I had no idea where we were going, or why. Because Misha seemed curiously reticent about imparting any information, I definitely had the impression that something was, as Sherlock Holmes would have said, "afoot." We pulled up in the middle of a broad flood plain, whereupon everyone decanted from the bus and proceeded to sit down on the grass. The bus departed and left us in this rather uninteresting spot.

The true purpose of the visit was revealed when a large orange *Aeroflot* helicopter clattered into sight and landed just in front of us. We boarded, and soon we were flying over the peaks of Elbrus heading toward its lee side. This, in contrast to the southern face, had a much higher snowline, and was a world of vast grassland plateaux and treeless high slopes. We descended onto a spur of pastureland with no dwellings or roads anywhere in sight. At this point Nuris, Misha, Eldar, and I disembarked. The others flew on to complete an air-photography mission. The weather was glorious, the silence total and all-embracing. The moment we disembarked, a Caucasian horseman in riding boots and Alpine fedora with feather drew close and invited us to ride. Nuris, carrying the blood of Genghis Khan in his veins, looked as though he were born to ride a horse. We snapped photos of each other on horseback against the magnificent backdrop of the twin volcanic peaks of Elbrus. Back on two legs we walked past extraordinary towering triangular rocks, known locally as the "Gateway to Paradise" in this otherwise totally grassy landscape. On passing between these rocks, one's wishes were said to be granted.

On the other side of the odd-shaped rocks, a gentle rumbling heralded the presence of an upwelling of hot springs in a series of rust-colored natural baths. This was our destination, and once more all clothes came off and we embraced the warm ochre water. Such was the force of the emerging spring that it held one horizontal. By my side,

Nuris and Eldar on the north face of Elbrus

looking at me with that unwavering stare, was Eldar. After the immersion, while the adults resorted to boiled eggs, cognac, and sandwiches, a totally naked Eldar zoomed off up the hillside to work off his stored energy. This not only felt like, but was beginning to look like, lunch on Mount Olympus. There was no one around, so this staggering beauty was ours for the day. Behind us a regal waterfall plunged from a cave in the middle of a high cliff face. We felt indescribably *alive*, and I wrote in my diary at the end of the day, "I cannot remember when I ever felt this *good*, or people treated me this well. The solitude was quite marvelous. I had forgotten that there were still places on earth without roads or people (except us, of course). The silence is intimidating by its almost palpable presence."

The First, and Last, Farewell

For my last evening, Nuris and his deputy Yuri prepared a fire to make *shashlik*, or shishkebab. Unfortunately, making fires was not one of Yuri's strong points, and when we entered the room the place was filled with smoke so dense that Nuris and I had to crawl along the floor. Normally you do this to escape a burning building, not enter it. Nuris and Yuri worked to get the chimney to draw while I tried to recover in the fresh night air on the balcony. As Yuri nursed the revitalized fire, Nuris started to show me slides of avalanches from the distant and more recent past. The power of these calamities was extraordinary, and more awesome still when the pictures were clearly from places where we had walked in the last few days. Then Nuris showed me slides of his time with the Soviet army in Afghanistan where he was retained as an adviser on avalanches to keep the one and only road to the USSR open. This conversation became eerie and uncomfortable since we were discussing something about which, until recently, we represented opposite sides in an armed conflict. The embarrassment was heightened suddenly when Nuris informed me that Yuri's son was killed while serving in Afghanistan. The mood started to get maudlin, but Nuris snapped us out of it by saying how stupid conflict was, which was something we could all agree on, though I doubt it made Yuri feel any better.

The conversation wandered through the universality of science, the essential goodness of people, and the monstrosity of war. As before, I could not believe that two people without a word of each other's language were baring their souls as frankly as this. We became very emotional, perhaps helped by the constant toasts taken with fine Armenian cognac, and we ended in a common silence of understanding.

My final day in the Caucasus saw the return of awful weather. To help me revive my spirits, for I was deeply sad to leave here, Olga prepared a dish of porridge and rice pudding. To show my appreciation for the efforts of this eternally happy and resourceful woman, I gave her my favorite pen. She returned with two small ceramic vodka glasses that she had fashioned and fired. I still treasure so personal a gift. Nuris, eyes shining and without a word, handed me a pair of the infantry boots I had really come to appreciate during our long walks. They were, he told me, to encourage me to keep walking in the mountains. I informed him it was going to be hard to put these boots to work in the subdued topography of Indiana.

Standing off to one side, as always like a silent spirit, was Eldar, watching all that passed from beneath his mop of blue-black hair. He studied his father as Nuris gave me the boots, his face saying nothing. Then he slipped out of the room and returned with a bright blue hip-pack, which, silently, he handed me. This was the most touching moment of all, and I was beginning to get hopelessly emotional about the whole scene. Finally, Nuris presented me with a Georgian drinking cup made from a horn which, he told me, was to be used at my forthcoming wedding. It was unique in that it would not stand up, meaning that the contents had to be drunk before the cup could be put down. I promised that I would toast him with it on the day.

The wedding, a week after I returned

In a quiet moment I mentioned to Nuris that I would be happy to invite him and Eldar to spend a summer with us in the USA. It would be a good opportunity for Eldar to learn some English, and it would give me the opportunity to repay their hospitality. Nuris thought at length.

"I really would like to do that," he said with a firm handshake.

"Remember this," I said, looking him in the eye, "for I am quite serious."

"I will," he assured me.

As we were to discover later, while Misha translated, that pair of eyes in the corner was taking it all in, and storing it away.

Our party boarded the university minibus for the long journey to the airport. We stopped to be photographed next to the artillery pieces that were used to induce avalanches before they became too large and threatening. We made a final stop for a local delicacy known as *kichin*—my third breakfast of the day. Just as we were about to reboard the bus, Nuris took my camera and asked me to stand on the steps for a last picture. Eldar was caught at this moment looking into the camera.

"Look," said Nuris, "I don't want to say good-bye over and over again. It is better to say it once and have done with it. Let us get it over with here and now."

I understood these sentiments precisely, since nothing so complicates a friendship as a protracted farewell. Nuris clasped me in a strong embrace.

"Don't forget my offer," I confirmed.

"I won't," he replied.

I shook Eldar's hand and boarded the bus.

I could not explain the terrible feeling of deep sadness I had as we drove through this wild place, and driving rain, the several hours to the airport. After all, I had known these people for less than a week; I could not speak directly to any of them; and yet I was so morose that I was not disposed to converse with anyone on the way back. I felt deeply and profoundly upset, though I did not know why. I kept on thinking how tremendously happy I had been there, and how much I felt for the man who had inspired me to do things I would, otherwise, not dreamed of doing. And that boy: he simply would not leave my thoughts. I felt depressed for hours like a teenager who had just said good-bye to his first infatuation. Though I had met many interesting people on my travels, somehow this felt different.

Eldar's Recollections, 1992

In the summer of 1990, when I was eleven, we, as always, went to Terskol. I could still ski in the summer because the snow is there all year long. In June my dad said that a person from the US was coming here for a visit. The visitor's name was Randall Baker; he was a professor from Indiana University. Since I didn't speak English, I couldn't speak to him. We went with him to many places, and became good friends. One day Randall told my father that it would be nice if I could come to the US and learn some English. But we never discussed this further, and Randall returned to the States.

The next summer (1991), we again went to Terskol, and my cousins from Uzbekistan came there for the first time. Melis is the oldest son of my dad's sister, and Albina is Melis's younger sister. We had a lot of fun there together. We went mountain climbing and skiing, and played tennis and other fun things. Melis is one year younger than I and Albina is two years younger. Actually Melis's name is really Mels, because the first initials of his name stand for Marx, Engels, Lenin, and Stalin. Albina was younger, and because she was a girl we would always get in trouble because we would make fun of her and tease her.

That summer I got my first moped. My parents had already bought it, but couldn't get it to our house because it was too far to ride there on it from Moscow!. I was waiting for it to come all the time, and thought of nothing else. I couldn't wait till the truck would arrive. One day it finally came without any announcement. I was so eager to ride it that I immediately went and put some gas in it, but NO, my dad said that I should read the manual first and then I could ride it. I finished reading the manual the same night, although I would never usually read anything in that way. My method was to get on and take off. But I was just bursting to try the moped. So the next day I went to the garage and started it. It started on the first try, and I thought, "Wow, that's pretty good!"

But guess what? I tried to go, and it stalled. I started it again and tried to go and it stalled again. Well later I found out that we had to do something to the clutch and gas before we could ride it; I suppose to stop kids like me from doing exactly what I was doing. So my dad said, "I thought you read the manual. How come you don't know how it works?" and didn't let me ride it for a whole week. I thought I would die. Finally after a week and a half I first rode my moped, by which time I could recite the manual like a religious text.

When my cousins were going to go back to Uzbekistan, so I asked my parents to let me go with them for a visit because we had become good friends. They agreed, got the ticket for me and I went with my cousins. When we got to Central Asia, Melis's father met us at the airport. By now, it was August, and school was due to start in September. But then my family couldn't get an airline ticket back home to Moscow for me, so I stayed there and started in yet another school. Since Uzbekistan was then in the USSR, everyone knew and spoke Russian, so it was not difficult for me to start a new school. I spent half a year in Uzbekistan, and then I went back to Moscow after finishing the first semester In fact, I had been to school in Uzbekistan before, when my parents were with the military in Afghanistan.

When I came back to Moscow in 1991, long after Randall's departure, and after a semester of school in Uzbekistan with my dad's family, my father was confirmed as the director of the field station belonging to Moscow State University in Terskol, where Randall had stayed. This station was, by now, in very bad condition because the last winter had been extremely harsh with many avalanches, and as a result of the chaos in the USSR, and its eventual collapse, there was no money to fix anything. The heating system was broken, all the pipes were frozen, and the first floor of the buildings was covered by a thick layer of snow and ice. My father suggested that I come with him back to the Caucasus, so I did, though my mother and brothers stayed in Moscow. I started the second semester in school in Terskol—another change.

Azau Research Station

The school there was very small. The average class had about 15 to 20 people in it, which was good because teachers paid more attention to individual students. I had a lot of friends there. I joined the ski team, and every weekend, and sometimes after school, we had practice and competitions. It would be impossible for a skier to live in a better place. In the winter, school was often closed because it's so cold there that the pipes freeze, or the teachers are sick, or we had a snow storm the night before and we couldn't get to school. Actually the University's station wasn't in the village of Terskol itself; it was in a place called Azau, which is about three kilometers from Terskol where the road to Elbrus ends, near the cable-car station at the foot of the mountain. We didn't have school buses, so I had to walk three kilometers to school and back everyday, occasionally through snow taller than I was. Sometimes, in clearer weather, I took a skateboard to go to school because it was downhill all the way to Terskol. One day though, I was going very fast and one of the wheels rode over a stone so I came flying over the skateboard and was sliding on asphalt on my left knee. That stopped the skateboarding for a while.

Everything there was like a child's dream—like being all alone in a theme park where all the rides are empty and free. I loved it. I got pretty good grades for the first time in my life. I skied all the time, because the slopes were right next to the station where we lived. The students in residence, the faculty, my dad and I spent our lives hiking, mountain climbing, flying down the slopes on skis. It was one of the happiest times in my life, and it all seems like a dream now.

One day, my father went skiing with two American professors who came to the station to set up an exchange program with students of Moscow State University and American students. They also loved skiing, but really had not become experienced in conditions like the huge slopes of Elbrus. When I came back from school, as usual, on 28 January 1992, I went, up the stairs to our apartment—it was just another day. However, the door was closed, which was definitely not normal, and, because it was never locked, I didn't have a key. I could not understand this, and went downstairs to try to find my father to borrow the key. But he wasn't there. One woman, my dad's colleague, told me something about my dad having been caught in an avalanche. She didn't have any details, but it explained why he was not back and had not opened the door for me. I ran up to the mountain as fast as I could go. There were many cars, and official people, and I saw the track of the avalanche very high up on the mountainside. The mountain patrol, which handles rescues, was already there. A person who was standing next to me had a radio; he turned out to be the director of the mountain patrol. I heard over his radio people up on the mountain saying, "The person higher up is an American and the person lower down the slope is Nuris." Later I heard, "One of the Americans is still alive, but Nuris isn't moving." When I heard that I started crying. Our friends, suddenly noticing that I was there, took me to their house in Terskol. I stayed there with them for two days, and was told that my dad was in the hospital in a really bad condition, but I could not see him. Then my mom and my brothers flew in from Moscow, and we returned to our apartment in the field station. Our best friend called me to his apartment and said,

"Eldar I need to talk to you. Your father. . ." He took a moment to think. ". . . is dead. He died right up there on the mountain. We didn't want to tell you this right away. We told you that he was in the hospital so that you would be prepared."

It was so sad because my dad spent all his life studying snow, glaciers, avalanches, and then he died in one. He really loved the mountains and he died there too. I still remember how we skied together, how many things he taught me, and how many lives he saved from avalanches, and how much people loved him. We had to get packed and go to Moscow. We had so many things in Terskol, which had been gathered there during my family's visits over thirty years. All three of my father's brothers came to Terskol to take his body to Uzbekistan for burial (he was a Moslem). We all went to Uzbekistan. We had a great funeral for my dad. Hundreds of people came to his funeral because so many people respected and loved him. I know I did.

Chapter 4
Making Contact

When Susan and I looked at the schedule for the coming summer in Bulgaria, alarm set in. We realized that our return to the United States would be approximately 10 days before the beginning of the new academic year at Bloomington's high schools. So, if the intention was that Eldar would spend his time in school in America, we faced a very tight timetable to get him settled in domestically, documented, set up at school, and so forth. In the back of our minds also was the fact that we would be in a certain amount of turmoil upon our return. We would have to move back into our house, unpack after three months in the Balkans, and get ready for the new university year that itself would be just two weeks away. This timetable seemed impossible, so we inserted a statement in our first fax to the effect that it would probably be better for Eldar to come in December. That delay, in the context of the teenage sense of anticipation, must have seemed like an eternity. Nevertheless, we felt more comfortable not having to deal with so many major changes in such a short time.

On April 1, not completely unconscious of the symbolism of the date, we sent the fax to its totally unknown destination somewhere in Russia. It was an odd experience not knowing really to whom we were writing, or the real circumstances behind this extraordinary correspondence. However, the machine emitted the usual shrieks indicating that many thousands of miles away the unknown fax machine was feeding our reply into a tray. We did not expect an immediate reply, for we had asked a number of questions that would require Eldar, or whoever was the sender of the fax, to search out some details.

The days went by in silence, and then turned into weeks. Meantime Susan and I were proceeding with our plans for my imminent departure to

Bulgaria (Susan following in one month), realizing the whole time that we were going to have to make some decisions well in advance of Eldar's coming if he was to have a bed in which to sleep, a room in which to live, and other domestic necessities. Nearly three weeks passed without any sort of response from Moscow.

By April 19 we were wondering whether the prospect of a brief period of surrogate parenthood was going to fizzle out after all. The process was rapidly moving to the point of no return in which we would have to make decisions that could preclude Eldar's coming at all. We preferred to resolve this issue while we were still in the United States, rather than try to communicate from Bulgaria, for we had no idea whether we would have access to international phones and faxes there. In a state of some alarm we called Voiko, the Bulgarian who had assisted with the translation of our reply into Russian, for we needed someone who could pick up the phone and talk with someone in Moscow who could clarify what was happening. At the bottom of Eldar's original cryptic fax he had given a phone number in Moscow. We were not at all sure whose number this was, but it offered us a chance of opening a second line of communication and of getting some answers to our many questions.

That afternoon, a warm, sunny spring day, Voiko came to our house. We did not need to brief him since he was as familiar as either of us with what we needed to know. He called the number in Moscow and heard the long single tone that so confusingly sounded like the US busy signal. The tone stopped suddenly and Voiko engaged in a short conversation quite unintelligible to us.

As he put down the phone he said "I got some old guy; I'm not sure who he was, but he said Eldar is out right now, though he will be back soon."

At least we knew he was around, and we could hope to get some answers. We decided to call back at 9 p.m. Moscow time, which was some seven or eight hours ahead of us, as best we could gauge from the international dialing book next to our telephone.

At what we took to be 9 p.m. Moscow time Voiko called again, and this time struck gold. We heard the name "Eldar," followed by a lengthy conversation in Russian. Frustratingly, we could not understand anything that was said, so all we could do was speculate as to what he must have said and learned from Eldar.

Eventually, after an eternity that did wonders for AT&T's share prices, Voiko replaced the receiver, and uttered a single word "*wow.*" We were not entirely sure how to interpret that as a summary of 25 minutes of international conversation, so we asked him to elaborate. As he spoke Susan dashed down a summary in rapid, stabbing strokes on a pad doing a passable imitation of Lois Lane.

"Ok, here it is," Voiko began. "First of all that was *not* Eldar, that was his natural mother, and her name is Ludmila. She sounded very intelligent to me, and we had a good talk. She said that they got the fax, but didn't know how to answer."

We were stunned. Susan's pencil was frozen. This was the first mention we had ever had of a living mother.

Voiko continued, "She definitely wanted Eldar to come—it was his father's wish; that was very important in the Central Asian tradition—and she thinks it will be good for him to attend and even finish high school here, *and then he can make up his own mind.*"

Her acquiescence to Eldar's coming here for several years came as a shock. Once more we were staring at the possibility of a completely open-ended commitment that could stretch off into eternity. At least now we knew that this was not simply an extended holiday.

Natasha Kosheleva

Voiko added, "Eldar is now 13 years old, and he has two brothers, both of whom are quite a bit older—in their early to mid-twenties or so I think."

Voiko was not sure whether the brothers were Eldar's natural siblings since, as he said, "there's a limit to what a total stranger, and a foreigner too, can ask over the telephone." He went on, "The family has been in touch with Natasha [my former student now living back in Moscow and one of the names I had given in the fax], who was teaching Eldar some English, since he speaks none now. His mother is still thinking in terms of August, by the way, though she said they could switch to December if it is absolutely impossible to come in summer."

Susan asked Voiko whether there was anything we could send to make life easier for the family, for the tales coming out of Russia at this time were appalling. Voiko suggested large jars of vitamins and aspirins, neither of which was readily obtainable there at the moment.

Susan scribbled, brows furrowed, mind racing.

Then she looked up and asked Voiko, "What does she mean by 'then he can make up his own mind?'"

"Well, she thinks he is too young to know these things for himself now at age 13, but by the time he is 18, then he will be in a position to decide his future," posited Voiko.

"Yes, but what does *she* think? I mean she is his mother; she can't be entirely without an opinion regarding the rest of his life?"

"I understand what you are asking," said Voiko, "but really, Susan, I cannot ask her these things. I don't know about the USA, but in Russia it would be very rude for a stranger to ask such personal questions. It would be better for you to ask her yourself, but unfortunately you cannot speak Russian."

Voiko had certainly put his finger on a real dilemma here. We were proposing an extremely intimate, potentially long-lasting link between two families who could not even tell the time in each other's language. We were going to be heavily dependent on our Russian-speaking friends and intermediaries if this was ever to work out. They would have to gain Ludmila's confidence if we were to proceed.

Where did that leave us? We would certainly need to become Eldar's legal guardians if he was to spend any time here in the public school system, and so Ludmila would have to grant written permission for that. But first, of course, we needed to get him to the United States.

Voiko told us that they were sending us a fax in reply to the one we sent; in fact they were just about to send it when we called. Susan and I hoped the fax would clear up any remaining points, and enlarge on Voiko's recollections of the phone call.

"Was there anything else?" I inquired of Voiko.

"Actually, there was some sort of complication," he responded cautiously. "It seems, from what Ludmila said, that in Russia it is not possible for someone Eldar's age to have a passport, and without a passport he cannot travel. It seems he can travel abroad only *with a parent*, and so Ludmila might have to come with him."

Susan reacted visibly. "But she can't! What would happen when she goes back? She can't leave him here without a passport, and we certainly cannot host the two of them on a potentially everlasting basis. This is ridiculous. It simply isn't possible to proceed with this if those are the conditions."

"I can see that," said Voiko, "but she has been looking into this with the authorities, and you have no idea what it is like to deal with the Russian bureaucracy. I really don't think it is her desire to come to the States to stay—but you should be careful—I don't know what is going on here. First a child sends a fax, which seemed unimaginable to me, and then it turns out his mother may have to come as well, and stay too! Move carefully!"

With that he drove off leaving us looking at each other in absolute confusion. This revelation really did seem to throw a monkey wrench in the works.

Eldar's Recollections, 1992

Before I went to Uzbekistan to my dad's funeral, I wrote a fax to Randall Baker, who came to Elbrus in 1990. In the fax I told him that my father was killed in an avalanche, and asked him if it would still be possible for me to come to the U.S. Before my father's death we had talked about it sometimes and he was going to write Randall, but he was very busy, because the station was in such a bad shape that he couldn't leave it. I knew that he really wanted me to learn English and get a good education, and he had planned to go with me to America in response to Randall's offer. I remembered that, and I thought I would write Randall.

When I came back from Uzbekistan, my brother told me that there was a surprise for me, and he would give it to me only if I promised to be good. So I did. He gave me a letter. I looked at it with confusion on my face and started reading it. It was a reply to my fax to Randall Baker. I actually didn't expect to get a reply. In the fax he said that he would like me to come. He suggested that I come in December to give me time to get everything done. He didn't know anything about my family, because my father never talked about them. He asked me all sorts of questions about how old I am, who do I live with, etc. He said that he is married; his wife's name is Susan Baker. They got married right after he left Terskol. They got married the same day and the same year that my middle brother did. He gave me names and addresses of people who might help me to get a visa and all the things I would need to come to U.S. I was very happy to get his fax and I was very excited. I showed the fax to my mom. She was very excited too. The next day we called to those people who Randall said might help us. One person, Roman Zlotin, was a professor at the Academy of Sciences, at the Institute of Geography. The other person, Natasha Kosheleva, was Randall's former student, who had gone to Bloomington to study at SPEA (School of Public and Environmental Affairs.) We didn't know her telephone number, only the address and where she works, therefore we couldn't contact her for sometime. My middle brother, Timur, is a student at MSU (Moscow State University), in the Geography Department, and he went to the office and found Natasha. Randall also wrote that it would be great if I could learn some English. He told me that Natasha speaks excellent English and that she might help me with that. He wrote a letter to her asking to help us with some things and maybe teach me some English. She is one of the best translators at MSU. She agreed to teach me. I went to her house two or three times a week for about two hours. She gave me homework; I didn't get grades for it though. She taught me the most basic structure of English, like how to make a sentence, some words, pronunciation, and so on. She told me everything about Bloomington and the U.S. in general. I'm really thankful to her for what she's done for me.

It was very hard living without a father. My mom didn't work and my brothers were in the university. I was out of school for a whole month because of my dad's funeral, so I was way behind. We had another funeral for the benefit of our friends in Moscow. Also, hundreds of people came to our three-room apartment. The door to the apartment was always open; people just kept coming in and out. I didn't want to stay there, because there were too many people and I didn't want to be in the way. So I went outside to see my old friends whom I hadn't seen for a long time. I was happy to see them after such a long time. Then, every day after school we would go out and have fun. We went to the woods next to our house, where we hung around and talked about different things. Almost every one of my friends smoked. So, I thought that I should, too. I had a girlfriend for a couple of months, her name was Natasha, but then we broke up.

I had very good grades when I was in Uzbekistan and Terskol, but somehow when I was in Moscow, I could never get good grades. I hated school even though it was right next to the place where we lived. Every week I would skip whole days of school at least twice, not counting the individual classes. I was barely making 3's (D- in Russia). At the end of each grading period I would plead with my teachers to give me a passing grade. When I skipped school, I usually went to the movies, which started about 10:00 a.m.

My friends and I then started to go out and buy beer or cognac and get drunk. We could just walk into a liquor store in Moscow and buy whatever we wanted as long as we had money.

On the 8th of March (Woman's national day in some countries), my friends and I decided to have a party at the family dacha (summerhouse) on the outskirts of Moscow, and invited some girls. We saved enough money to buy food and alcohol for a whole army, though

Eldar at the family dacha near Moscow

not that many people showed up. We had a great time, even though my mom and brothers found out, but they didn't say anything.

Later I started getting in trouble with my mom and brothers and even ran away from home and lived in the Moscow railroad station for three days when I borrowed the car to go to a party. Of course this was illegal, and my Dad would never have allowed me to do this. Even though the car was fine, I parked it facing the wrong way, and my brother knew right away what I had done. I'm not sure why I suddenly became so wild. Maybe because after my father's death there was no strong hand to look after me, though I think my brothers did a good job.

Now I think in a funny sort of way, that those were some of the happiest times in my life, because I had so many good friends, even though they got me into trouble. But I knew I could not go on like this.

Chapter 5
The Hand of Fate

After three days Eldar's promised fax from Moscow arrived. During those three days we thought of little else. When we had it translated we learned of one change in plan; Ludmila now suggested that Eldar come for one year to "see how things go." After all, he knew me for less than a week, had never met Susan at all, and had never been outside the Soviet Union. With all those unknowns, perhaps he would not be happy here in such totally strange and frightening circumstances. After all, we could not even communicate with him. And what about us? Susan and I had, as I mentioned earlier, never had children, and were now more or less resolved not to. How would we react to having a teenager around the house? A one-year trial did seem, on reflection, a more reasonable arrangement for both sides than waiting until Eldar reached 18 or so when he could "make up his own mind." Eldar's fax went on to say (in Russian),

> *Thank you and your wife for responding so warmly to our pain. We have thought and consulted a lot and have decided that it would be better if I come there. It will be hard of course for mother to part with me, but nevertheless she thinks that if I come there I would receive a good education. My father also wanted that for me. My parents always dreamed about a good education for their children. My brothers are already studying: my oldest brother Roman is studying architecture, and the second one, Timur, is in the geography department at Moscow State University. . . . If it turns out to be possible, I would like to finish school in the USA. While father traveled in Afghanistan, I changed schools a lot and this is difficult. . . .*

Personal data: I am 13 years old, in the 8th grade. Name Eldar Nurisovich Urumbaev, born September 27, 1978, in Tyrnauz in the Kabardino-Balkarian Autonomous Soviet Socialist Republic. I live with my mother.
Mother: Ludmila Vasilievna Urumbaeva born in Tomsk, Siberia.
Father: Nuris Arypkhanivich Urumbaev, nationality Kazakh, deceased.

We checked at the exit visa office. They told us that if a child is younger than 16, he can't have a passport and the first exit occurs only with parental accompaniment.

Our hearts sank when we read the last two sentences. We were of course powerless to change Russian passport and travel laws, and it looked to me as if Eldar was telling us that he could not come because of his inability to get a passport. I remarked to Susan that it seemed that the only way he could come would be to travel with his mother.

"But that's ridiculous!" she responded. "If he doesn't have his own passport, what is supposed to happen when his mother goes back?"

The answer was not obvious to me.

"Because we certainly can't house him *and* his mother for a year. That's out of the question." Susan's face creased into a mass of confused emotions.

It was beginning to look hopeless to me, and I said so. Susan remained undaunted despite the barriers falling across our path.

"Oh no. We'll get him here. He *will* come," she insisted.

As we both stood there, I had a sudden idea about someone who might be able to help us. In 1990, as I mentioned earlier, I had been one of two hosts to an international conference on the environmental destruction of (then) Soviet Central Asia. After an organizational frenzy and a financial nightmare, people had come from many parts of the USSR. One of them, Roman Zlotin, had hoped to return to the United States to teach a course. A geographer by profession, Roman directed an institute attached to the USSR Academy of Sciences in Moscow. On that previous visit he had

The Soviet passport cover was already out of date when Eldar contacted us

wanted to see the Hoosier National Forest south of Bloomington, and was taken there by a similarly exuberant, fly-fishing-obsessed wetland specialist. They communed among the trees exchanging excited taxonomic comments in Latin, which must have sounded like a medieval gathering of churchmen. This faculty member had recently asked me to help arrange for Roman to teach a course at my school at Indiana University. Originally, he was due to come for the current spring semester, but had to postpone his arrival to the fall. Thus here—amazingly—was a person who would be traveling from Moscow to Bloomington in late August. This was precisely the time Eldar would be due to travel. Here was the first of *many* intriguing coincidences that came to typify this remarkable tale as it unfolded.

I decided to send an express package of documents to Roman Zlotin, though to be honest, I was not absolutely sure I remembered him that well, and did not know how he would react to this approach out of the blue. I included a mention of the Eldar story because I imagined Professor Zlotin might well have known Eldar's father Nuris, who was also a geographer in Moscow—though not at the same institution. As it turned out later, he did not know Nuris, but Roman Zlotin was very moved by the tragic tale, and understood Eldar's wish to come to the States at this turbulent time in his life. Once he received our overnight package, Roman wasted no time in replying. On May 7 I found the following fax in my box at work:

Dear Randall,
I received your express mail and think your idea to get Eldar is brilliant and I'll help both of you in this. I met his parent immediately, discussed all questions and understood what she agrees, to send him alone with me. So, I'll try to get a passport for him in my Academy of Sciences. That can be possible, probably if you send me an invitation for Eldar, and a second letter to me with the remark "in time of your SPEA arriving bring Eldar with you. He is my personal guest"...

The meaning of this was not exactly clear to us, especially with regard to how the Academy of Sciences, Russia's most prestigious institution of learning, could have anything to do with getting a passport for a 13-year-old boy who had nothing to do with that body. But we were willing to go with any option that presented itself, for it was clear that we could do nothing to oil Russian wheels from Indiana. We didn't even know what teeth were waiting to grind us, and our project, in the jaws of bureaucracy. At this point we completely abandoned the idea that Eldar might come in December, which would have given us some time to recover from Bulgaria and organize ourselves for this dramatic change in lifestyle. Now we had to face the prospect of a late summer of barely controlled frenzy.

I was still trying to place Roman Zlotin in my mind among the mass of people at the conference in 1990. I talked to his friend on my faculty, and then I recalled who he was. I saw in my imagination a short, stocky, bright-eyed and slightly gnomic individual with a zeal for nature. He reminded me of a Disney caricature of an Irishman rather than that of a noted Russian ecologist. But it was clear that Roman, whose English was actually offbeat and rather good, would make a successful teacher. Just how energetic and resourceful he really was I was to appreciate soon enough when he emerged as the central figure in determining whether or not Eldar's wish would ever come true. We had no idea, back in rustic Indiana, of the Kafkaesque maze he had entered and through which he tried to navigate in search of (true to his leprechaun image) the pot of gold represented by a passport and an airline ticket for Eldar. At this point he had no idea, either, as to what gymnastics would be involved.

We now had less than a week before I had to leave for Slovenia, Croatia, and Bulgaria for an entire summer in the Balkans. We took heart from Roman's short fax, but we were now in a real dilemma. Very shortly both of us would be in Bulgaria: Europe's equivalent of the dark side of the moon. We would be there until August 16, then we would come back to face, in a couple of weeks, the new academic year at Indiana University, which would involve dozens of social and study-related meetings. The high-school year, we found out, was scheduled to begin on August 25, so if Eldar really was to come with Roman we'd have just *10 days following our return* in which to unpack, get settled, and prepare for his arrival. He in turn would have one day before school started! When I worked this out on the back of a grocery list, I was stunned. Of course I should have realized it, but I had never thought out the implications of all these things coming together.

Susan, ever determined that Eldar would come whatever the circumstances, said—alarming me even more, "We need to think about reorganizing this house *now* if he is going to live here. We need to get him a bed, make a room for him, and find some place for him to store his clothes, and so on."

I was more hesitant; I felt that we were tempting fate very badly if we proceeded to set up a room for him. Well, to be honest, there was a little more selfishness to what was churning round in my mind. A quick review of the geography of our home turned on another flashing red light in my head: the only conceivable place that would work as a bedroom was my study, and I really didn't want to give up my office. As you can see, Susan and I were perfect foils for each other.

"I don't think we should be hasty about this," I responded. "We must be realistic." I felt like a reptile as I said it.

The hard, bright light behind Susan's eye did not diminish, so I guessed I was out of a study. Even though both of us wanted Eldar's visit so much, the chances of his coming, as I added up the hurdles, seemed slim, and I was not sure we should rush into the expense of making a commitment to changing the house, and especially converting my study, until the situation was a *lot* clearer.

"It may mean some frantic rushing around at the end, sure, but I think we should hold off,"

I tried as a final gesture in the direction of my status quo. But, less selfishly, I was worried that Susan was getting too far into this prospect emotionally, and this would increase the very real disappointment she would feel if the now almost legendary, Eldar failed to turn up. Foolishly I thought I had convinced Susan to leave things in the house as they were for the present. Dream on. Had I learned nothing in two short years of marriage?

Ludmila receives part of the nightmare of paperwork

My departure date for Bulgaria, May 16, drew closer alarmingly fast. We sent a package of material express mail to Ludmila in Moscow. It was necessary for Ludmila to sign some forms to enable us to become Eldar's legal guardians once he had arrived. Without that authority he would not be able to attend school. With two days to go before my departure, to add to the general atmosphere of lightly-concealed pandemonium, I had still not received the money for my Fulbright. I had also been informed that, since Bulgaria had no system of personal bank accounts, traveler's checks, or personal checks, it would be necessary to take funds for the entire three months in cash! I now faced the prospect of trying to scrape up sufficient money in the absence of my travel grant and then packing it around my person like ballast.

At that moment a letter arrived from Belgium. It was from my former student Natasha. She was attending a meeting there, but had earlier made contact with

Eldar's family. I had asked her to go round, introduce herself, and try to teach Eldar a few words of English. She wrote her impression of the situation:

> *I met with the family of Nuris. I loved Eldar a lot. The wife of Nuris is a nice lady, but now she needs a lot of support and advice. . . . I find myself in an awkward position as I'm not old and experienced enough to give her advice. I asked in the visa board [office] about the way to get a visa for Eldar as he is not yet 18. He needs some adult relative to go with him. The best thing is that his mother goes with him. . . . She is worried about the conditions in the USA; it will be great if she sees everything herself. I told her to write you everything as it was. I don't know what she has written exactly, but she didn't feel quite comfortable to tell you everything. The prices in Russia are incredible now, so she can't even think about asking you to pay for the tickets for her and Eldar. She was brought up when the USA was accepted as the enemy country and the country with very bad living conditions. So she is now afraid whether Eldar can get a good education in the USA.*

Now here was something quite new. We had not counted on elements of the Cold War entering the picture; it had never occurred to us that Ludmila might question the quality of the United States' education system. We rushed to reply by fax right away to deal with these fears. We stated that we could not afford to sponsor both Eldar *and* his mother, and so it was now essential for Professor Zlotin to find some way around this problem, else, as far as we could see, the visit would not happen. I had no choice but to leave for my trip with everything in the air. On May 16, Susan drove me the fifty or so miles to Indianapolis airport, where I departed on the first leg of my flight to Sofia. Normally this would have been a time of great excitement and expectation. But now I was leaving a situation full of uncertainties (except for the Fulbright money—which, fortunately, had arrived at the last moment). Susan would follow me one month to the day. I had no idea what the circumstances of my life would be like when I returned home in August. How long would my office survive being turned into a bedroom once I walked down that jetway?

Chapter 6
Corridors of Power

By way of the lovely Alpine state of Slovenia and the neurosis that was Croatia, I had arrived at the edge of Europe where it threatens to fall into Asia, and was now established in my fifth-floor apartment in Sofia. I felt about as remote as it is possible to be in Europe: isolated from almost everything—especially the capable organizational talents of my wife.

What was going on in Moscow regarding Eldar remained, most of the time, a mystery. Fragments of information filtered out, but now I had several additional problems: (a) I was moving around several Balkan states that were engaged in various stages of warfare, (b) I didn't know what news Susan had received, and vice versa, and (c) I didn't know what kind of communications were possible between Sofia, (Bulgaria's diminutive and totally charming capital), Moscow; and Bloomington—surely one of the more bizarre triangles outside Bermuda.

To fill in this gap I relied on the colorful narrative of Roman Zlotin and an extremely feeble-minded red Bulgarian telephone. Roman was pitted now against the tyrannies of one of the world's gold-medal bureaucracies. He wrote:

> *I have two problems: biggest is passport, second is ticket. It is impossible to get the overseas ticket without a passport containing much-prized US visa. At same time, also no ticket without formal letter of invitation, even though you had sent me the money. I was starting to work with the officials of the Academy of Sciences. I have many friends there and they can help me. This is [the] Russian way my friend. You see, there are different rules for the Academy of Sciences, certain privileges you might say, because we need to travel quite a lot to conferences and so forth. For this, we have, within our Academy, a special department of foreign*

affairs. We don't have to deal with the central machine as it were. He has informed me that I must go and see a top-level bureaucrat in our Academy who, alone, can make this happen. I have never before met this top-level person, and so I have, so to say, constructed a ladder of ever-ascending functionaries. The end of the ladder is, by coincidence, just in front of the door of this most elevated man. I have jumped from level to level, and the excellent news is that I have seen this solver of problems.

I know, very well, a lady in that foreign affairs office. I have been to the USA several times, as you know, and so she is familiar with me and my ways.

I said to her, "I am going to the States, and I would like to take with me a certain boy who has no passport," or words to that effect. She has informed me that I must go and see a top-level bureaucrat in our Academy who, alone, can make this happen.

I explained to him the sad story of Eldar, and stressed that the boy is going only for a visit.

"Most surely he will return," I assured him. To my considerable surprise this gentleman informed me

"That is not a very serious question for me. I will do it."

What has happened to our old bureaucracy that existed only to explain why this matter, or that matter, was absolutely impossible?

Roman

The Bulgarian Triangle

In Bulgaria I was established in Sofia right next to what was, and maybe remained, the headquarters of the Bulgarian equivalent of the KGB. I was here to help a new university work out a graduate program in public administration. The university itself was a somewhat informal and movable feast, and right now it was situated in a suite of dimly lit rooms over the local grocery store. But these were early days in its formation, and this was a fascinating community of scholars intent on bringing about change.

I also had to work closely with a body called the Center for Administration, which was headed up by a red-haired dynamo named Emilia Kandeva[4]. Emilia had certain characteristics that, when put together, looked like the answer to nuclear fusion. These qualities were: (i) she felt she was letting herself and the world down if she were not working on three things simultaneously; (ii) despite

---

[4] The story of this summer, remarkable in itself, was published as another book entitled *Summer in the Balkans*. Kumarian Press, West Hartford, Connecticut. 1994.

this she always had time for my most minute and absurd domestic needs. Her short stature and red hair, coupled with the constant certainty of her advice, made me feel like I had Dr. Ruth on a full-time consulting basis; (iii) she drove like Jehu, often conducting conferences in the car while so doing. She, poor woman, became my surrogate Susan as I tried to resolve all the Eldar problems in my head during this time. Many long hours she sat and heard the latest twist or turn. Often this patient counseling was conducted in her summer home tucked away in a spectacular valley north of the capital. Like Susan, she too was eternally optimistic that Eldar's coming was going to happen. We sat as she shelled peas or cleaned the mushrooms we had gathered that morning on the hillsides up among dozing shepherds and the restful gentle echoing of sheep- and cow-bells. In more practical terms, both Emilia and the university had fax machines. The fax was to be our lifeline for the next three months.

My apartment, provided for me by my hosts at the New Bulgarian University, had an engaging charm, perched as it was over the red tiles of the local skyline. From the kitchen I could sit and watch spectacular thunderstorms roll in from the dark mass of Vitosha Mountain, which provides the backdrop for Sofia. Other times I felt like Madame de Staël conducting her salons, as off-beat intellectuals gathered to discuss the fast-changing issues of the day over heady Bulgarian *Rakia*, the local variant of brandy. No visitor escaped without, at least, a brief update on the Eldar situation.

The most immediate link with the outside world resided on a shaky wire-frame table in the hallway. This was the red telephone. It looked to me as though it were made by the Fisher-Price company. From time to time it emitted a frail tubercular ring that occasionally went on to reach full ringing potential; at other times it never got beyond an agitated buzz. I never learned how to place a call to the USA on this machine, since phoning overseas was something that had to be reserved with the international operator well in advance, and then your life had to be given over to a monastic format, dedicating yourself to a state of total servitude to the telephone company until they decided to call you back. On the other hand, providing it had not rained in the last 24 hours, in which case the underground cable channels flooded completely and the monastic order went Trappist, taking involuntary vows of silence, it was possible for people in other countries to call me. Most of the time, callers—whether from overseas or across the street—sounded as though they were being held hostage in a cellar in Beirut and had been allowed one call with the sack still tied over their head.

One morning the phone rang at an hour that I had never previously suspected to exist. It was Susan who told me that she had received a form from the Russian embassy in Washington that had to do with inviting minors, and she had found it terrifying in its complexity. As a professor of public affairs, I understand the procedural nuances of these things and was able to offer informed advice.

"Trash it," I said, knowing that submitting such a form would just complicate matters inordinately.

Susan had also been thinking over Natasha's letter, and she said:

"I think we should just go there, to Moscow, and help Eldar's mother to do all this paperwork, get tickets, and so on. We can't leave her to handle all this on her own." Susan suggested. "How soon could you go?"

This was a five-alarm statement. How was I supposed to drop everything in Bulgaria, having just arrived there and started my Fulbright? Like most Europeans, I have a mortal fear of the telephone, agreeing with Andrei Codrescu, who once remarked that it was invented only to get bad news to you faster.

"No, I don't think so," I replied. "Even in the short time I was in the Soviet Union, I realized that Russia was a place quite beyond my comprehension. Everything was done under the surface through favors, barter, networks and so on. We would be absolute novices at this. Roman Zlotin had said that he would take care of it, and I think we should trust him." I prayed quietly.

"I suppose so, but Eldar's mother has never met me or you, and I have never met Eldar. I just thought it would help. Well, let's leave it to Roman for the moment."

I directed the conversation down more neutral and less threatening avenues. My tenure in the Balkans was, for the moment, safe.

Meantime Susan had met with a Russian-speaking graduate student who, during a visit to Moscow, took time out to meet with Eldar's family. It was so strange to be dealing with other people who were meeting the family while, to us, they remained quite unknown. It reminded me of a situation when I was growing up in Wales. Each time I visited my aunt and uncle there was often present an elderly, but very alert, lady present by the name of Mrs. Bevan. On one occasion, when I was about 20 or so, I went to tea with my aunt, and Mrs. Bevan was there. We got to talking about the family, and my much-married grandfather. As my aunt pieced together the elements of the family, Mrs. Bevan would correct her. This intrigued me, until eventually, when my uncle slipped into the kitchen to make tea, I joined him.

"How is it that Mrs. Bevan knows so much about the family?" I asked.

He looked at me rather strangely, but, without losing a stroke, said "she ought to, she's your grandmother."

Nobody had ever pointed this out to me, and since she had married again and had a different name, I had never made the connection.

The student Susan had located had brought back from Ludmila the necessary documents to help us establish ourselves as Eldar's legal guardians when he eventually arrived. One of these documents was his school record, which showed us he had changed schools an astonishing number of times moving between Uzbekistan, Moscow, and the Caucasus. Indeed he was shown as attending three schools in this year of 1992 alone. The record also demonstrated that Eldar appeared to be no Einstein, or at least that he had been performing at an indifferent level for some time. Bill, the returned student, told Susan that Eldar had met him at the subway station when Bill went to visit the family, giving the two of them a chance to talk on the stroll to the apartment.

Bill asked him directly, "Whose idea was this for you to go to America?"

Without hesitation Eldar replied "Mine."

Bill also said that he got the impression from Ludmila that Eldar might decide never to come back. He could not elaborate on that.

Susan, meantime, had been playing aggressive tennis to take her mind off the topic of Eldar, for it was beginning to obsess us both. Round and round in our heads it went: "He's only coming for a year, or maybe until he's 16 or 18, when he could decide about his future. . . .or maybe he will never go back."

On the morning of June 6, resting on a desk in the perpetual gloom of the Bulgarian university's sitting room/office, I found a one-line fax from Roman Zlotin telling me that he had "booked a flight for Eldar on August 24, the same flight as me [Roman]." This simple untarnished proclamation, however, camouflaged an uncommonly Byzantine process that I never appreciated until he told me about it months later, over dinner:

Again I have two problems: money and the passport. The ticket requires $500. I would have to illegally sell your dollars in Moscow, for I did not have this sort of money of my own. Also I did not know exactly how much it would cost because of the inflation. At the same time I could not wait for Eldar's passport as this operation needs 45 days. Without a passport he cannot get a visa, without passport and visa you cannot buy ticket. Big problem.

So I start to do everything. First problem, everything booked solid on Aeroflot, and I have to fly with Aeroflot, and Eldar has to fly with me. We have no time to wait for passport. Must find other way. Now, we can buy tickets from two agencies. One belongs to the Academy of Sciences; the other is available to the regular common Soviet people. So, I work in both directions. I visit the Academy office and ask them to reserve two tickets for me. They can do nothing without passport. Then I go to the regular agency, and there we have about 20 to 30 women selling tickets. They ask for official letter of invitation, passport, the works. They said they will put me on a waiting list. I understand in

> *this last case, I will get nothing. I try to meet the director of this agency, but it is extremely hard for he sits behind five doors, each of them locked independently. It is like five borders. But one day I opened all these doors, met him and found him to be a not very bad person.*
>
> *He and I, we find some common areas for conversation: I love his family that I have never seen; he loves Eldar whom he has never seen either. Soon he puts me on the list and said that everything would be ok.*

I know Russia better than that, and told him

> *"No, wait, please call directly and put our names there and give me a guarantee."*

He did. Amazing.

> *In this moment I have two things: a document to get a ticket with both names on it, and a promise of action on the passport, which, my friend, is a much tougher act. So I start to go all the time to our Academy foreign affairs office, sometimes with flowers, always saying*
> *"Hello, I'm Roman. Remember me?"*

But all those theatricals in Moscow were unknown to us in midsummer 1992. By now it was almost time for Susan to leave Bloomington and come to join me in Sofia for the rest of the summer. Just before leaving, she decided to make the plunge, and with the assistance of Voiko and other friends, she bought a bed for what would—she was convinced—be Eldar's room, and moved my computer into what we used to call the music room. The first I knew of this was when, somewhere toward the end of another frustrating, static-laden phone conversation, she added parenthetically,

"By the way, you're going to love the things I've done to the house!"

It seemed that Eldar's arrival was fated to happen. I realized that I should accept the inevitable. Once Susan's steel-trap mind had been set, resistance was futile.

Chapter 7
Crisis in Vienna

My temporary Bulgarian bachelorhood eventually came to an end one Tuesday afternoon. Emilia drove me to the airport like the early English queen Bodicea slicing through the Roman legions in her chariot. I was nervous with anticipation because, distractions apart, I had really missed the one person without whom life was pretty empty. The madcap frenzy of the last month could not disguise my loneliness. Several cups of hundred-octane Turkish coffee at the airport did not help calm me down. Then, more or less on time, through the glass of the customs hall in Sofia's decrepit airport, I saw the slight, familiar figure, and dark determined eyes of Susan, full of energy and determination, making her way for the exit. Hugs, kisses, and much love and affection traveled among the three of us. I certainly needed Susan's organizational skills, grit and sense of resolution. Most of all, I just needed *her*. I had been going soft in Sofia, falling into lazy and indolent ways. In short order she fired up, and while bouncing around unrestrained in the front seat of Emilia's Russian car she briefed me on what had happened via an unremitting stream of consciousness. The news was mainly that she had totally restructured the house "ready for Eldar." I sat there in the back of Emilia's gray Moskvich hatchback biting my lip and staring at Emilia in the rearview mirror. A knowing smile had spread across her face. She looked more like Dr. Ruth than ever, and she knew for sure what I was thinking as Susan poured out her pure energy.

"I am sure it looks just lovely, my dear," Emilia said to Susan looking me right in the eye.

I mentally intoned the last rites for my study, lately transformed into a teen's bedroom, but I was wiser than to put my thoughts into words.

"You've caught some wretched weather," I observed, feeling a need to avoid any further revelations about my changed domestic arrangements back in Bloomington.

The Energy, once we were back at the apartment, continued unabated, and was soon channeled into unpacking, inspecting, equipping and strategic planning for the remaining weeks.

"What on earth have you been eating? You have everything here to cook meals, but there seems to be no food."

"Well, I have had such a busy schedule. . ." I offered lamely.

"Let's go!" she said, and we started day one of the renaissance.

After Susan arrived, although this may sound like an impossibility, my life calmed down a bit. At the same time, we entered an information blackout on events in Moscow, and all we could do was wait as Roman Zlotin tried to scale the bastions of bureaucracy. We could not claim in any way to have forgotten about the Eldar story, but in the absence of new information we became even more boring on the subject, as we endlessly rehashed tired news.

The pace quickened one morning with a call from the New Bulgarian University to say that a fax had arrived from Roman in Moscow. We dropped everything and made our way through the streetside shoppers, trams and derelict cars to the office. There we read the fax that told us Roman had, indeed, secured the ticket—though he had not managed to get his hands on a passport yet—and one without the other would not do the trick. The problem now, he went on to say, was that he needed 45,000 rubles, which at this time was around $450. What was more, he needed it right away in order to secure Eldar's ticket. Unfortunately, Roman had forgotten to alert us to the fact that he would need the money well in advance

Prof. Zlotin and unlikely friend

of the planned departure from Moscow. Although I was carrying half the US Treasury strapped around my waist, I had no way to get it to Moscow. There was no modern, international banking system that I could discover in Bulgaria capable of performing this task. What could we possibly do?

Then Susan recalled, as we sat there at the Formica breakfast table fretting over this new hurdle, that an acquaintance of ours in the Indiana University geology department, Michael Hamburger, had mentioned he would be leaving for Moscow some time soon. We jumped up, rushed out, and I managed, through the good offices of the New Bulgarian University, to phone my secretary Kathleen back in Bloomington. I tried to convey the urgency in my best "drop everything" tone. She called around and discovered that the information was correct: Professor Hamburger was leaving for Russia—*the next day!* Though I knew Dr. Hamburger on a rather casual basis, I was about to test that acquaintanceship to the limits by asking him to take $450 of his own money—in cash—and to hand it over to a total stranger in Moscow. He, however was an old hand at the convoluted workings of the former Soviet Union, and he readily agreed. As soon as this information reached me back in Bulgaria, I rushed round to the other office and faxed Roman in Moscow with the details of Professor Hamburger's arrival so that they could complete the transaction. More and more this was beginning to feel like something Oliver North might have organized. Over a home-cooked dinner, we stared out across the ancient red-tiled roofs of Sofia, and wondered how all these arrangements were ever going to work. Only one link in this chain needed to break and we were sunk.

Susan and I were about to depart for a week-long conference on public administration at the magnificent Hofburg Palace in Vienna. After that we would move on to spend another week visiting a family who had lived in Bloomington for a year, and who now had moved back to their home in Slovenia's delightful miniature capital, Ljubljana. We anticipated a break from worrying about the situation in Moscow. Besides, it really did look like everything was moving now. Only the passport remained, although that could be the most impossible barrier of all. We had no choice but to leave Roman to deal with that, however. There was nothing whatsoever that we could contribute now. Or so we thought.

Everything was packed, Susan had checked all her departure lists, and we were standing in the hallway waiting for our ride to the airport. Just as the car arrived, there was a muted stutter from the red phone. It was Roman. It was a perpetual mystery how he could always get through when people round the corner had a less that fifty-fifty chance. Maybe it reflected the former position of the USSR over Bulgaria? We were pleased to hear Roman, because his calls nearly always meant progress.

"I got the money, thanks. I called Dr. Hamburger at his office and I said 'Hello, I am Roman.'

He said, 'Ok, what Roman are you?'

I told him, 'I am the Roman who is interested in $450,' and he told me he had it and I collected it."

That was good news since everything seemed to have gone according to plan. But then, Roman continued

"There is a small problem, my friend. It appears that Aeroflot may raise its fares and I may need more money. In fact I may need another $400, and I must buy the ticket in the next five days. I hope this is not a problem."

We froze.

It certainly *was* a problem, for even in Vienna it was barely possible to get money to Moscow reliably in that time, in cash. Roman did not want this money appearing through any official channels since he was not allowed to trade in dollars, and if he did not trade them on the street he would not get a reasonable rate of exchange. And today was Sunday.

All through the Vienna conference this logistical problem continued to haunt us as we investigated ways to get the extra money to Roman in time for him to buy the ticket without losing the reservation, especially after all the run-around it had cost him to get it in the first place. It seemed hopeless. He could not use money transfer, wire, checks or any of the normal international transfer methods. We were down to the ends of our fingernails with only two of the five days left to the ticketing deadline. By now we were left hoping that Roman could raise the money among his friends.

I had come to the final event of the conference, during which I would present my own paper. The people assembled were specialists on government in Eastern Europe, but I simply could not pay attention because my fevered mind was consumed with the eternal money problem. Then, we were at the final wrap up session, and the chairman was taking questions.

A speaker from the floor inquired, "Would it be possible to obtain further copies of the paper you mentioned?"

The chair, an Englishman, responded, "I would be happy to send those to you, but it will take a week or two because I shall be out of the office. *In fact I am leaving for Moscow tomorrow.*"

The effect was electric and I sat bolt upright in my chair. Emilia from Bulgaria, sitting next to me, jumped sideways and must have thought that I was having a heart attack. I immediately cornered the diminutive Englishman who promised to be my salvation, before anyone else could divert him, and hastily I explained my dilemma. Would he be willing to take the money?

"Of course," he replied. I agreed to give him the money that evening in his hotel room, for we were both staying in the same hotel. At 8 p.m. Susan and I, clutching a long envelope stuffed with bills, knocked at his door, then knocked again, and again, until, eventually Mr. Paul Collins appeared, clad in bath towel and trailing water. This procedure had now taken on the feel of a low-budget espionage movie. I thought back to the *Third Man*, and remembered that, at least, we were in the right city. Mr. Collins, disconcerted, accepted the money, and now more than ever, we felt that Sidney Greenstreet or Peter Lorre should appear from the shadows behind the door. Once more it seemed the hand of fate had saved us. However, a colleague at the conference, just arrived from the States, informed me that, as of yesterday, my secretary, Kathleen, had quit to follow her husband to a university in Ohio, so there was nobody holding down the Bloomington end of the triangle now. One door opens—another closes.

Final Tensions

Back in Bulgaria we could only hope and wait. In Moscow, Roman's exertions continued with vigor. We knew that their air tickets were booked for August 24, but there was no news on the passport. There was, in fact, no development in the story for the remainder of our time in the Balkans. I worried instead about how on earth we would communicate with someone who spoke no English, as we spoke no Russian. Finally, I asked an American colleague who had a teenage son about this question.

"How old is the boy?" he inquired.

"He will be almost 14," I responded.

"No communication problem there," he reassured me. "At that age they wouldn't speak to a parent in any language."

I was not reassured. Susan and I scouted the alfresco second-hand book market just up the street from where we lived in Sofia, for a Russian phrase book that might help us in the early days if—or *when* as Susan would say—Eldar came. Some of the more useful phrases in this book, printed in 1964, were

> *What are your trade-union affiliations?*
> *Where may I meet a representative sample of working people?*
> *Did you know that my county has consistently supported resolutions aimed at liberating oppressed peoples from colonial bondage?*

All these looked like useful ice breakers. I also drafted a long letter to Eldar's mother, Ludmila, trying to address many of the concerns that must be going through her head. If we are worried, what must she be feeling? Emilia's daughter Ivona translated it into Russian for me. But the high spot of the remaining time in Bulgaria was when we received our first communication from Eldar himself. He was working on learning some rudimentary English with Natasha and so was able to write, on the back of a photograph of his father, a short note saying that he was looking forward to coming to the

USA. It was charmingly headed *Deer Randall*. And so we waited for news from Roman. In Moscow Roman too was waiting. Later, over dinner he recalled the time vividly:

> *No one would normally, in the USSR, present you with a passport containing a visa until one day before you leave. So you were supposed to wait on your ears until the last moment before your departure. It is a typical Communistic tradition, to keep you in a situation where you are nervous. Then, in the last several hours, you receive your passport like a gift from God. The last evening, it was 6 o'clock, and I was sweating, when I got the call. But there they were—my old passport and a newborn one with Eldar's photo. I could not believe it.*

The last hurdle had been jumped. Or so it seemed.

Eldar's Recollections, 1992

Professor Roman Zlotin, who had been introduced to us by Randall, wrote a fax to Randall saying that he could probably get me a passport. He said that we would need an official invitation. He was going to Bloomington in August, and I could go with him. Otherwise they wouldn't let me on the plane by myself. We knew that it wouldn't be easy at all. We even started to doubt that it would be possible.

Bill Wood, Randall's graduate student, came to Moscow and visited us. He brought some money from Randall for a ticket. We gave him my school records for grades 1-7. He was really nice, he also spoke pretty good Russian. He was the second American I've ever met in my life.

Roman asked me for all necessary documents and photo for my passport. I came to his office to bring it to him. It was the first time I had ever met him, before that I had talked to him on the phone or my mom had met him. At one point Randall and Susan thought to come to Moscow to help us with everything. They were so worried, because the situation sounded impossible. Randall had already left for Bulgaria and Susan was still in Bloomington. She started rearranging the house, and preparing my room for my arrival. She was probably the only one who always believed that I could really come to Bloomington.

Finally one day, sometime in late summer, I went to see Roman with my mom. He said that he had a surprise for me. He handed me a brown bag on which it said: "For Eldar." I opened it, looked inside, and took out a Soviet passport; the first time I have ever seen a Soviet passport in my life. It was so strange because I was only thirteen, and we don't get a passport in Russia till we are sixteen. The second thing in the bag was a ticket. The ticket was for the 24th of August. I was so excited that my hands started shaking. I was so thankful to him, because he had done an impossible thing. He gave flowers and presents to people, so that he could get the passport for me.

In July I went to Leningrad to see my mom's relatives, and say good-bye. I showed them pictures of Randall and Susan, and everything. They were happy for me. They thought that it would be a wonderful experience for me. When I was going to the airport, my brother's car broke down. It was quite scary because we were supposed to be in the airport in half an hour. Somehow I didn't panic. (Actually I never do because I'm a laid-back personality.) Roman (my brother) called to his friend to ask him give us a ride to the airport. It was so hard to leave Moscow, my family, and my country.

Chapter 8
August 24, 1992

Our journeys through the Balkans at an end, we arrived back in Bloomington to face a terrifying schedule. In ten days we had to unpack, start work, collect Eldar and not only get him into school, but work out what he was supposed to study. We were frazzled by the whole thing. Susan's lists had proliferated dangerously. *The* day was upon us before we could really say we were prepared for it.

All through the hours until Eldar's scheduled arrival we were in a state of hopeless agitation. For me this derived from a mixture of Eldar's impending knock on the door of our lives, and of some equally impending, much-needed root-canal surgery scheduled for two days later. Feeling much like I had lost a Tae Kwon Do round with a mule, I existed in two conditions: the first was without codeine, in which case I was irascible, unreasonable and sometimes dangerous; the second was with codeine, in which case I felt as though I was suspended several feet above the ground floating on a pale lilac cloud. I alternated these conditions to be fair to my friends and to Susan. Furthermore, this was the week during which hoards of students would arrive to start the new academic year, and I was scheduled for all sorts of speeches and social events.

Our minds had been in a whirl ever since we had returned from Bulgaria. First we had to unpack from three months of living out of suitcases, then deal with the mountains of mail and with getting back to work, and finally we had to put the last touches to "Eldar's room," as it had already been named. I bade farewell to my old study, now laid out with a single bed, a chest of drawers, a cupboard. Ready. *Waiting.* My entire work existence had been transferred to the former music room where, at least, I had a view out across the yard. Susan had a very definite "I am so glad I had the foresight to do this" expression. I was beaten and I knew it.

We had had some late-breaking news from another of my students, Susan Cutting, who had been in Moscow for the summer. She went round to see Eldar's family several times, and became quite friendly with them. She corrected Bill Wood's earlier observation that "Ludmila is living with some older guy, maybe a boyfriend," by telling us that the person in question was Ludmila's own father, Eldar's grandfather. She told how Eldar was wild with excitement when Roman delivered his passport to him in a brown paper bag. We learned, also, that Ludmila thought that it was important for Eldar, at this time in his life, to have a male role model. Eldar had now moved from being a major topic of conversation with many of our friends to being the *sole* topic.

Susan Cutting also carried with her a letter from Eldar's entire family:

Greetings Dear Randall and Susan

We send this letter kindness of your graduate student Susan regarding the quickly-approaching departure of Zlotin and Eldar (in our country where documents are being processed up to the last minute we can't be sure that it will be a departure until it actually happens).

First of all, all of us (I mean the mom and our children) want to express our deep appreciation for your warm relations with our Nuris and for the gentle kindness you have shown to Eldarik [a diminutive form of Eldar]. Nuris was always so open to other people and to life. Eldar's character is so similar to his dad's, and we wanted him somehow to continue some of Nuris' ideas—at least his attitude to life.

Eldar's character is soft, and it seemed to us that in view of the warm attitude you have toward him, there shouldn't be any problems. But at the same time, 13-14 years is not an easy age and there may arise some unexpected manifestations and changes in his character. If Eldar does go in August, we want to correspond frequently with him. If there are any kinds of misunderstandings, we could settle them through correspondence. It is possible that life in your family will be very different from ours, and Eldar may be a little lost in the beginning, but children get accustomed to new things very quickly. . . .

Ludmila Vasilievna, Roman, Timur, Eldar.

On the 21st of August, Susan had phoned the high school to find out just what a non-English speaker does to get established there, and learned that he would have to take regular classes supplemented by *one* special English course for students who were learning English. We worried about how he would manage in school since we had no idea how much English he had picked up in the past few months. We also met with two professors from Moscow who gave us their impressions of the situation. They believed that he would almost certainly want to stay. "But," they counseled, "be careful not to get too attached because the day may come—and almost certainly will, since his family is all back in Russia—when he must go home."

On Monday, August 24, or "E Day," as we were calling it, when Roman and Eldar were supposed to show up at Indianapolis airport, all we knew was that if we didn't try to work through our normal daily routines we would most surely go crazy. We at least tried to go through the motions, but it was almost impossible. By now everyone we knew was fully aware of the significance of this day, and Susan, always hyperactive, was exposed to something like a late pregnancy phenomenon as friends asked how she felt, saying "When is he due?" By noon her stomach started to churn uncontrollably, as in some grotesque parody of morning sickness. I found myself talking incessantly about Eldar's arrival, like any expectant father would do.

The plane was due at Indianapolis at 9:40 p.m., so we had the prospect of a long period of agitation at home after work before we needed to depart for the fifty-minute drive. Before long we could stand no more of it, and left early. We had to be doing something—anything. On the way up I said to Susan

"You know what's really strange? This could well be the last moment of our old existence. After tonight our lives may never be the same again. It really is like the drive to the maternity hospital. Is this actually the end of the road that began with that limp piece of fax paper back in February, or I suppose, with that visit to Caucasia in 1990?"

Driving north through the last traces of the day, I ventured a question

"Did you really believe that this moment would ever actually happen?"

"Always," Susan replied—staring straight ahead at some point on the horizon approximately where the airport was situated.

But, of course, I knew that.

Roman and Eldar were flying, as only *Aeroflot* seemed to, via Iceland and Newfoundland. At the airport, the indications were that their connecting flight was on time. Our anxiety levels moved into high gear—Caucasia, Sofia, Vienna, and now, finally, Indiana. We were positioned at the end of the jetway, by the gate. The agitation built to insupportable levels, and we chattered vacuously and apprehensively to relieve the nervousness.

"What are we going to do when he comes through?" said Susan suddenly.

"We should try to make him know that he is really and truly welcome. Give him a big hug. That's what Brezhnev used to do," was all I could think of by way of advice.

I was not sure that Susan was a hugger, but it was worth a try.

The plane taxied in absolutely on schedule. An eternity passed, during which I noticed that Susan—eyes fixed maniacally on the jetway—had grasped my hand in a crunching vice-like grip. Slowly, a trickle of passengers started to emerge. Since this was a domestic connecting flight, most people were business types. Little did they suspect what magic and mystery was moving with them.

"THERE THEY ARE!"

Susan literally yelled, and started bouncing like a crazy ball, without once letting go of my now bloodless hand. Roman appeared in the throng some distance down the jetway. He was not easy to spot at first because he is rather short. Once he spotted me (Susan's face was still unknown to him), he was already full of smiles and was waving like Father Christmas arriving with the ultimate gift. Next to him, and to my astonishment, rising above him, was someone very different from the wraith of the Caucasus mountains whom I had left behind that soggy, mist-laden morning in June 1990. He had filled out, was much taller—just an inch or so shorter than Susan—and the mop of black hair had been shorn. I was, momentarily, astonished. I don't know why I expected him to look exactly as he had two years before. He was not smiling, but was doing his very best to look dignified after 20 hours in the air.

Then came the smile, and Susan was lost forever.

"I knew instantly," she wrote in her diary that night, "that we will come to love him quickly, and that we hope that he will be able to stay with us for more than a year. He is quiet, maybe exhausted, but terribly charming and likable."

The avuncular and jolly Roman, decked out in denim, gave me an even-more devastating hand crusher, and said with a splendid flourish and sweep of the arm,

"Here is Eldar. *Finally*!"

At which Susan and I proceeded to hug the lad. He was rather stiff and unyielding at this stage in the face of such an onslaught, especially from people he barely knew. His face was encompassed by a totally endearing, horribly embarrassed, smile.

"Hello. How are you?" he asked.

His voice was much deeper now (though he could not have spoken more than 10 words to me while I was in Caucasia, so my basis for comparison was limited). I noticed right away that he still fixed you right in the eye when he talked to, or acknowledged, you. Whatever else may have changed, that had not. Susan had turned to Jell-O.

For his travels he was clad in a Mickey Mouse T-shirt and a pair of white jeans, both of which were too small for him. The clothes were also rather ripe after such a long period of travel. Susan, meticulous in all matters of personal hygiene, rolled her eyes as she recovered from the rather clumsy hug. I could see she had plans for him.

After we loaded our bags in the car in the airport parking lot, Susan asked the three of us to pose for what would be Eldar's first photograph in the United States. We then headed out of the airport. There were a million things we wanted to ask and say. We, however, were too excited to think straight, and they were too exhausted to comprehend much as far as we could tell. Roman was, of course, translating everything for Eldar, so we really didn't know to what extent he had learned some English. He was still revealing nothing in his extraordinarily set Soviet expression, though he seemed reassured at the sight of at least one face he knew from the past in these totally unfamiliar surroundings. He asked no questions and he showed no strong emotions. This was hard to read, especially for Americans who have a strong need to be liked instantly and demonstrably. On the other hand he was probably exhausted.

Since he was in the USA we decided we should probably plunge right into the American culture and stop at a McDonald's for a snack on the road from the airport. In Moscow, at that moment, it would have been necessary to queue at Russia's first McDonald's on Pushkin Square for four hours for this same culinary delight. I had a drink to accompany my Excedrin since my root canal problem was awakening rapidly, probably as a result of all this nervous excitement. Eldar was confounded by choice at the counter, and I remember vaguely some love affair between him and ice cream, so I selected a frozen yogurt for him. The cone is an impossible piece of unstable engineering piled absurdly high. Roman broke into laughter at the sight of it, and Eldar's face creased into a quiet, controlled smile, and genuine anticipation of so much pleasure. As Susan snapped a second photograph, this time of him with Roman and frozen yogurt, he recovered his solemn and unsmiling official pose.

It was too dark to see anything on the drive home, though much the same could be said for this journey in the daylight too, as the area north of Bloomington is dispiritingly flat and featureless. It is only as Bloomington gets closer that the diminutive hills begin, the woodland starts to multiply, and the horizon closes in to a more intimate and cozy distance. Bloomington is often called an oasis in the rural expanse of southern and central Indiana, and it certainly is. It is, of course, an archetypal campus town dominated by the limestone edifices of Indiana University, and set about with the glories of its meticulously maintained campus. Not only is it an oasis, but it also has the qualities of a timewarp, for this is still Norman Rockwell's America: the main drag (that teenagers still cruise on Friday night), the courthouse square, a decidedly southern pace, and a sense of secure well-being upset only by the collective angst of so many prima donnas and intellectuals perilously gathered together in such a small space. On the other hand, Norman Rockwell's small-town America probably did not have two Tibetan restaurants and 1400 classical music performances, including full-scale grand opera, every year.

When we got home I took him through the front door, and the smile on his face was all the reward we needed. Our house had been our greatest source of joy. Utterly unpretentious from the outside with no architectural merit, inside it is made warm by its all-wood interior, glorious rugs, and the accumulated bric-a-brac of a lifetime. The main room belies the small exterior of the house, and is solid glass on three sides. Around three of the walls are arrayed tiers of tropical plants lit from below. I find the whole effect timelessly beautiful, and the only thing I find more beautiful is to stand out in the darkness in the acre of yard, under one of the 50 trees and look in through the great windows. It looks like an elaborate theater set. In addition, all the remnants of my earlier life in Britain are here too, having traveled with me in 90 boxes back in 1985 when I made the commitment to come to America forever. Most of all I love the totally un-European phenomenon of being able to live on this acre of ground with its majestic trees only seven minutes from my office door. It was terribly important to us that Eldar also felt this house could become his home. Quite often, and quite spontaneously, Susan and I would say to each other, "I love this house." We never tired of saying that we loved it.

We ushered Eldar, and his huge black bag, down the corridor to my former study. When shown his room his happiness was more than evident, and he opened the big, black travel bag and started to put out pictures: a large portrait of Nuris; a picture of Nuris in Red Square; a picture of Nuris in Afghanistan, several large black-and-white enlargements of family groups—some clearly Russian, others Central Asian. Now I felt base and mean for having resented the appropriation of my erstwhile study. Susan was suffused with a glow of what looked dangerously like maternal warmth, probably mixed with deep satisfaction at my guilt over my previously ignoble behavior. How could I deny anything to that smile?

By now it was close to midnight. Roman had agreed to stay overnight to help communicate some of the basic items that Susan and I would have to discuss with Eldar in the morning. Even though at that midnight moment both travelers must have been close to catatonic, they held up well, and we cracked open a bottle of champagne to toast our new house guest—and the man who made it all possible. Eldar went once more into his huge, formless black bag and drew out a Russian shawl for Susan, a chunk of rock crystal, several art books, and last of all something totally indefinable that was about eight inches long and half-cylindrical in shape. We had absolutely no idea what it was, and he asked us to guess. We were mystified, and confessed ignorance. Then Eldar told Roman in Russian what he was holding. Roman was clearly astonished, his eyebrows shot up, and his mouth formed a perfect "O" of surprise. He looked at the object with new respect.

"Here is something amazing" he said. "It is part of a woolly mammoth tusk that Nuris found in the Siberian Arctic."

I was so touched by this that I really didn't know what to say. Remembering my experience in Russia, I gave him a big hug. He seemed to think that was ok. But he remained as wooden and embarrassed as before.

By 1:30 a.m. Eldar was finally in bed. He had said very little, and even when he gave us the gifts the ceremony was mostly one of actions rather than speech. But now we had the first real chance to talk to Roman face to face.

"You know," he began suddenly before we could say anything, "I don't think he will ever leave. You have met him before, Randall, and you know that he is no ordinary boy."

I wasn't absolutely sure I knew what that meant, though I had to agree that Eldar was unlike any other child his age that I had met. Then Roman told us of his final nervousness regarding the departure, about which he had previously said nothing. This involved putting Eldar's new passport to the test at Moscow airport. He took a cognac and started:

First, I am full of nerves about what would happen at the airport, because we have to go through immigration in Russia when we leave too. We had to get up at a terribly early hour, and Eldar's brother [also called Roman] had offered to drive us to the airport. He is there on time, but on the way to the airport his car broke down, and is totally dead. I can't believe that we have made it so far just to give up now. I called a friend, and he came rushing round in his car, found us on the roadside, and took us the rest of the way just as fast as he could go.

Next I am nervous about immigration. I do not have the same family name as Eldar, and Eldar's passport said that he is not only from the Academy of Sciences, but that he is Academician. That is our highest rank you know, and even I do not have this. How do you imagine this 13-year-old got it? Maybe a genius? Also, he is 13, and the youngest age for a passport is 16. This could be the end for us, right there and then. But, nothing happened. In fact nobody asked me anything. Usually we get lots and lots of really stupid questions from the KGB frontier police.

On this occasion the guy just compared the photographs with our faces, and waved us through. I could not believe it.

Eventually, we were all too exhausted to proceed even with this exhilarating tale, and reluctantly gave up our hold on this, possibly, most important day of our lives. The clock had abandoned it hours since.

I said, half jokingly, to Susan, "I think you have fallen hopelessly in love with this boy."

"It is impossible not to," she replied.

I knew she was right. Before finally going to sleep Susan wrote in her journal—a habit she had maintained since she was seven:

He makes us want to make him happy and make him smile. I think, and hope, that he will be happy here, and that we will do a good job of nurturing him and teaching him. He clearly is a special person, and for us to be entrusted with him was a tremendous honor and privilege. Both Randall and I get the feeling this was, somehow, destined to happen; it just seemed so right. How lucky we are.

The first days

Unfortunately, our first full day with Eldar was somewhat complicated by the fact that I was scheduled for root canal surgery at 9 a.m. Some days later we decided to take Eldar to the dentist for a regular check up.

"When you come home from school tomorrow I will be here to take you to the dentist," I informed him.

"Why?" he asked, "I am not in pain!"

That morning I also had to give a speech to newly arrived graduate students at my school's orientation. Susan would stay home from work to see Eldar through his first acquaintance with Bloomington. Things were going to have to move swiftly for him because he appeared to have almost no clothes in that capacious bag, and we had to become his legal guardians before he could start school. In fact school started officially the day after his arrival, but he would just have to miss the first few days as we got him some clothes, took him to have some required vaccinations, and to choose his courses with his school counselor. He would not have much time to relax. Fortunately, Emilia, our great friend from Bulgaria, was also a visiting professor that semester at Indiana University, and she spoke Russian fluently. She would be joined by her youngest daughter Martina, who was also starting in the same high school, but a year ahead of Eldar.

We decided that clothes were the first priority: a closer look in Eldar's bag revealed only two pairs of underpants, two pairs of socks, a few shirts and pairs of pants that already looked too small, and a winter jacket. We took him on his first foray into the world of big-time shopping. When confronted with the "young adult" section of the clothing store—for Eldar was too big for the children's section even though he was only 13—it soon became clear that he was wholly confounded by choice. Susan exhorted him to buy some things that he *really liked*, and he stood there like a fish out of water.

"Come on, Eldar. Do you like this?" Susan inquired, holding up item after item, to which there was a general nod of approval, but no sign of any conviction.

I don't think choice had featured much in his world up to this point and he had not yet become a motivated consumer. We could only work back from the null hypothesis, for he was eventually able to tell us what he strongly disliked. I was alarmed as this would mean selecting by eliminating every other item in the store. That was a rather backwards way of doing things. In addition it would take about four months. Furthermore, he seemed astonished when we suggested that he try things on before we bought them, but he did, disappearing into the changing room and emerging to model his new attire. Eventually we had a basic wardrobe, and we never saw Mickey Mouse come out of his closet again. Then, when one of my colleagues presented him with a pair of khakis, we knew we were beginning to get somewhere when we saw a real gleam of appreciation. The spark of consumerism had ignited.

At school we faced a similar problem, when he was confounded by the huge list of courses and options. In Moscow the program had been, to a much greater extent, settled for him. Here, Emilia and Susan worked with him, in the company of his school counselor—another new and bewildering concept for us— to establish his new program of study. Eldar was bemused to find that he would be taking six courses, and not 13 as in Moscow. The process also was slowed down, rather than accelerated, by his amiable willingness to take everything suggested. Some, clearly, were totally mysteries to him: "Study Hall?"

At double-quick time, at lunchtime, the entire Bulgarian/Russian/American ensemble poured into the car and headed off across campus where documents were lodged with a lawyer to transform us into his legal guardians. Things were really moving along. Emilia's effervescent daughter Martina, something of a veteran of the US high-school system, bubbled away in Russian to an Eldar who seemed to have moved to another planet. We were not sure whether it was culture shock, or the attention of the utterly vivacious Bulgarian redirecting his life from so very close. He was going to be 14 soon, after all. She described the courses jabbing at the printout. He watched her face, not her finger. Were we going to have trouble?

Amid this frenzy, on a truly beautiful late summer day, Eldar made it clear by gestures that he would like me to go with him on a walk around our subdivision to get some feel for his new surroundings. We were fortunate to live in what the realtors call a "mature" area, meaning it has magnificent towering oaks, spruces, and in the case of our yard also, a lone, wonderful elm. As we strolled in the glorious sunshine, I explored the extent of his English. Despite his limited exposure to the language, he showed no hesitation in trying it out. As we walked he stared at the ground, his face a picture of intense concentration as his brain assembled a sentence from the very limited number of parts available. We had to name each tree, dog breed, car, and object along the way: the sight of a familiar breed or species brought forth "We have that one." Susan and I had decided some time back that we would be most comfortable if he simply called us by our first names, and I was happy to see that he showed no reluctance to do that. As we progressed other marvels were revealed, especially when dogs came bounding across lawns only to stop at some imaginary electronic boundary. I gathered from our walk that he had a moped back in Moscow and had a powerful yearning to achieve the American dream of motorized movement. He surprised me by using the term "fox terrier," when describing his brother's dog. Momentarily he fell silent again, while the assembly line in his mind was in full production. Then, as we passed a sycamore that reminded him of the ubiquitous Russian white birch tree, out came his first full sentence:

"Why there are no tall buildings in Bloomington? In Moscow we live in tall building."

I was astonished, and muttered something to the effect that this is a small town and the people don't wish to see the skyline disrupted by huge geometric shapes. I am not sure how I put that in words of one syllable.

"I see," he responded.

I felt like a proud parent whose child had just uttered the first words. It certainly beat "Dada."

In the afternoon he phoned home to his family. From the lounge, we heard him shouting wildly into the receiver. Like all good, modern, parents, we immediately became frenziedly neurotic with anxiety.

"Eldar," said Susan, slowly and clearly, "Is anything wrong? Do you have a problem with your mother?"

Everything had gone so well that we could not imagine problems at this stage.

"No mother," he responded.

We gathered that the person on the other end was his brother Roman.

"I see. But what is wrong?"

The reply was totally incomprehensible to us, and we started to worry even more. Eventually Eldar ran from the room. Susan and I exchanged confused glances, not knowing what to do. As we stood there Eldar rushed back into the room clutching a book and staring intently at one page, his finger running up and down the printed words. Suddenly the book was thrust in front of us, the finger glued to a point on the page. The book was a dictionary, the word was *deaf*. At that moment I learned two things: (a) Roman was deaf; (b) Eldar is a nail-biter. Neither condition was to improve.

School: Into the Deep End

Having never had children, and having grown up overseas, neither Susan nor I knew the ropes about daily life at an American high school—lockers and the like. We had worked out what a school bus was because there was always one in front of me when I desperately needed to get somewhere fast, and we knew, more or less, how the system functioned. Eldar was enrolled at the northern of our two high schools. This is curious as we live on the south side of the city, but it appears that some years ago when there was some difference between the two schools, some chicanery had been conducted to encompass the tiny outlier of our subdivision into the northern catchment. At 7 a.m. on the overcast morning of Thursday, August 27, we huddled round Eldar, whose misfortune it was to be one of the first pick-ups on the school-bus run that takes an hour before it disgorges its cargo. His misfortune was compounded by the fact that the bus also collected the children for the middle school whose presence was infinitely demeaning to those on the Olympian heights of high school status. He boarded and was gone, and we really felt like parents then. People standing around must have wondered why we were so uncertain and excited about putting a child on a school bus—especially when the child was 13. Where had he been all these years?!

Getting him home, however, would be another matter. Susan took some time off work to drive to the school, capture him before he could get lost, and steer him to the correct bus out of the dozens lined up around the building. As she waited, the tail end of hurricane Andrew clouded the skies, roused the wind, and then unceremoniously dumped inches of water from a quite literally *green* sky on the emerging hoard as they discharged from the school. Eldar's first day ended in something akin to the apocalypse. His initial class had been in stained glass; a concept that mystified him totally, but which, we learned over tea, he seemed to have enjoyed, though we had no evidence of any prior interest in decorative work. In his English class, it slowly emerged, he wrote four complete sentences. His progress was astonishing already. We had a genius on our hands. And probably Michelangelo too. Best of all was his evident comfort with the way the day had gone.

We had invited jolly Roman Zlotin to come and translate the day's events for us. It seemed that Eldar was taking this all in his stride. He had no problems, and no questions that Roman could discern. Overall, he still remained rather serious, introspective and quiet—though a vocabulary of about 60 words will do that to you. All that changed, however, when of all things, he and Roman discovered in a drawer, a book entitled *The World's Tackiest Postcards*, and they were both helpless over the table in no time. Eventually this distinguished academician and a 13-year-old boy he barely knew were shedding tears over a picture of a pig diving off a springboard into a swimming pool. Humor is universal.

When they were eventually able to speak again Roman put his arm around Eldar's shoulder, and said,

"Well Eldar. Here is the end of your first day. How do you feel?"

"I feel like ice cream," he replied without hesitation.

This was wonderful. Here was someone who could express my innermost thoughts about things I would never dare mention in our regulated domestic environment of balanced food groups. Baskin Robbins was the beneficiary of this new surge of international solidarity. But all the time I was wondering, as we spoke to Eldar mostly through Roman, and later through Emilia and Voiko, how on earth was it going to be possible for him to continue his education when he spoke almost no English? And he was taking regular classes in English with native English-speakers! It was not too surprising, then, when he came home with his first test scores. He had zero across the board. Of course, this only served to raise in me a whole new wave of doubts: Wasn't this just going to make him frustrated and unhappy? Should we take him out of school and try to give him more English? How would he cope? What were we doing to him?

Eldar's Recollections 1992

When we flew over New York city, it was a very different from Moscow. I saw big houses with swimming pools, boats, etc. When we were changing the planes, we had to go to the different airport, it was the first time I've ever heard people speak English. The airport in New York was so crowded, thousands of cars, buses, etc. When we got to our new gate Roman decided to call Randall, but there was no one home. Professor Zlotin and I arrived at Bloomington after a long day of flying. It took us about 20 hours. On the night of the 24th of August I came down from the plane in Indianapolis. Randall and Susan met us at the airport and we drove to Bloomington. I can't remember much about the ride, because I was exhausted from the long trip. On the way back we stopped at the McDonald's, I wasn't very hungry, but I couldn't resist to have an ice-cream cone. I can't really remember my first impressions, because I was really tired. The house seemed very big and very nice. Not a lot of people in Moscow live in houses; they usually live in apartments. Except some people have summer houses, which are usually not in Moscow but outside the city, where they go for a vacation or for a weekend. Though we had a summer house very close to our apartment, which is very lucky for Muscovites.

I slept well the first night. In the morning, for a minute, I couldn't tell where I was. Roman stayed the night with us. Breakfast was quite an experience, it was the first time I had cereal; I quite liked it. I even ate it for lunch; but not for long. I was very eager to see Bloomington. Susan took me and Roman to Roman's apartment. I was very nervous, because I couldn't say very much in English, especially after Roman left, because he was the only person I could talk to. Even though I knew some words, I was scared to use them.

Welcoming the new arrival

Chapter 9
Settling In

In a remarkably short space of time Eldar was part of the family, just as the cliché has it. It really seemed as if he had always been there. Susan and I discovered our respective parental qualities. Susan was ever watchful of his homework, his personal hygiene (deodorant was a novelty to him), coming-home hours, and the like—even marking shower days on the kitchen calendar to Martina's amazement and Eldar's everlasting humiliation. As for me, I was always wanting to indulge my own childhood fantasies such as the impromptu ice cream, taking off for nowhere in the car, strolling the main drag for no reason whatsoever, in other words, doing the things first my mother, then my wife,

Voiko captures the family in its native habitat

steered me away from in my "best interests." Almost from the beginning it was clear to me, that there existed a solid bond between the two of us. There was never any question of building up trust, gaining his confidence, or any of the other problems associated with taking in an older child who was, more or less, an unknown quantity. He always wanted to do things with me, and was always ready just to sit and talk—insofar as we could at this early stage. But as the hours went by we came to know each other just a little better with each encounter. I also continued a tradition that his father had begun, which was to give him a ritual back rub before bed. This was when I discovered that years of skiing had left their mark, for he was built as though from granite without one ounce of fat or loose muscle. Most of all I felt that, ridiculous though it sounds in such a brief time, we loved each other and positively enjoyed being together.

He was plainly a person who had great inner strength, but revealed none of his private emotions. Never once, for instance, did he give any indication of the deep sense of loss he felt for Nuris, though it was evident from the number of photographs that appeared on his walls, he did have such feelings. I also remembered clearly how Eldar had hung on every word his father said. But he never seemed to suffer outwardly from homesickness or disorientation. We never found him sad, contemplative, or remorseful, or musing on days gone by. He simply seemed to have devoted himself inwardly to the challenge of moving on. Much later he hinted that in fact, he did have to contend with such feelings during the early days, and, on reflection, it would have been extraordinary if he did not. He was just remarkably skillful at concealing his emotions from us and everyone else.

In all respects he turned out to be a parent's dream (though I am convinced all parents would write the same even if their child turned out to be a homicidal maniac). First, Susan discovered, to her great joy, that he ate *everything*, even though he declared to her it would be no bad thing if we had meatloaf every day from now on. This did not mean that he *liked* everything, but at least he was willing to try it. He devoured fruit as fast as it could be replenished. As a result of her four years in the Peace Corps in the Fiji islands, Susan was adept at conjuring up Indian dishes, and she and I were both partial to hot, spicy meals. Probably as a result of his time in Uzbekistan, Eldar would match us, chili for chili, at those culinary championships. He was partial to meat, but would eat vegetarian casseroles just as happily. Susan was astonished that despite the fact that he had the normal teenager's genetic antipathy to anything green, he liked broccoli and cauliflower, although beans and asparagus fared less well. Some struggle was involved in preventing them from being left to last in order that he might declare, "I am so full I could not eat another thing." Especially as this was usually followed by "what's next?" After hearing one of our friends state she was a vegetarian, Eldar asked her what that meant. When she explained, he thought about it for some time, and then declared, "I am dessertarian."

Slowly but surely, too, his earlier confusion and indifference about clothes began to yield to an awareness of what passes for fashion in the teenage years although, mercifully, he never acquired the peer-pressure driven addiction to advertised designer name brands that has replaced religion among American teenagers. Nevertheless, there were still moments of adjustment, such as when we came to do the laundry at the weekend and, on opening his laundry bag, Susan found only *one* pair of underpants! She took care of that with a short but forceful instruction on the need to change these daily. He was mystified, clearly attributing this drive for cleanliness to some sort of incomprehensible American paranoia. Nonetheless, from time to time the underwear count would fall, and Susan would repeat her injunction by placing the one, or two, items on his bed with a suitably inscribed *Post-It* note attached. They communicated in this way, by underwear, for some time.

Most astonishing of all was the speed with which he acquired English. Indeed it was so rapid that we barely noticed him learn. He was, on the other hand, rather quickly, appalled at the ungrammatical English he heard. When a school instructor asked him, using a classic Hoosier grammatical form, "Where is Mike at?" Eldar could not resist the temptation to reply "He's *at* inside." Our all-time favorite Hoosierism was, without doubt, the statement, *"If I'd knowed I could have rode I would have went."* Each day we were able noticeably to communicate a little better. We placed great emphasis on eating together so we always had a chance to talk and be a "family." We loved this new experience, and I could not imagine why we had dismissed it so easily before Eldar entered our lives.

He passed through a number of language phases on his way to fluency. In the earliest phase he worked mainly through the use of single words, but that rapidly yielded to short sentences. Of course, at school he had no medium of communication other than English, since at least as far as he could tell, there was no other Russian speaker there. Martina, like all Bulgarians, spoke a little Russian, but she was a year ahead and rapidly becoming the focus of adoring attention by most of the school's male population. One fascinating and rather bizarre way Eldar coped with the language problem, at this early stage, was to use an armory of incomprehensible and fantastic noises to fill in the gaps and maintain the flow and momentum of what he was trying to say. Chief among these noises were frantic— but very convincing—imitations of Donald Duck interjected at critical moments. For several months we learned to live a sort of cartoon existence not unlike that of the detective in *Who Framed Roger Rabbit?*

Ivona (l) and sister Martina, the other Bulgarian factor

Another device with which we had to become familiar was the tense indicator. Since Eldar knew only the present tense of major verbs, he had a problem when it came to putting accounts into the past or future tenses. This he eventually achieved by pointing his finger forward to indicate the future tense, and, with his thumb, back over his shoulder for the past tense. Soon, meals became something that Victor Borge could have scripted. In these curious ways did we come to know each other. Each mealtime became an idiosyncratic affair in which we would hold conversations with a duck using American Sign Language. But you get used to anything given time.

Back in Moscow, Eldar had seen almost any film that made it to Bloomington, mainly as a result of his cutting so much school. So, after two months we trooped, as a family, to see *Batman Returns* (something else we would have been unlikely to do before). As we made our way through the press of people coming out of the cinema, we asked Eldar what he had thought of the film.

After a moment he informed us earnestly "The role of the Penguin had many defects."

That immediately reminded me of a time when I had been in the Orwellian world of Albania back in 1977. As I browsed around a bookstore that seemed to sell only the 19-volume collected works of Party Secretary Enver Hoxha, I made conversation with the ten-year-old behind the counter.

"Do you speak English?"

"Of course" (with steely glare)

"Is that your English book?"

"It is, would you like to see it?"

I did look at it and it was an archetype British colonial period book full of middle class white people chasing their dog around the yard.

"How do you find this book?" I asked the young Albanian.

"It is perfectly adequate for a bourgeois-liberal text" he told me.

It had never struck me that way when I used it 30 years earlier.

But it was in the realm of homework that the language problem became greatest. Naturally we could help him with his English classes by trying to explain the meaning of words, though this became a nightmare with abstract concepts like *meaning*. Then we resorted to the heavily thumbed and dog-eared Russian-English dictionary, though it was extraordinary how little we used it after the initial few months. Every evening until bedtime, apart for a break when we ate, was given over to slow, laborious explanations of the meaning of the homework questions or assignments before he could attempt to answer them. The day then ended, almost always at 9 p.m. with a backrub. There was one exception. One night he yelled out in panic, and I rushed in to find him backed up on top of his bed. He was staring out at an opossum, which was returning his gaze through his bedroom window. He had no idea what it was, and fancied it to be the world's most gigantic rat.

As each week passed, however, the homework tasks seemed to become a little easier, and then we began to notice that he came to us only with specific questions, not with the entire homework, before he returned to his room. Eventually he did not come to us at all, and the link remained only through Susan's frequent exhortations, such as

"How many projects do you have? When are they due? Don't you think you should take a break from the computer games?"

Our parental joy knew no bounds when he came home clutching his algebra test complete with an A+. We pointed to the grade with animated pride.

"What does it mean?" he asked.

In his English class, the teacher assigned five idioms each week, such as to "put your foot in your mouth," or "twist someone's arm." At first he found these incomprehensible, but we helped explain them and he usually did well on the weekly idiom quizzes. Susan, who had an MA in Applied Linguistics, was fascinated by his progress, and marveled at Eldar's ability to hear a word once, then remember it forever. It was just like first-language acquisition. We had been warned he would be too old to learn English properly or easily, but, happily, as it turned out, he was not. After only two months he stunned us by saying that he was already thinking and dreaming in English.

One of the major differences with which Eldar had to cope was that of living in the suburbs of a small campus town (Bloomington has around 100,000 people—of whom 35,000 are nomadic IU students). His previous existence had been in one of Moscow's vast high-rise apartment blocks. There he was surrounded by children, and could walk to school with his friends. Now, in our neighborhood with its one-acre plots, he was surrounded by the mostly childless professional classes or older retired folk.

We had come to realize that Eldar was, deep down, a very shy individual when it came to making friends, though he appeared, probably as a result of his time with his father, to be perfectly at home with university students and professors at dinner parties. For example he soon discovered that *nothing* in the United States is impromptu or spontaneous. If you want to meet someone, then you telephone ahead, and this he could not bring himself to do for many months. In Moscow people did not call each other, they generally just dropped in—something I remember vividly from Wales. On the other hand, Eldar was not hesitant about answering the phone, and it took me quite a while to get used to this low, accentless voice saying "Hello, followed by a silence," when I called home. Furthermore, so many American parents seem to be mortified by often inflated and ridiculous accounts of child molestation, assault-rifle attacks and so forth (some of which may be true for the larger cities) that they become paranoid about their offspring's safety. It takes a long time to cut through this, and naturally it was at first all totally incomprehensible to Eldar, whose *modus operandi* was just to get up and do something, not plan it three weeks in advance. Even sport was not spontaneous, and he had a season or so of soccer, but that was conducted in a manner that ensured that no human contact whatsoever would ever take place among the participants. The children would arrive together in their parents' cars five minutes before the game, and were then rushed off by the same suffocating parents immediately afterwards. I was astonished to find that there was no recreation period at school in which children could mix, and that physical instruction was satisfied by one miserable semester of participation. Perhaps Susan and I were cynical because we did not grow up in this culture, or did not become parents in the slower, more conventional way, but it did seem to us that the "American Way" tended to deprive the children of the pure joy of just being children and indulging in anything spontaneous. Occasionally children need something that is not supervised or organized, for that is what being a child all is about, but here spontaneity was taboo, and all green spaces in the city were filled in as quickly as possible with a passion by the mayor. I suppose we simply do not trust children ever to be alone, or to be children any more. It is not surprising so many become neurotic since they grow up stifled and bored. Given such a different context, we really worried about how Eldar would be able to develop solid friendships.

A Gathering of Friends

On September 27, little more than a month after his arrival, Eldar was to become 14, and this was an opportunity to thank all the people who had helped in bringing him here. He had already gained some fame by being featured—in full color—on the front page of the local newspaper with an accompanying article titled *Tragedy Brings Teen to Bloomington*. For days afterward he affected to cringe at the expression "Oh, you're the little Russian boy . . ." Secretly he loved it. The article also served a useful function in letting his teachers and schoolmates know something of his background, for he would rarely initiate a conversation.

The night before his birthday, thanks to Eldar's regular and mercifully early retirement hour of 9 p.m., Susan worked on a cake for him. In the Russian tradition we put a small present under his pillow soon after he fell asleep. Before going to bed Eldar had called his family in Moscow. As usual in these conversations, he clutched the phone and occasionally said *horosho* (good, or OK), while the amount of news he actually seemed to convey was

Eldar makes the local newspaper

minimal. It was still extremely curious for us, knowing he had this other family out there, most of whom were completely unknown to us except from the photos on his bedroom wall. He almost never talked about Moscow or Russia, or home. One exception was occasional mention of his deaf brother Roman, who was a most accomplished skier and who had competed in the deaf Olympics in Canada. Where Roman was concerned, Eldar nursed the typical teenager's admiration for an older brother.

Susan and I had planned to get up early, something that was anathema to Eldar, so that while the birthday boy was still asleep Susan could ice the cake. She was furtively engaged on this exacting task when she was almost propelled through the kitchen skylight at 8 a.m. by a silent intruder who shouted "BOO!" and threw his arms in the air. Susan screamed fit to raise the dead. It turned out he had been up most of the night in anticipation of the day, and he was already wearing the "Kiss me it's my birthday" pin that Susan had concealed under his pillow—though he would die sooner than allow anyone to do that.

"Get out of here right now!" the still-startled, but laughing, Susan yelled, chasing the chuckling Eldar out of the kitchen and round most of the house before confining him to his room.

His first birthday present had him in such a state of agitation that we were barely able to control him until it was revealed. Through the good offices of a colleague in the school we had arranged to take Eldar up in a sailplane. The fortunes were certainly with us as we had a near-perfect day, the sky azure, the temperature high, and the thermals forming visibly in ascending clusters of wispy clouds. He was ecstatic as he soared and fell over the Indiana/Illinois border, until his pilot, a man in his mid-60s with a perverse sense of humor, dropped the glider into a stall-spin causing Eldar to come close to losing his lunch. We matched him heave for heave as we watched from the ground. But it was all contrived—or so they said later.

That evening the key players in the Eldar story gathered around the cake and a bottle of champagne that Eldar had produced from his black bag cornucopia from Moscow, which was to continue to yield surprising things for months, little by little. Here were Emilia, Martina and Ivona, who nursed me through the pangs of surrogate fatherhood in Bulgaria, Voiko who made the initial contact, the Hamburgers—furtive money carriers who arrived with a lady geologist from Tashkent, Roman Zlotin—architect of it all, Susan Cutting, the student who had met Eldar and his family in Moscow, and numerous new aunts including Blanca, a Spanish dynamo whose staccato flow of accented English flew incomprehensibly round Eldar's head like a flock of wild birds. I toasted them all for making this happiness possible, and then we toasted Eldar for his having achieved the magnificent age of 14. A special moment was reserved for a presentation to Roman Zlotin, who, more than anyone, had really made all this possible.

The Future

Several months had gone by since Eldar arrived, and he was firmly and comfortably at ease in school and at home; in no small part due to an extraordinary English teacher, Ms. Black. He was now conversing freely in English, though he still had no idea how to study from a text book. He would read pages and pages but there would be not a note in sight. Always lurking in the background was the idea that he would finish high school and then decide what he might do with his life. This was obviously the best plan, but we needed to be clear what that involved in terms of his visa status, our role as guardians and the like. A major problem was that no one seemed to have *any* idea exactly what rules applied, or what they meant. Then a

Bob Rund

friend at the university's International Services Office recommended to us that we contact a specialist in this arcane area of the law—a Mr. Rund who was based in Indianapolis. If only Mr. Rund had known.

We made an appointment to see Mr. Rund in his office under the flight path of the international airport. Robert Rund, a stocky, rather lugubrious man, disappointed Susan at first as a consequence of a limp and indifferent hand shake: a key factor in Susan's human evaluations. She was dead wrong in this case. But, he appeared drawn into the tale we had to tell, and intrigued by its unusual nature. Most of all he seemed genuinely touched by the story of what had happened to Eldar. Much of the time he came across as a benign professor of classics, rather than someone in the cut-and-thrust of immigration and visa law. Fairly quickly that afternoon, we discovered that life was more complicated than we imagined.

"Eldar may stay in the United States as a student for many years, and you may remain his guardians. No problem there," Mr. Rund assured us.

Susan manipulated reams of paper arrayed before her and responded,

"That's good, because we have discussed this with his mother, and we think the best idea is for him to finish his high school education here, and then he can decide what he wants to do. Right now he is too young to make such a decision for himself of course."

Looking more doleful than ever, Mr. Rund shuffled his papers and spoke directly to them.

After a few false starts, he then declared,

"I'm not sure what you mean by *decide about his future.* Once he finishes his schooling, at whatever level even if he goes to college, he will still have *no right to stay here.* He is, after all, a Russian citizen. He does not become a US citizen, or gain the right to apply for US citizenship, simply by staying here, however long that may be."

It appeared, from what Mr. Rund explained, that Eldar could continue with his studies, and we could continue to be his guardians, but during such time Eldar would never acquire any rights whatsoever to remain in the United States once the period of study was completed.

"Well, you mean that whenever he finishes, he *must* go back?" Susan asked animatedly, eyebrows aloft.

"That's correct. His F-1 visa allows him to stay here as long as he continues to be a legitimate student, but once he's out of school—be that high school or college—he'd have to return."

Since this was the third time Mr. Rund had said the same thing, we gathered that there was not much to debate on that score.

"So, how do we give him this option to decide his future, which was what his mother had in mind when he came here? I mean, is there any way?"

Susan inquired, biting her lower lip and gripping the file in her hand very tightly.

"Certainly there is," Mr. Rund reassured her with a smile, "**You would have to adopt him.**"

A total silence swallowed up the room.

My mind went into hyperdrive. *Adopt him*? He already had a family for Heaven's sake.

Susan, composure returned, mused for a moment and said,

"I see. By the time he finishes high school we would all know each other much better, and that might be a reasonable thing to consider by then. He would be old enough to have the situation clear in his head. On the other hand, we have not really thought about this issue much (*much?*)—after all we didn't expect to do much about it for several years. We certainly have not discussed this issue with him, and it is a *huge* step for him to consider. After all," she went on, echoing my thoughts, "He already *has* a mother, and a family. Still we should tell him about this, even at this early stage, and then he can have it in mind as the years go by. He should certainly finish school here because he told us that he would get no credit back in Moscow for what he was doing in Indiana, and would have to repeat the courses taken in Bloomington. He is doing well, and having gone this far he might as well get his diploma, and then we can see."

The whole time Susan was disclaiming Mr. Rund was poised, waiting anxiously to interject. But, once Susan is up and running, challengers are few. After studying the table very closely for a while as Susan enumerated the points, Mr. Rund, realizing his chance had come, jumped in and said,

"Ah, I'm afraid it's not as simple as that. You see, once he is 16, an adoption will serve no purpose with respect to his eligibility to get an immigrant visa and stay in the United States, which would be one of the major reasons for the adoption. Your problem is that we have two separate sets of laws running interference on each other: immigration and adoption, one of which is federal, and the other, state, as if things weren't already bad enough (*eyes roll toward Heaven*). But adoption of a child is determined by the law of the residence of the child at the time of adoption. In the case of Eldar that means the United States, and more specifically, Indiana. It is not determined by the law of the country where his birth parents reside. Also, Eldar must live with you as your ward for two years before he can be adopted."[5]

---

[5] In fact this was not, as it turned out, strictly correct, and Mr. Rund was simply giving us his initial general overview of the situation. It *used* to be the case that a two-year legal custody had to be fulfilled *before* the adoption, but that law was amended in 1986 so the two-year period could be before or after the adoption to qualify for immigration purposes. He informed us of this later.

"Wait a moment!" said Susan, furiously scribbling notes and looking frazzled, "Let me see if I understand. If he has to have been our ward for two years, and if, once he is over 16 an adoption will serve no purpose for immigration, this gives us between September 1, 1994 and September 27, 1994, to conduct the *entire process*. He has to decide his whole future in *just those four weeks!*"

"No," responded Mr. Rund shaking his head at the foolishness that anything could be as simple, if impossible, as that. "He has to decide his future *before* then, so we can gather all the documents from Russia and have them ready to go in that short window of opportunity. Also, there are a number of steps we must take here since this would be a US adoption. You should be thinking about this *now*."

It seemed we *didn't* even have a year to see how things would go, never mind four years of high school. If he was to have any choice about his future, we and his family in Moscow were going to have to make some irrevocable decisions about the remainder of his life right now. None of us had contemplated the process being telescoped in this way. Could Eldar possibly know what he wanted at this stage? Could his mother possibly make such a radical decision at this time? And, were *we* ready for this?

Eldar's Recollections 1992

Probably the first two things that I found were very different on my arrival in America were lots of amazingly overweight people and the number of stores and things in the stores as well as the time people spent shopping. Also people were very friendly. Whenever I would go for a walk people whom I didn't know at all would say "Hi, how are you?" which you would never hear from a stranger in Moscow.

I went to school the third day of my arrival. It was very hard for me. I didn't know almost any English. I couldn't talk to anybody. I was lost in school because it was so huge. First day, Susan wrote a note for me, which said: "Hello, I'm Eldar, I speak very little English." I showed it to every teacher, and they said something, which I couldn't understand. At least I could say: "I don't understand." Then they would point at the seat, and I would go and sit down. My first class was stained glass, and I didn't really need English for that. The teacher would just show me what to do and I would repeat it. English class was much tougher; though the teacher did a good job of explaining things to me, and other students would help her. Day by day I was learning more and more.

It was very hard to make friends, because they had different interests mainly television and sport. I couldn't speak English, and I didn't know how to make friends in this country. Sometimes I felt very lonely and isolated. We lived in a neighborhood of Bloomington where the houses and yards are very big, and people who live there are mostly retired people or professors in the university, and they don't seem to have any children. In Moscow people live in big apartment buildings and their children go to the school nearby. So there were always lots of people milling around all the time. We didn't have to take the bus to school, since it was right there. If I wanted to go out with my friends, I wouldn't need to call them a week in advance; I would just drop by and ask them to come out. Or I would go outside and check out who was around. That is impossible here as there is never anyone around.

Although I didn't know much English, I still did well in school. I didn't have any C's. I mostly learned English like a baby. It's like throwing a person who can't swim in the swimming pool, and he would learn or drown. I had no choice: I had nobody to speak in Russian to. I heard a word said many times, and I would try to figure out what it meant. I used my dictionary, but not that often as that was too slow. Soon after arriving, I had to take a test in English, which would tell if I could go to a normal English class or stay in English as second language. I got zero on it, as I expected. At the end of the first semester I took it again and got 44 percent, and you need 55 percent to pass, so I stayed there for a second semester. But at the end of the second semester I got 89 percent. Then I took it again, after one month, the day of the final exam, and got 98 percent on it.

I guess I was learning something after all.

People welcomed me very warmly. I began making friends slowly after a while. The strange thing is that all of my friends were either foreigners or students in the university. I played soccer because that seemed like a good way to meet people, but it was very organized. Whereas, in Moscow I would usually go and play soccer outside without parents watching every move you make, here it is like a military operation. We went as a family to different places in the US and Canada. My favorite place is probably Seattle, because it has mountains with snow, sea and the city all together. I met Susan's family. Randall's family is in Wales so I haven't met them yet.

Chapter 10
Defining the Options

With the prospect of adoption now both immediate and substantive, we both knew how much we really wanted to do this. This was not for purely altruistic reasons to give Eldar choices, a future, whatever, but because we loved him dearly. He brought us so much happiness, and he seemed so much part of our life now. But, it was necessary and unavoidable that we sat down and discussed the future with him, though it seemed terribly unfair, only three months after he had arrived here, to ask him to think about making such a commitment. Then we had to consult with his "other" family. Susan and I decided it was best to approach the question obliquely by asking him first how he felt about continuing his education into the next school year, and perhaps, avoid the adoption issue at this stage. He had responded well to a very caring group of teachers, and his progress as a freshman was nothing short of astonishing. His grades were climbing steadily to a point that would take him very quickly to being an A student in the school's top 10 percent.

In fact, precipitating the discussion, Eldar unexpectedly brought up this topic of continuing his education in Bloomington at dinner one evening by saying:

"It would be crazy to change now when I am doing so well, and I really like the school system here. Also, I don't think I would get credit back in Moscow for what I am doing here. Back there we take 12 to 14 subjects at once; here only 6. Since I have gone this far, and may not get credit, I might as well finish everything here or everything will be wasted."

He had reached the point where he had to make course selections for the following semester, but when he brought back the form from his room he had filled in the options, not only for that but, to the end of his senior year. It was evident that, at least for the foreseeable future, he considered America to be his home. It seemed to us that if he was not truly happy he would never have learned English so astonishingly fast.

He was also learning the joys of capitalism, exercising his undeniable charm on our neighbors to induce them to use his lawn-mowing service. However, never having grown up in a consumer- and service-oriented society, he had some difficulty handling this responsibility. His perception was, quite clearly, that the local lawns would happily accommodate the nuances of his personal calendar, and fairly soon calls started to come in asking why he had not been around. In a letter his mother had written to us soon after Eldar had arrived, she stated,

"There is some danger for Eldar to lose his head, so don't overindulge him. Make him help you in family and household matters. He used to help at home too. Eldar, like the rest of us here, was not very well organized and not very prompt in his work and life."

This, we suspected, was a universal portrayal of the genus *Teenager*, but he certainly needed to be jump started on each job. At the same time he showed genuine joy and astonishment as the money piled up in his savings account. He no sooner opened the savings account, however, than he left the passbook and card in the first store he entered after leaving the bank.

Eldar's mother, meantime, had written to us again. Her letters were irregular because she, in common with everyone I ever met in Eastern Europe, did not trust the postal system, relying instead on people who were going to the United States to carry and forward mail from her. Sometimes these people forgot, and her letters were delayed for weeks. I often wondered which was the more unreliable system, friends or the post office? On the other hand, we indulged in the same practice if there was anything of any value to be sent to Russia, since letters sometimes arrived with part of the contents removed from the envelope. Ludmila's aim was still that we should meet, and that was more of a priority than she realized in view of the fact that very soon we would be asking her to think about what we were already calling the "adoption option." Frankly, it seemed totally ridiculous to imagine that she could make an irrevocable decision about her son's entire future, as a result of which he would become the legal child of two people she had never even met. Regardless of whether she had Eldar's prospects uppermost in her heart and mind, it seemed inconceivable to imagine she could take a risk like that, or ever bear to let him go. Were we not just wasting a lot of time and money here?

In the Russian Orthodox tradition it is very important for the family to mark the first anniversary of the death of a relative. This was done, often, at the physical site of the death. And so Ludmila wrote to tell us that she and Eldar's two brothers, Roman and Timur, would be going to Terskol, where

Nuris had perished, and from there to near Tashkent in Uzbekistan where his family still lived. The only person missing from this group would be Eldar, and so Ludmila wondered if we could take advantage of this moment for both families to meet. This seemed entirely appropriate since it would allow me to pay my respects to Nuris, allow Susan to see the wonderful Caucasian Alps where Eldar spent so much time, and permit both families to work out some form of understanding about Eldar's future.

More Pitfalls

What seemed to be an admirable solution to our problem was put firmly on ice when we started to look into the details. The problem was Eldar's legal status in the USA. His documents allowed him to go to school, and to continue to go to school, without complication—despite the fact that his passport was a Soviet one, which meant it was from a country that no longer actually existed. On the other hand it did not exist when they gave it to him in August 1992 either! But the real difficulty came if Eldar tried to *return* to the USA at the end of our stay at any place abroad we might visit together. We learned that, with the exception of visits to Canada, Mexico, or the Caribbean, Eldar would be unable to travel outside the United States without having to *reapply* for a new visa from the US embassy. Bearing in mind that it was a miracle he got a passport at all, we were very much afraid of putting him through all this again. This seemed to turn any trips to Russia or Europe into a real problem, and we didn't relish the prospect of spending most of our time standing in enormous lines outside the US embassy in Moscow to try and ensure Eldar's return to the United States. Even more worrying, an immigration official, writing from Moscow, reminded us that "It is *by no means* guaranteed that the boy would be readmitted. Each case is taken on its merits."

This was altogether too risky. Of course Susan and I could go, but that would leave Eldar alone during school time in late January. It quickly became evident that we would not be able to take part in the pilgrimage to commemorate Nuris, and this upset us considerably because he was the common bond between the two families. And since the anniversary came during the semester, I would have difficulty finding someone to cover my classes at that time.

For his part, Eldar showed no outward sign of wrestling with these immense problems. He went about his, by now, daily routine, his day starting with a frenzied scramble through the door just microseconds ahead of the yellow school bus. He brought home evidence of remarkable skill at forming stained glass into boxes, eagles, art nouveau plant holders and the like. His gentle nature and ready smile won over all our friends, but his profound shyness kept most potential teenage friends away. Normally he was very expansive about his artistic work at school, but with one project he was very furtive until one day in November he opened his backpack and announced he had something to show me. Then, his face a picture of deep concern and disappointment, he rushed off to his room clutching the backpack and disappeared completely, leaving me waiting and wondering with heightened anticipation.

"What is it?" I inquired from the living room after an eternity.

"Ah . . . nothing," came the distant reply from his room-cum-landfill, and I was left in the dark.

The next day we went through the same ritual, only this time he emerged from his room clutching an uncommonly accurate glass likeness of Dolli, our calico cat, whose comfortable life of undivided affection had been swiftly ended by the entry of a sturdy nonfeline rival. I could not believe it, but Eldar had captured the very essence of the cat in multicolored glass.

"This is for Susan's birthday," he announced with undisguised pride.

"Why, it's the absolute image of Dolli; Susan will love it. But what was going on yesterday with all the panic and secrecy?" I inquired.

"I sat on my backpack coming home on the bus, and that broke some of the glass, so I went into class early and replaced those bits. Now, you cannot tell anything ever happened to it," Eldar said with a smile.

Susan, needless to say, was ecstatic with parental bliss and pride as she placed the cat, now known as Vitreous Dolli, a corruption of Boutros Ghali[6], in one of the big south-facing windows.

One facet of Eldar's character that I found particularly endearing was his willingness to do "boring adult" things with us. We understood that most teenagers would sooner die than be seen in company with anything resembling a parent. But Eldar came with us to receptions, on one occasion meeting a group of Russians who complimented him repeatedly on his excellent knowledge of their language! Eventually he had to start naming little-known landmarks of Moscow to convince them he was a fellow countryman. He happily accompanied us to adult dinner parties, much to the astonishment of some of our hosts who were, nevertheless, delighted to have him come along. In part, we realized, this was a result of the difficulty he had, because of his bashful nature, in making friends among the established groups in school, and not entirely because of our electrifying personalities. Eldar clearly loved small children, but still we saw absolutely no evidence of his having made any real friends. He had no interest in American sports, and rarely watched television, except for an undying love for Danny Kaye and prewar black and white romantic comedies. He was, quite possibly, the

---

[6] At that time, Secretary-General of the United Nations

only local teen carried away by Charles Laughton and Deanna Durbin. His time was spent overwhelmingly with us, and this started to make us nervous. Just like most efforts at matchmaking, the few introductions we engineered fizzled out. Despite having a collection of English and Russian books, he almost never read, but loved to be read to. He did, however, develop a passion for Calvin and Hobbes, taking Calvin as a major role model in his life. His time was spent more and more with his computer, which he came to refer to as his "girlfriend."

We were adapting rapidly to the role of parents. Diligently we attended the supreme mysteries of parent evenings at the high school, somewhat like amnesia cases for we, unlike all the other parents in the room, did not have the collective experience of all the preceding years of their child's education. As we sat there in those diminutive desks, Susan and I exchanged looks of surprise, guilt, and astonishment at the incredible micromanagement some parents seemed to effect over the lives of their offspring. We were intrigued, too, at the way so many teachers went to lengths to convince us that their classes were *fun*. I was not sure that fun was what it was all supposed to be about. "Oh you are Eldar's guardians. He is such a *lovely boy*" seemed to be the universal comment.

But what about his school work? It was also clear that he was unable to break the Russian tradition of the teacher as an authority figure with the mission of drilling information into the student's head. "*Fun?*" So, he remained largely silent in class. We wondered when those interminable teen phone calls would start, but they never did.

1992—The First Christmas

We were beginning, as new "parents," to fantasize about our first Christmas with Eldar. During Halloween we went out and bought pumpkins, carved them and placed them on the porch—something we would certainly never have done without him. In fact, before Eldar came, the festive seasons passed without much visible recognition in our home—except for Christmas, which was often a family gathering. Now we faced the prospect of the first "family" Christmas in which we participated as equal parental partners, and not as Yuppie onlookers somewhere on the periphery beyond the inner circle of drooling grandparents. We wanted to take care not to overindulge him, though he never expressed any interest in material goods at all other than new, and more complex, computer programs. Christmas provided him with his first opportunity to meet Susan's parents (mine both passed away many years ago) who had flown in from Toronto, Canada. You will remember that her father, Peter Hobbs, is a descendent of the Wheelwright family that gave the British such a hard time in Boston that they were thrown out of the colony and went off to found parts of New Hampshire. Retired now, Peter was formerly a senior administrator at the Business School at the University of Toronto, putting his Harvard MBA to good use. Susan's mother, Verity, might have been born in the mind of Richard Wagner, for she had a "commanding voice" and an unmistakable presence. Part of her family was in America eleven years before the *Mayflower* ever left Leiden. She went to Wellesley, as did her mother, Mitzi.

Susan, Grandmother Mitzi, and Mother Verity

This occasion was, I felt, something of an odd experience for them, for they secretly hoped that their daughter (in partnership with yours truly, I presumed), would provide them with grandchildren. They were profoundly into grandchildren. As it turned out, Susan's younger brother, Michael, who worked for Microsoft in Seattle, had already beaten her to that prize twice. How would they take to the "instant teenage grandchild?" We were rather jealous that Eldar, who was, of course, not our child in any biological sense, should get a fair deal in the veneration and idolization stakes. This situation, we appreciated, was not so uncommon, since people marry other people with older children from earlier marriages all the time. Fortunately Susan's parents fell immediately under the spell of Eldar's winning ways and open character. Christmas also provided Susan and I with the excuse to get a Christmas tree for the first time, which we decorated carefully so that the cat would not destroy it. We almost saved the cat that necessity when the whole thing started to fall in slow motion. A swift flying tackle from Eldar saved the occasion.

Eldar's earlier performance on his birthday was but a pale shadow of the delirium he developed on Christmas Eve. Just like any small child he was desperate to know what we had bought for him, and just like any child he did not want to lose the element of surprise: in short he drove himself crazy. He had been counting, and recounting, the number of boxes under the tree on an hourly basis, and was stunned by the sheer profusion. Susan and her parents constructed a treasure hunt for Eldar to follow. This tested both his ingenuity and his recently acquired English proficiency skills. As expected, the computer-related presents won out in terms of excited response. We, in turn, became the proud owners of a remarkable stained-glass panda, and a stained-glass landscape of Mount Elbrus showing Hut Eleven and a setting sun. Nothing he could have bought us would ever have matched the pleasure of receiving the gift of his own imagination and creative talents.

We pulled out all the stops with a traditional Christmas dinner, but the spirit of internationalism was preserved by a combination of Soviet champagne, Caspian caviar, and Ben and Jerry's *Rain Forest Crunch*. At Emilia's apartment the cosmopolitan tradition continued in the evening with plum pudding and Bulgarian *feta* salad washed down with fiery *Rakia,* as always powerful enough to strip paint from walls.

The first Christmas together

A visiting Russian professor from Moscow University's Geography Department was passing through Bloomington, and over dinner he informed us that on January 28, 1993—exactly one year to the day that Nuris died—a massive avalanche thundered down the mountainside and buried parts of the village of Terskol, where Nuris had lived, killing several people. Then, two days later, another huge wave of snow crashed down on the very research center where Nuris had been the director. It thundered through the surrounding ancient pines in the night, and broke over the building where I had stayed, burying and killing several students, some of whom were friends of Timur, Eldar's middle brother. Meanwhile, Ludmila and the rest of the family arrived in Uzbekistan to commemorate the ritual of the first anniversary of the death of Nuris. At that precise moment, to the day, Nuris's elder brother, who was hosting the events, died suddenly and without any warning. Eldar's grandmother had now lost two of her sons in the last year. Tragedy compounded tragedy.

Chapter 11
Where Next?

Shortly after Christmas, following a contretemps with her landlady, Emilia's 16-year-old free-spirited daughter Martina moved in with us for a while, thereby consolidating the Slavic phalanx. She was still effervescent, radiantly beautiful, and outgoing; a direct contrast to Eldar's shy and reserved nature. In no time Martina had introduced Eldar into her circle of friends and he finally began to build those links that had eluded him for so long. He attended his first party, and then he started to go visiting. On one occasion as I was trying to choose a picture frame at a local store, I noticed an extremely red-faced Eldar cornered by two girls. I caught only the phrase "You look so cute today." I had learned that he abhorred the idea of being thought *cute*, but as a result of his extraordinary good looks it was a word he had to endure all the time. Then, while at one birthday party he called us, asking if his 10 p.m. deadline could be extended.

"How about 10:30?" suggested Susan.

"How about 11, and then I would love you forever?" responded Eldar.

Hard to resist that. Returning from another party, Martina, who was driving Eldar in her mother's car, was stopped by the local police for having pulled up two feet over the white line at a stop sign. Noticing her dark features, the policeman decided that she was "Hispanic" (though, of course, she is Bulgarian), and wrote this in the appropriate box on his form, much to Martina's amazement. He asked Eldar some questions, and decided that he was Hispanic too. It is true that Eldar has a dark complexion, thick black hair, and dark eyes, but his partly Central Asian origins are unmistakable. This categorization as *Hispanic* was particularly ironic since Eldar, by virtue of his birth in the Caucasus, was probably the only genuine *Caucasian* this policeman had ever seen!

We were able to provide Ludmila with a continual stream of good news about her son. He phoned from time to time, and helped convince his mother that he was truly happy in America, and was doing well in school. However, the time had come to present the options to his family and to initiate the process of determining his future in terms of those options, as we now understood them. This was going to be really tricky because we did not want to give Ludmila the impression that we were trying to force the issue for selfish reasons. After all, we were a childless couple and it was easy to see what sort of interpretation could be made of any pressure on our part. Adoption was never on the cards when I had discussed Eldar's coming here with his father; nor did it ever arise in the subsequent discussions with his mother concerning Eldar's coming here for "one year in the first instance." On the one hand I had to convince his family that he was welcome in case he decided he wanted to stay forever, and naturally they would wonder how we could know that in such a short time—less than six months all told. On the other hand, Eldar had to convince them of what he wanted, though they could also be forgiven for thinking that a 14-year-old was not really in a position to know such things. The only bridge, because of language, was Eldar himself. It seemed like an impossible task to discuss issues of such complexity without a common language, using the principal subject as interpreter, and having him make such a profoundly difficult decision at this stage of his life.

Susan and I sat down and composed a long letter to Ludmila, much of which was devoted to explaining in detail the various ways in which, to us, Eldar appeared to be happy and comfortable with his situation. I stressed his strong school record, but I was also honest in mentioning that he did not seem to be making many serious friends, except for an older-brother-type relationship he had developed with Voiko. I wrote:

There is something you and Eldar will want to think about. He needs to consider where he wants his future to be. He is doing well in the school system here, as we have said, and I am certain he will be an excellent student. I am also certain he will get into university easily. But the real question is where he wants to make his future: here or in Russia? If he wanted to stay here there would be only three options that would eventually allow him to stay in the United States. They are

1. If he had special skills that could not be provided by a citizen in the context of a specific job.
2. If he married a US citizen.
3. If he was adopted by us.

We went on to outline other problems such as the fact that, as a foreigner, he would have to pay high out-of-state fees if he went to university, and that however long he stayed here he would gain *no right* to remain. The latter was something, we believed, that was seriously misunderstood in Moscow. I knew this was going to be hard to explain because I was aware of a Russian saying that states "every house has two doors," meaning that every rule in that country is there to be circumvented. Because of this, I feared the Russians would not look at these American rules too seriously, preferring to adopt a "wait and see" attitude. We made the point that the longer Eldar stayed here, especially when we considered how rapidly and completely he had adapted, the more difficult it would be for him when he went back to Russia. We concluded:

> *Once again, the point is that he can continue to study here indefinitely—no problem. The real question comes with respect to what he wants to do after that. This is something only he and his family can decide. But let us tell you that we shall be happy whatever he decides. Of course we would hate to see him go because he makes us so happy. But we will go along with whatever is best for him, as decided by the two of you [Ludmila and Eldar]. We have no intention of turning him into an American or changing him in any way. He is wonderful the way he is, and is very proud of his country and family. So don't worry about that. He will always be Eldar, and he will always be your son.*

Susan and I had an overall sense that Eldar's continued stay in the USA seemed unrealistic, upsetting though that was to us. Placing ourselves in the position of Ludmila and the rest of the family, the adoption proposition seemed crazy. In short, we had no blood ties with Eldar, the two families had never met, and here we were proposing that Eldar settle down in a country that has, historically speaking, been an enemy of theirs. At the same time, lurking in the back of my mind, more and more, was the feeling that Eldar had slipped so comfortably into the way of life here—for instance, he spoke English, after only six months, without any trace of a Russian accent—that I feared the longer we kept him the more cruel it would be if he was eventually forced to go home against his will. The image of the "Baby Jessica" case on the television did not help. I resolved in my own mind that if the adoption possibility was not acceptable to his family, then Eldar should return to Russia at the end of that current school year. But Susan, the eternal optimist, did not see the need for this. When I was briefly in the Netherlands I mentioned my concern. Susan immediately replied by e-mail:

> *It is totally unnecessary to send him back this soon. You are forcing him into the most terrible decisions. He likes high school here, and he is doing well. Let him benefit from that, and let's do what we agreed originally. He should finish high school. I think you are being very hard and dogmatic. He is only a child.*

I was surprised at the powerful conviction in her tone, and it was evident that she thought I was entirely wrong on this score, and just being unreasonable. I responded:

> *I understand what you are saying. But if he stays here and completes school, and then is forced to return to Russia, what have we done to him? I don't think that is expanding his choices, I think that is being very cruel. He believes that much of his school credit here will not count in Russia. You have seen how much he has slipped into the life here. Do you want to be around when he is forced to board that plane to Russia: a country in turmoil that he will not have seen for four years?*

The best we could do was to agree to disagree, since the matter would not be resolved until we heard from Ludmila.

We now knew we had to raise this issue with Eldar, not least because his mother was sure to mention it in a future phone call and he must be prepared for it. I broached the question of a possible adoption with him one evening. To be honest I felt totally unsure of myself, and had no idea how to start this conversation with him. On the other hand, our relationship was totally open, and I always felt I could talk about anything with him without fear of his retreating into a shell.

He was sitting in his room at his desk working on a school assignment. I was still not sure how to begin such a devastating conversation, so I started rather dryly by explaining how the law of the United States severely limited our options, and his, over time. At first he found this heavy matter easiest to deal with by continuing to destroy fast-flying aliens on his computer screen. I could not cope with this, even though I knew it to be a standard operating procedure for teens talking "seriously," and so I gently persuaded him to return to this cosmos and turn off the computer. I started off with an explanation of how law and bureaucracy were forcing him to grow up extremely fast. Then, I went on:

"You understand that it is not our intention to *replace* your family in Russia. It is ridiculous, I know, but we found out that you will not be able to wait until you are older to make a decision about your future, because once you are 16 the options disappear and even if you stay to continue your education, you will have to go home once you stop being a student. If we were to adopt you it would be to give you *another* family to add to the one you already have. Now, the law of this country says that you have to be our son, and *only* our son, but it is what all of us think and feel that really matters. You would, as far as we are concerned, have two families in a sense, and we would make sure that you have every chance to spend time with both. You understand what I am saying?"

For once in our relationship he was not fixing me with his full eye contact. This was a formidably difficult thing for either of us to deal with, and I could see his mind was in turmoil. That made two of us. On the one hand, it was clear that he fitted in perfectly here, and envisaged staying for a long time. On the other hand, he was being put in a position where, if he jumped at our offer, it could look, particularly to his mother, as though after just a few months in the USA he was ready to reject his natural family and all that they had done for him through the years. It was clear to him, as it was to me, that this would be the greatest decision of his mother's life and he did not want to hurt her feelings. And so he kept his comments to monosyllables, staring at his desk as I continued:

"Another problem is this. We think it is important, even if you stay here, that you maintain contact with your family in Russia. If you return any time with your current visa, there is no guarantee we can ever get you back here. In fact we have heard officially that the chances would be poor. As it is we cannot really travel anywhere while you are here because of that visa situation. This is not something someone your age, with a family—or, indeed two families that love you—should have to decide. Of course your mother never sent you here on the basis that you would be adopted; just that you would have enough time here so that when you were older and could cope with such a decision as this, you would have a choice. I have no idea how she will react when I present this new option now, when you have been here only a few months and have just turned 14. I know it is going to be extremely hard for her—maybe impossible—but I would like to know about *your* real feelings. Maybe you don't want to make such a decision, or just can't, and I can understand that, and it is perfectly possible for us to leave it so that you finish your education here and then go back to your family. Why don't you think about the possibilities over the next day or two, and then you will be better prepared to speak to your mother honestly when she asks you for your views, because she is bound to want to know exactly how you feel about everything."

This was heavy stuff, and Eldar remained stoically impassive throughout my short discourse. I could read no signals in either his expression or body language. It was evident, though, that he was wrestling with something truly awful. I tried again:

"Well, what do you think?"

"Why can't I just finish high school and decide then? I thought we had decided that is what we are going to do" he asked, mystified by the whole thing.

I explained again the arcane legal reasons that precluded this.

"I'm just don't know. I want to finish school here—I do know *that*."

I told Eldar once more to think again, reiterating that he was free to go whichever way he felt was right. It was absurd for me to expect him to come up with an answer to such a devastating question immediately without any notice or warning. What child could make such a decision off the top of his head? I tried to imagine when any child had been forced into such a corner at such an already difficult time of life. Most of all I did not want to look as though I was trying to make the decision for him, and so did not give him any hint of what Susan or I wanted. We both knew what we would like the decision to be of course, but it was not our right to impose or promote any suggestion of that. This wasn't how we had imagined the process would be at all. To be honest, we were as unprepared for this enormous change as he was, and certainly none of us was going to have to grapple with anything as difficult as the problem it posed for his mother.

Our letter to Ludmila in Moscow had been sent with a member of the faculty of education on January 9, 1993, and we expected that this would yield another long delay, not least because the issues raised were so fundamental. By now Roman Zlotin was back in Moscow, and we prevailed on him, and on Natasha, to give Ludmila a true picture of life in the United States to help her make up her mind. Furthermore, Roman Zlotin had seen Eldar in his new environment in Bloomington, and knew us rather well, so he could provide Ludmila with a first-hand account from a sympathetic and unbiased Russian source.

The same faculty member who had taken the letter to Ludmila returned, bringing with him a large box full of Eldar's personal items. These included pins, coins, and some books in Russian that his mother hoped would encourage him to maintain his knowledge of his first language. Occasional visitors from Russia gave us various accounts regarding Eldar's Russian. Some said he was developing an American twist to some of the distinctive Russian sounds. Others said that he was forgetting some basic words (like "birthday" on his birthday!) Ludmila described his language on one occasion as "speaking English in Russian." In this same packet from Moscow was a letter which we looked at with considerable anxiety, knowing it must be a reply to our "adoption letter." It was frustrating beyond words not to be able to read the reply instantly, since of course the letter was written in Russian. We knew we needed to get the letter expertly translated since its contents were vital to us and we could not afford to miss any nuance but we could hardly ask Eldar to do the translation. Then, a couple of days later, we obtained a very accurate rendering from a visiting Russian student. This was what we read:

> *I am always glad when I receive not only letters and photos from Eldar but also the detailed descriptions of your caring for Eldar.*
>
> *In January I went to Nuris' home. I saw many of his relatives and friends and we talked about Eldar's life in your family. We all appreciate that you care about him. . . .*
>
> *Eldar is a very kind person of ready sympathy and we are pleased that you live with him as a son. It is you, Susan, and your friends who contribute to Eldar's progress most of all. Despite some abilities and talents, Eldar did not make much progress and maintain good relations in the Moscow school as he does in his new school. We're sure it is you who has created the good conditions for Eldar. Of course he had many friends, especially in Gazalkente [Uzbekistan] and Terskol, but not in Moscow. We could not do anything about this. That is why we are so glad for Eldar now. Certainly we are not going to destroy that which you have done for him with such love and care. We understand that there is nothing good for him here, and since you enjoy living together, we would like Eldar to continue his studies and life with you. Difficulties we would meet when he comes of age we still did not realize in full. We are simply not ready to decide anything about Eldar's future. We spent the whole year on recovery of our life after the tragedy. Our children helped us a lot in this. Now we are beginning a new period in our life when we will have enough time to decide about Eldar's future. We are looking forward to seeing you this summer.*

What were we to make of this? There was no specific mention of the various options, but rather a restatement of the original "wait and see" approach. This was what I call the default option and, in effect, it meant that Eldar *would have to return to Russia.* The only question was *when?* Were we to let it go at that? Or, were we to assume that in Moscow the meaning of the immigration law had not been understood—or perhaps not taken seriously? We realized we had better be careful with our emotions now because it looked like Eldar would *not* be able to stay with us indefinitely since the adoption issue had been skirted over. Remembering my fears about the disorientation he would feel when he did return, and that this would get worse the longer he stayed, I strongly advised Susan, again, that his return should be at the end of this school year.

"I don't think that's necessary," she said with considerable determination. I had seen that look before.

"Let's not get possessive," I urged. "He is not our son, and whatever his mother wants we simply have to agree to."

Inside I shared the exact emotions I knew Susan was feeling. It looked as though Eldar's stay would be cut short after all.

Chapter 12
Indecision and Confusion

As Eldar's school performance continued to improve, we had to wrestle with the still unresolved issue of getting an opinion from him about his future. Though it seemed Ludmila felt he was too young to make such a decision, she had indicated that his wishes were ultimately paramount, and so we needed to know what they were. Or, at least we needed to know if *he* knew what they were.

In another long conversation with him, I again tried to discuss the question of options as Mr. Rund had laid them out to us. Once more I explained that any adoption would enlarge, rather than divide or split, both families, giving him a sort of extended family. It was evident from his expression that this was a tortuous decision. I tried to reassure him:

"We will make sure that we don't try to turn you into an American rather than a Russian, nor will we force you to switch from one family to another. This is just to give *you* the largest number of choices in making decisions about your future."

I just wished there was some way we could have had this discussion with all parties present. Maybe that was the best plan, but how were we to do that given the visa situation? Eldar did indicate, tentatively, that he thought the adoption road seemed to make the "most sense," but said nothing much more than that in terms of his personal attachment to any option. The choices were threatening to him, and deep down he just didn't want to make any choice at all.

Susan and I decided that it was quite impossible for Eldar to make any decision without long consultations with his mother, because he was clearly now even more concerned about how she was going to feel about any decision of his to become adopted, regardless of the fact that she had continually said that everything should be his decision. But what child of 14 is asked to choose between two mothers? That is what it looked like to him, whatever we said about extended families. Furthermore, his mother's latest letter clearly indicated that the family in Moscow had *not* been able to make a decision at present, and so the burden on his shoulders had grown heavier since he had no guidance from them. Rather than being asked to support something his mother proposed, he instead was the one having to propose something to his mother. In the light of that terrible responsibility, Eldar was extremely unlikely to go out on a limb, whatever he might secretly want for himself. Part of the problem remained that, as always, he never revealed his innermost emotions. "He was always a mystery" his mother was later to say and, indeed, as you will have realized by now, he was frustratingly hard to "read."

Then, in early spring, a most remarkable Armenian professor, whom I had met on my 1990 visit to Moscow State University, arrived on a visit from Russia. We had been told he would be carrying a letter from Ludmila. We were delighted to receive Mr. Batoyan as he was one of life's more colorful characters—tall, dark, and lean, and looking for all the world like a Mafia hit man. During a trip I had taken with him once, on the overnight express to Leningrad (as it was then called), he astonished me, for as far as I knew we were going for only two nights, by boarding with three suitcases—two large and one small. I soon discovered that one large suitcase contained two VCR players, the other was totally alcoholic in content, while the third, very small one, contained all the necessities for the trip. While in Leningrad he managed to get me an entrance into a closed museum by telephoning the director and saying that I was the president of Yale University. His speech was curious

Prof Batoyan, an eternally surprising fellow

mixture of English sprinkled with random Spanish words derived from his time in Cuba.

I met Mr. Batoyan at Indianapolis airport. Almost the first thing he did was to hand me $10,000 in cash, saying he would like to take back some computers and scientific equipment. I hastily deposited this enormous wad in the local bank, probably arousing suspicion of some illicit drug deal. Eventually, true to his word, he did attempt, as only he would, to take back *seven* computers as hand luggage—and not laptops either! Our last sight of him was a face surrounded by cardboard boxes that filled the entire rear of the airport limo.

As promised, Mr. Batoyan did indeed bring a reply from Ludmila to our long letter. We were really nervous as we opened it, and then of course we realized that, once again it was in Russian. In fairness we could not ask Eldar to translate it since it was probably about him. Mr. Batoyan was not close enough to the family in Russian terms to ask him to become involved in their personal affairs. And so we had to wait until later that week my student translator produced a carefully worded English version. Ludmila wrote:

> *. . . Probably the time has come for us [in Moscow] to understand in detail what are the necessary measures on our part to set up Eldar that we should take as his relatives, and what we would "lose" in consequence. . . .We would like most of all to put all the responsibility on you. That is why we would like to receive a letter from you and Eldar with many details and instructions. Meanwhile we just wish you all the best, and probably soon you will take all the necessary measures for Eldar to stay in school for the next year.*

We were still confused. This letter seemed to be saying that *we* should decide whether or not Eldar should take the adoption route. At the same time it asked for details of what the real implications of such a course of action would be for the relations between Eldar and his natural family in the future. I could certainly reassure the family about our intentions regarding adoption, but I was still hazy about the legal consequences and implications of the citizenship situation. The United States does not really allow for dual citizenship, except in very rare cases, and adoption would clearly not be one of these exceptions. If the adoption law was as absolute as it seemed in transferring all rights to the adopting family, then what rights would Eldar have to visit Russia? Would he become a US citizen upon adoption? Could he have dual citizenship under this arrangement? Would he have full rights to reenter the United States if he left to visit some other country? The more we thought and inquired, the more totally confused we became. Clouding our thinking on this already baffling issue was the fact that because we loved him, emotion was influencing us on the issue of whether he should stay or return. Nevertheless, we were going to have to solve some of these riddles—and soon.

Back in October of 1992 we had contacted Mr. Rund simply to find out what, broadly speaking, the "Eldar options" were. Now, half a year later we contacted him again to determine the details involved in actually pursuing the idea of adoption. We explained to him that we did not have consent, or anything resembling consent to adoption. We desperately needed to explain to Ludmila what was involved and, as she put it, what she "might lose." Once more Mr. Rund gave us the impression of being both extremely interested in this case and fascinated by its rarity. He tried to set out the position as clearly as he could:

"You have to understand that this is not a common, straightforward adoption case, though adoption law is adoption law," he told us.

"First of all, most adoptions involve infants who are not, as you might say, 'developed persons' at this point. They would then develop and grow up in their new family. In your case the adoptee is already formed, and is 14. Apart from anyone else, *he* may have to give his *own* consent to this. Secondly, when older children are adopted it is often the case that there is some bloodline connection—grandparents, uncles, aunts, that sort of thing—who are engaged in adopting orphaned related minors. This boy is Russian, an adolescent, who has no connection with you, and has a living parent. This is most unusual, most unusual."

"But is it *possible*?" we inquired.

"Oh, I definitely think so, though the timing is tight." Then he surprised us: "Mercifully, the Russian authorities will have no part to play in this. In this case, Eldar's adoption would be a purely American legal issue to be resolved in the county court."

I could hardly believe the simplicity of what Mr. Rund was saying.

"How can this be?" I asked, confused. "I have a neighbor who spent weeks and weeks in Bucharest wrestling with the Romanian bureaucracy to get his now-adopted child. It was an absolute nightmare as I hear it."

"No doubt" Mr. Rund replied, "but the difference in all those cases is that these children are still in their native country. The problem is to gain legal possession of them there, and then to get them to the United States. But Eldar is already here; you don't have to get him out of Russia. Had he been an infant it would probably have been much more difficult. No, all you have to do is process the same forms as though he were coming from Idaho or Minnesota. His mother must give legal consent to a document that I can prepare for you, and that we must have translated exactly into Russian. Fortunately, I have a Russian-speaking assistant who can help you with that."

The consent form, which he showed us in its generic form, was surprisingly direct and blunt for a legal document.

I wondered how Ludmila would react when she read:

> *I hereby consent to give my son, Eldar Nurisovich Urumbaev, to the care and custody and control of Randall and Susan A. Baker, who have given my son a proper home and who have promised to continue to do the same; that I hereby authorize them to initiate legal proceedings to adopt my son in the court of the appropriate jurisdiction, and I hereby consent to said adoption. . . .*
>
> *That I understand that the execution of this Consent to Adoption will result in a complete termination of my parental rights to my son upon the entry of a final Decree of Adoption, and that when the Court so decrees, my son shall be and become child of the adoptive parents. . . .*
>
> <u>*THAT I UNDERSTAND THAT THIS CONSENT IS FINAL AND IRREVOCABLE UPON MY SIGNING OF IT*.</u>

There was not much room for ambiguity there, and the capitalized, underlined last sentence certainly got the message across bluntly. Mr. Rund went on to explain that Ludmila would also have to submit a family medical history, Eldar's birth certificate, Nuris's death certificate and . . . well, that seemed to be about all.

"Ah yes, there is one difference. She would have to take all these documents—several of which need to be in English and Russian—to the US embassy in Moscow in order to sign them and have them authenticated for the courts here. From there on, it is just a basic adoption, except of course that since Eldar is over 14 he would have to grant his own permission. But, please let me correct one thing I might have told you that is not accurate. Eldar does *not* have to have lived with you for two years before you can petition for adoption. That rule only applies to citizenship. It is very hard separating the immigration and adoption parts of these cases and this is what caused some confusion initially. At any rate, you can apply for an adoption at any time before Eldar's sixteenth birthday."

We breathed a huge sigh of relief. At least now we would not be going through a wild scramble to complete an adoption petition in the three-week period between the two-year anniversary of his arrival in Indiana and his sixteenth birthday. Even so, there was little enough time to spare to get the documentation together, assuming Ludmila and Eldar agreed to the adoption, if the process was to work its way through the system.

Susan and I decided to explain all this to Ludmila, even though we would have to tell her that we could not accept the responsibility for deciding Eldar's fate alone. In our own minds we knew exactly what we wanted that fate to be, but that was *our* secret for the moment. The best plan seemed to be to start the paperwork anyway, regardless of what was decided, so that if we all agreed on the adoption route, then at least we had started the process moving. It did not commit us to anything, and it cost very little. Our aim was to make a start in the summer of 1993 because Roman Zlotin was due to come back to Bloomington to teach in the fall, and, if it all worked out, he could be the courier for the legal documents, and bring them back with him. Certainly we would not want to commit such important papers to the mysteries of the Russian post office. Most curious of all, perhaps, was that once we had a handwritten authoritative Russian translation of the Consent Form, Eldar offered to type it. This he did, becoming—perhaps—the first child to type his own adoption papers! The man who translated the form, though not in any way personally involved in this process, remarked that one reason his people might have difficulty over the whole idea of this adoption was that during Soviet times those who left were regarded as traitors.

"My own grandfather, for instance," he told us, "on principle would never read the works of Russian émigrés. Traitors, he called them."

We added this latest piece of obstruction to our long list, and returned to main discussion:

"One real benefit of this adoption," I mentioned to Mr. Rund in passing, "is that it will allow us the freedom to travel. Right now we can hardly go anywhere outside the USA because of the fear that Eldar might not be readmitted, and because of the nightmare of his having to get a new visa each time."

Mr. Rund looked at me for a moment, then remarked, "It isn't quite as simple as that, I'm afraid. You see, his becoming your legally adopted son—even though you are both US citizens—*does not automatically make him a US citizen!*"

"What?"

This was a real shock. How could this possibly be? We were then told that Eldar would have to go through the same waiting period as someone who had, for instance, married an American. Our hearts sank at this prospect, and Mr. Rund, to confirm this, left the room to deliberate with a colleague who had been a consular officer in the US Foreign Service.

"Correction!" he said on returning. "No, he would have to complete two years residence with you as his legal guardians, then he would be eligible to apply for his green card. He can then petition for citizenship right away. By the way, if he does become a citizen, he should be aware that he would have absolutely *no* rights to bring any other members of his natural family over here to settle."

We didn't think that Eldar would have a problem with any of this. We never had the impression that he wanted to bring anyone to the States from Russia on a permanent basis, and his family had never shown any interest in that. We did find it curious, however, that we could become the legal parents of a child who remained a Russian, and who, should he go to foreign parts with us on vacation, might not be guaranteed re-entry to the United States. This was truly bizarre, but that was how the law determined it should be.

"But, even more curious I feel," continued Mr. Rund pulling another rabbit from his copious legal hat, "is the fact that when Eldar *does* become a US citizen, he would be a *born* American. I mean you would get a birth certificate for him, showing he was legally *born American*. Since, Randall, you are a naturalized American, he would be, strangely enough, *more American than you!* This is even though he gets his citizenship through his parents! Maybe, though I am not certain, he could be president, but you could not."

This was the least of my worries.

"I think," said Mr. Rund, as we prepared to leave his office, "that, in all honesty, nobody envisaged a situation such as yours when these laws were written. I can see why they would not want you adopting foreigners over 16, for then it could become a business, you know, $50,000 per adoption to get people into the States. But all this complexity appears to stem from the fact that he is in this 14-16 window. With infants, the citizenship seems to go right along with the adoption. I don't think there are many people out there looking to adopt unrelated adolescents from Russia, or any other place. Good luck."

We left better informed, though maybe just a little more confused at this bizarre situation.

"How the heck can you have a son who is a foreigner?" inquired Susan. "That's wild."

We had learned from Mr. Rund that if we wanted to have a fair chance at the adoption we would need to have all the documents in hand, signed by Ludmila at the US embassy, by September at the latest. It was already late April, and we needed to know what Eldar and Ludmila were really thinking. From Eldar we needed something more than "I suppose it seems to make sense," with regard to a decision reshaping the rest of his life. As for Ludmila we still didn't know whether she was prepared to make such a life-changing decision, or if she really wanted us to make the decision for her. Neither of these options was very helpful, but I fully appreciated what a strange situation she was in. Many of my colleagues remarked, "But how can you expect a mother to *give away* her child?" which was a fair comment. In fact, this was almost always the reaction of everyone who heard the story. My answer always was that I didn't expect anyone to *give away* anything. This was not a commodity trading arrangement. I expected only to *enlarge* Eldar's options He would have two families.

Roman Zlotin was in constant communication with Eldar's family, helping them wrestle with the decision they had to make. It was obvious now that the only way to resolve the issue was to bring all parties face to face during the summer. Since Eldar could not go to Moscow (or perhaps not get back into the States if he did), the logical alternative was for Ludmila to come to Indiana. We were more than willing to underwrite the cost of the journey. I then received an e-mail message from Roman saying that Ludmila still really felt that she could not decide, though it would be easier once she had spent time with Eldar and ourselves in August. But she was now thinking that Eldar's two brothers should come along too and help her make the decision. The cost of doing that would be extremely high, and we were not sure such an arrangement was practical. But we could understand very well that she needed help and support in coming to such an important decision. So I wrote to Roman:

> *We would be happy to receive Ludmila in our home during August—better it should be in the early part of the month because Eldar must start school on the 24th. They need to talk, to have time together, and come to a decision. We are not trying to push any particular option—only the one that they decide together. We love Eldar, and he is welcome to spend the rest of his life with us. But if it is resolved that Ludmila does not want to decide on the adoption, then it is probably better that Eldar goes back with her before he becomes more acculturated to the US way of life, school system, etc. I believe that this summer must be the time of decision. The best plan is for Ludmila to have the forms, understand them, and then she can sign them after her discussions here with Eldar. But it is best that she gets the forms right away, and at least completes them. Then they can be signed here. We cannot wait to begin this process until she leaves at the end of August. But she makes no commitment by completing the forms—only by signing them.*

To get a US visa she needed a formal letter of invitation from us to reassure the embassy of the purpose of her visit and that she fully intended to return to Russia at the end of it. At this difficult time in Russian history there was a flood of people trying to leave the country for the US, and many of these cases were contrived. It was the embassy's job to sort out the merits of each case, and the onus was on the applicants to prove their case. I provided for Ludmila, as convincingly as possible, our assurances regarding the temporary nature of her stay, her reasons for returning and so forth, and sent it off to her in Moscow to take along to her interview. We were both convinced that if Ludmila could meet us, see Eldar in his new environment, and talk to everyone frankly, albeit through translators, then we might be able to come to a final decision. Otherwise, I didn't see how we could resolve the situation.

Her response came sooner than expected. On my computer at work, I found an e-mail message from Roman Zlotin. *"The news is bad I'm afraid,"* he began. *"I should tell you some unexpected developments. Yesterday Ludmila was in American embassy and tried to get entry visa for USA. The conversation with an official was very difficult and serious for Ludmila. She has not got permission for coming to USA. She could make the next attempt only three months later. Officials at embassy put in Ludmila's application the next sentence 'You have not shown that you have sufficient strong family, social or economical ties to your place of residence to ensure that your projected stay in the USA would be temporary.'"*

Now, in light of this shock, how were we supposed to make a decision about Eldar's future? Time was running out fast, and we had to do something otherwise the decision would be made by default and Eldar would have to go back. And what impression would Ludmila have of the United States when it slammed the door in her face at this critical time? This was a real blow.

Chapter 13
The Hand of Fate... Again?

Upon learning the news of Ludmila's visa rejection, I immediately sent a fax to the consular affairs section in Moscow. In reply, I received a telephone call telling me the case would be reviewed, and that Ludmila could reapply. They told me her visa was denied because, since she was a widow with little income and a grown-up family, she did not convince them that she had a strong reason to return to Russia. It was hard to know how Ludmila could disprove these impressions, since in fact they were undeniably true. In addition, it was made clear to me that third parties were not influential in this sort of question. In other words, it didn't matter too much what I said or wrote. She had to convince them herself. I could not see any easy way for her to provide the sorts of assurances they wanted. Still, she was going to try again; in fact she had to if we were ever to resolve this issue.

The situation looked bleak. But one day, as I was rummaging through the mail on my desk, Tom, the silent Mercury of the post room, glided in and deposited a page on my secretary's desk. Kathleen, now moved to Ohio, had been replaced by tall, hyperenergetic Maggie, who was already totally inducted into the mysteries of the Eldar movement. She perused Tom's delivery: a fax from Moscow State University that was signed by someone completely unknown to me, a Professor Kozeltsev from the economics faculty. Remarkably, it was a formal invitation to a conference sponsored by the mayor of Moscow on the environment of the greater Moscow area.

Being a true academic I was unintimidated by the fact that I knew nothing whatsoever on this subject. But, I pondered, to be in Moscow would be extremely valuable at that precise moment. The conference was to be held at the end of June—just three weeks away—which did not allow much time to get visas and plane tickets, but it could be done. Through Roman Zlotin,

I announced my intention to go to Moscow and visit Ludmila, who was delighted to hear that I was coming and invited me to stay with the family. This seemed like a natural way to work things out, although for the first few days, I had to stay first at the hotel booked by the conference.

And so I left for Moscow, via Frankfurt, on June 27, 1993. I was first there in 1963 during the period of Mr. Khrushchev. My second visit was in 1990, when the Eldar story began. My principal impression in 1990 was how very little things seemed to have changed outwardly. At Frankfurt airport there was nothing to capture the imagination, and it was merely a matter of killing time until departure. I was surrounded on the flight by American oilmen off to the wilds of Siberia. One of them, an extremely fat man with a smattering of Russian, who had been in this game in Russia for a while, was very loud. He warned the others of the dog-size mosquitoes, the amazing capacity of the local oil people to drink (something contagious, from my observation of him), and the total absence of anything else to do. At Moscow we arrived after what had obviously been a very severe downpour, for everything was exceedingly wet, although the sun was shining by the time we landed. We taxied in alongside Aeroflot's newly repainted fleet (the Russian flag having replaced the Soviet one on the tail). One plane at the end of the line had been painted yet again to replace the Russian flag with the glorious Russian double-headed eagle.

The only difficulty at the airport came in gaining access to the immigration area since various corridors fed into one central point and there was absolutely no sense of queuing order. Somehow people seemed able to put up with all this. I was a little nervous at this point because my visa was not actually valid until the *following* day, June 28. The reason for this was that the official invitation to the conference specified the dates of the conference, and the Russian embassy in Washington would give the visa *for those dates only* as though one were able to arrive by air on the morning of the conference's first day, which of course was totally impossible. However, I had asked Eldar to write, in Russian, at the bottom of the minister's letter (as though in the minister's own hand), "We shall pick you up at the airport at 5:15 on the 27th June" (which was today). This did the trick because the immigration officer showed the letter to his superior, who pointed to the Russian PS at the bottom, and waved me through.

I departed the customs hall with my suitcase, which I found already trundling around on the carousel, and made my way into a gigantic crush of bodies totally surrounding the exit, all waving placards which made it look like a normal day outside the US embassy in Teheran. But there in the far left distance was a very official printed card with the name of the conference and my name neatly inscribed below. The bearded gentleman who greeted me took me to his aged BMW, told me that he worked for an environmental movement here in Moscow, and proceeded to give me 10,000 rubles ($10), which was my honorarium. This was about two week's salary for a professor, and was my first introduction to how things had changed since 1990, when you could live for three weeks on just 350 rubles. In 1990 the biggest bill I ever saw was a 50 ruble note. Now there was one worth 50,000.

Then, just before we got in the car, I noticed to my astonishment that my watch was gone. I could not imagine how this had happened, since I remembered checking the time while we were waiting in line. If someone had relieved me of it then it was a very professional job. I then recalled that the person standing next to me at customs was asked by the officer to hand over his pen as a "gift."

I was driven through a Moscow that was now incredibly polluted. I had forgotten just how dreadful the stink of unleaded gasoline could be. The whole place reeked of it, and it turned the air quite blue. Most of the sidewalks were in serious disrepair, and it was clear that there was a serious shortage of either money or motivation to do anything about the problem. The cleanliness of the American urban atmosphere—even Los Angeles—seemed remarkable in comparison.

Our destination was the new International University, one of the hosts of the conference. The building was pleasant, in traditional ocher-colored brick, the typical hue for Moscow buildings in the last century. I noticed one strange thing—there was a shoe factory right in the middle of the residential neighborhood, something that could not happen with zoning laws in the USA. It seemed that most of the industry now in the midst of urban Moscow had been swallowed up by the tremendous expansion of the city with in-migration from other parts of Russia.

At the hotel, the lady receptionist was charm personified—something I certainly did not remember from my earlier visits. She showed me to my spacious quarters with functioning bathroom (and *hot water,* something else I definitely did not see last time). I fancied it was worthwhile unpacking since today was Sunday, and I would be in the hotel until Thursday morning. My only priority then was to avoid jet lag by getting some sleep to make an easier transition onto Moscow time. Unfortunately, I could not tell what time it was, because I now had no watch.

Despite that problem, I woke up on Monday—the first work day—in good time and enjoyed the blessed relief of a good shower, then dressed formally for the opening ceremony of the conference. All the time I kept thinking how strange it was that the family of the boy who had occupied our house and our hearts for half a year resided just a few miles from where I was standing. A knock at the door broke this reverie, revealing the lady who had been at the reception desk last night (who must have worked an extremely long shift), to tell me that breakfast would be at 8:30 in the dining hall. I arrived promptly and was ushered into what my hostess called the "special" back room where I met my companions for the next few days. There was a charming German businessman from Munich, a professor from Guelph, Ontario, whose accent immediately revealed him to be Welsh, but who did not speak the language, a geneticist from New York, and an Indian professor from a university in Pennsylvania. We were to meet each of the next several mornings over an identical breakfast of two fried eggs, wonderful bread, and Russian tea. We all liked each other instantly and that made for a good start. The Indian related how he had found a Chinese restaurant and somehow managed to spend $50 on a meal there. That was two month's salary here.

At 9 a.m., after a certain amount of anticipated confusion, we entered an aged bus and sat there for some considerable time until we realized that the driver did not know where to take us. We, for our part, had no idea where the conference was to be held for we had never seen a program. Salvation came from the geneticist, Professor Bloom of New York, who somehow, alone among us, had in his possession an English agenda for the conference. This revealed it to be in the *Mairie* or City Hall. With that we were off.

The Mairie was the original COMECON building housing the Eastern European equivalent of the "EEC" in the days of the Soviet empire. Now it had no purpose and so had been taken over by the Moscow city government. It was an enormous tower block next to the "White House" that featured so vividly during the August 1991 coup (and was subsequently the pyrotechnic scene of Mr. Yeltsin's confrontation with the opposition in September 1993). We had to pass the guards to enter. For this we needed a badge, but the badges were issued at registration—and that was inside. Happily, we were met immediately by our host, Michael Kozeltsev of the Economics Department at Moscow State University. He was a nervously hyperactive,

Roman in front of the "White House"

exuberant, chubby man who was always trying to perform many tasks simultaneously. I registered and was rewarded with the plastic badge that I needed to pass through security. I took the opportunity to ask the woman at the registration desk if she would help me try to establish contact with Roman Zlotin. As she was writing down the details of his phone number, I suddenly noticed that he was right there, standing behind me, beaming and resolutely denim-clad amid a sea of suits. He would be my lifeline for most of the conference period. We were delighted to see each other, but almost immediately had to make our way into the hall for the opening address by Russia's minister of environmental protection.

Over the course of the conference we were to learn that the average life expectancy of 14-year-olds in Moscow was now eight years less than their US counterparts, and that life expectancy in general, along with the overall Russian population, was actually falling rapidly. Furthermore, more than half the city's children were sick at any one time, and over 30 percent of these were chronically ill. It was astonishing to learn that male life expectancy overall had dropped to 60 years, which meant that it was now less in Russia than it was in Indonesia or the Philippines.[7] Also, the number of children born to each woman had dropped from an average of 2.17 five years ago, to 1.4. Deaths in Russia had exceeded births the previous year (1992) by 800,000. These appalling figures had a special, and very personal, relevance for me now, and I was better able to comprehend Ludmila's wish that Eldar grow up in the USA at this moment in Russia's history. It was not hard to understand the environmental mess when one considered the amount people smoked, the air they breathed, and the water they drank. Also, the stress of living through tremendous inflation and unemployment was certainly not helping—especially in a country that had not known either for three generations. The tale was dismal, and the cost of doing anything about it was totally beyond the means of industry and government. The Ministry of the Environment routinely issued fines to gross polluters, but had no way to make them pay or shut them down, which is what would happen if they did enforce the laws. Thus it was all empty gestures of one sort or another, for if the fines were imposed most of the factories in Moscow would close. Furthermore, since nearly all the factories were state-owned, the fines would mean that the government was prosecuting itself, and so was unlikely to comply, or even take the matter seriously.

In the evening after a most depressing day, Roman Zlotin and I walked to what used to be called "Gorki Street" the last time I was here, and I

---

[7] By 1995, this figure had dropped to an even more astonishing 55.6 years, which meant that a child born today can expect to live a shorter life than his father or grandfather.

marveled at the prominence of French perfumeries among all the confusion and economic pandemonium. From here we secured a taxi to Roman's flat on Krupskaya Street (still named after Lenin's wife). There I met Roman's wife, Sonya, who would be coming to the USA with Roman in the fall. She was charming, but knew very little English as yet. Their son Alexei (Alyosha), tall and very earnest, hoped to attend a university in the US in a year or two to pursue Arctic studies. His English was extraordinarily good and made everything flow well. Roman, clutching vodka and cognac simultaneously, helped things to flow too. The apartment contained, rather surprisingly, the skeletal remains of many animals, and had at one time boasted a live scorpion. On the balcony a small aviary housed various brightly colored birds. Roman's desk was topped by a large collection of miniature frog figurines. This was a most eclectic place as befitted the rather Pickwickian figure of Dr. Zlotin. Dinner was accompanied by Uzbek and Spanish wines: a combination that was a first for me. During the course of the evening Roman phoned Ludmila and arranged for me to visit Eldar's family for the first time the next evening.

The Zlotin family with son Alex

The following day we had a free afternoon so the German professor and I took a stroll to see the heart of the "new Russia." First we paused at a private hole-in-the-wall cafeteria where we had a reviving cup of tea for 10¢. Then we riffled through the CDs at the record shop next door, but there was little there to interest us because most Russians seemed to want to buy Western pop music. Then on along Arbat Street. This used to be where all the hawkers in creation sold their wares, but now they had been given their marching orders and told to go to the Ismailova Park, since definite evidence proved that the "mafia" had taken over this street and were demanding protection money. The mafia, through its general ascendancy over the civil *militsia* or police, now had enormous power, and the new wealth was evident in the hugely expensive cars on the streets— one vast Mercedes astonished even the distinguished professor from Munich. "My God! I can't see enough money around me in this city to pay for that!" he muttered subversively to me. In reply, I described the period of transition to him as moving from "*Tovarich* (Comrade) to *nouveau riche.*" That about summed up what was happening in the minds of most Russians. The German was in pursuit of a rather superior *matrioshki* (one of those endless Russian stacking dolls), and was apparently willing to pay anything to get the best. We saw every known variety, following the best Teutonic principles of shopping, and he ended up buying one for $350 (a total fortune in rubles) that contained 30 nesting dolls, all exquisitely painted with scenes from Russian fairy stories. I managed, rather more modestly, to find a photo album with a hand-painted lacquer cover for $7 and some small curiosities. We came upon an informal Georgian art fair in an upper room, where the only painting that caught my eye—albeit a very beautiful small one of a Turkish-style house and mosque in Tblisi—turned out to be $600! That was a true fortune in this city. At the end of this stroll—a word the German liked greatly and continued to play with in conversation during the leisurely perambulation—we came across a T-shirt for $6 emblazoned with the grand Imperial Russian eagle: one head looking west, the other east. This was more tasteful than the one showing Lenin with a Big Mac (MacLenin) or another with the red Soviet flag in tatters above the expression "The Party's Over." One curious thing stemming from the runaway inflation was that the old cash registers couldn't cope with numbers greater than 999.99 rubles (for which one could buy a car three years ago). So to buy a 6,000 ruble T-shirt the seller had to ring up the price *seven* times! I wanted to see my German colleague's 40,000 ruble *matrioshki* doll—go through the cash register, but mercifully they found some way around that.

Eldar's Family

That evening Roman Zlotin and I walked again to erstwhile Gorki Street to find a taxi. This was my first visit to Eldar's family. It was an odd situation for me; something akin to meeting the in-laws for the first time, and I confess to being just as nervous as a prospective groom as we drove along *Vernadskogo Prospekt* on which they lived. The taxi eventually pulled up outside an apartment block indistinguishable from the hundreds of others in the area. I noticed that Roman was handling me just as the best man copes with the groom on his wedding morning by carrying on a humorous mind-diverting, nerve-settling badinage about nothing in particular. After passing through the grim entrance hall of the apartment block, we ascended in a graffiti-covered elevator (why are graffiti *always* in English?). At the tenth floor the machine stopped uncertainly and we exited, turned to the left and found ourselves in front of a set of double glass doors. This was it. Roman rang the bell. There was an immediate sound of frenzied movement somewhere deep within the flat, a ruffling of the curtains, and then the door was opened by Roman Urumbaev, Eldar's oldest brother. He had the same slightly eastern cast as Eldar and, like him, had not one ounce of surplus weight. Most noticeable here, in conservative Russia, were his earring and pony tail. In the United

States he would have been taken instantly for a Native American. He seemed nervous but was fastidiously polite and ushered us into the Urumbaev home. I kept thinking how familiar this would look to Eldar, and how foreign it was to me.

Eldar's brother Roman who could be an Apache

The apartment consisted of a hall running right and left from the double doors. To the right the corridor was totally festooned with books piled high up the wall. Beyond that were the kitchen, shower and what the architects call the "usual offices." To the left the hallway opened out onto a suite of three rooms: further to the left, through another set of double glass doors was the dining/living room, sporting a very upmarket Sony television and video; straight ahead were two bedrooms. What suddenly struck me were all the photographs of Eldar. This drove home the fact that this apartment was his environment, which he might well still regard as "home". Of course I should have expected to see his photograph, but suddenly seeing him here was odd and unsettling, since this whole period of his life was an unknown to me. This was a new experience for a parent.

The family was marshaled in strength. Roman introduced me to his brother Timur, who looked like a wild, free-spirited Bohemian in a white jacket, with eyes that told you he was ready for anything. His wife Tanya was also there, looking lovely and not at all Bohemian. She was an English-speaker who had translated some of our correspondence for Ludmila. Her father was a professor; almost everyone I met had academic affiliations. Also in this group was Ludmila's father, Vasili Ivanovich Filin, a retired schoolteacher of mathematics from Siberia who was working on some project that I was never able to divine. The last member of the group, Professor Michael (Misha) Bogomolov, a professor of geology and a former schoolmate of Nuris, Eldar's father, was unknown to me. He had glasses and a white goatee beard, and looked the true intellectual. Gradually I came to realize that he had been cast in the role of counsel to Ludmila concerning the Eldar question, probably because of his close former association with her husband. I also learned to appreciate that he had been a counsel, quite sensibly, for caution, and it was *his* analysis of Eldar's future, I fancied, that would present me with my greatest challenge. Also, as an English speaker he was going to be the medium through which my message would have to pass most of the time, since no one in Eldar's immediate family knew English.

The only person missing from the assembly, I realized, was Ludmila herself, and she, I was told, was putting the finishing touches to dinner in the kitchen. Presently, after we were all seated, she entered. I knew her, of course, from Eldar's photographs, but she was shorter than I had anticipated, and since his photographs were black and white I was not prepared for her ice-blue eyes that provided a sharp difference from all three of her sons. We kissed in the Russian fashion on the cheeks, and I suspected she was at least as apprehensive as I. However, she deflected this by concentrating on the domestic details of the mammoth meal set out before us and backed up in the kitchen. She had a transparently open soul, though much confused by the recent domestic and political events that had sundered her previously comfortable life. She was also ill at ease with being cast into the role of decision maker in the family, a role that had previously, very clearly, been held by Nuris. Nonetheless, she seemed genuinely determined that I should have a good time.

L to R: Roman Zlotin, Timur, Misha, Ludmila, self and grandfather

Somehow we became comfortable with each other very quickly, perhaps because we had a common friend in Roman Zlotin. I spent a lot of the time trying to see resemblances between Eldar and his mother and brothers. Sometimes I could see it, sometimes not. Timur, in his early twenties, was an undeniably dramatic and turbulent-looking fellow, whereas Eldar had a tranquil composure that showed clearly in his face. Natasha, my former student and now a classmate of Timur, had assured me Timur's wild look was matched by an equally turbulent personality. They were both in the Geography Department at Moscow State University, but he had also a part-time job fitting out apartment buildings with reinforced steel doors. The fact that this was growth industry was a definite sign of the times. Roman Urumbaev was also shorter than I had anticipated from the one or two photographs I had seen in Eldar's room. Overall, Roman was rather taciturn and apparently quite the opposite of Timur, though his participation in the conversation was impeded both by his deafness, and because everything had to be translated. Everyone, at the same time, constantly rushed around trying to make the guests feel at home.

Fairly quickly the eating began. The table was already set when we arrived, which is an eastern-European tradition and had been the case in Bulgaria and Macedonia when I was there. First came the champagne that Timur let fly with a huge explosion and an expansive gesture suited to his appearance. Then came the first of innumerable toasts—a Russian tradition of which I retained a hazy recollection from the earlier visits— ("welcome, and thanks for what you have done for Eldar"). Fresh salad was accompanied by fish and Azerbaijanian cognac. Most of the first hour or so was consumed by my description of Eldar's life, school, activities, size, behavior, etc. This, I felt, was the evening of information, rather than substance or strategy. I was shown a video by brother Roman that his father took during my visit to Elbrus in 1990. I had almost forgotten how stunningly beautiful it was, and how small Eldar was in those days. He was really a child in the video, running around in tracksuit and sweatband, waving his arms, making faces at the camera, and being determinedly hyperactive. This was a very different Eldar from the quiet, shy and introspective teen ensconced in our home. I marveled at the change.

As the evening progressed, broken by toast after toast, we started to learn more about each other. Soon I felt really comfortable with them, and it appeared that confidence was shared on both sides of the table (Roman Zlotin and I sat on the bed against the wall that served as a bench). Everything came to a merry and joyful end as Misha offered to take me home well after 1:00 a.m. We had not really resolved anything on the adoption front, but then we never expected to approach that issue at the first moment of contact. At least they had now come to know who I was, and had obtained some personal knowledge of both sides of the Eldar situation. Previously their only information had come through Nuris, Eldar, phone calls, photographs, and letters. The main impression I gathered was that the link of friendship between Nuris and I was the principal point of confidence for the family. I learned that, before his death, he had intended to come and visit me in the USA, and had actually made plans for travel. That was something I had not known up to that point.

On Wednesday, the last day of the conference, the people at the hotel celebrated either our impending disappearance, or the accumulated joy of having had us around, by slightly modifying the breakfast so that there was a little jam with the bread. The heated discussions at the conference continued in the plenary session, though most of the attendees had left by now. The Russians had an interesting variation on the style of public conference speaking. While the person was making the presentation from the podium, people with questions wrote them down, then walked to the front and left them on the podium for the speaker to address afterwards. There was no real cut-and-thrust; it was all too structured for that, much like the US Congress in fact. The chair, however, was a master of crowd control, and did not allow any dissenting voices to get a grip on the proceedings. In the true style of the old regime he had already written the recommendations of the conference, and read them extremely fast.

After all was done, the German professor and I headed for the front door, where we had arranged to meet Roman Zlotin's son Alexei, our guide around the city for that day. By now all my colleagues were true initiates of the "Eldar Saga," as one of them christened it. Alexei was there waiting, and so was his father who presented me with my agenda for the rest of the week. It ended with the words "Sunday: departure, tears, despair . . ." We took off again pausing at a mini-cafe for tea, squishy cakes, and some salami sandwiches. Our next stop was a bookshop, where I bought some Russian classic hardbacks for Eldar (total cost $1) and two wall maps of the former USSR and the world. Unfortunately, the one section of the bookshop that I wished to examine was closed for "inventory." (This reminded me immediately of Bulgaria, where most of the retail institutions seemed to be permanently involved in inventory activities—always during shop hours!). Then down into the metro and off to unknown parts of the city to find another bookshop and stamp shop (I confess to that juvenile weakness). But when we eventually got there the shop was closed for something totally mystifying called "sanitary day." Alexei explained that this was common, and it just meant that they were cleaning it. Once more this demonstrated the fact that the store served the state, not the shoppers.

Our primary mission aborted, we retraced our tracks and passed, en route, a run-of-the-mill general department store, where it seemed appropriate to look for a watch to replace the one I had lost at the airport. I found a rather handsome *Zarya* for just under $2, accompanied by a leather strap for 8¢.

This allowed me to return to Roman the monster-sized blue wristwatch he had loaned me. It was very functional and could, as he observed, double as a useful weapon under the right circumstances. I also managed, at this ultracheap emporium, to buy a decorative cutting board, though I am not sure why. Exhausted by all this retailing, Alexei and I found a small kiosk where we bought some remarkably good Russian beer, sat on a trash-filled concrete structure of indeterminate purpose, and discussed the ways of the world. Actually we spent all the time discussing the nature of America, and what made it fundamentally different from Europe: my favorite theme. It was a very enjoyable chat, and quite mind stretching to think of these very fundamental questions that normally we never address.

I returned by taxi to the haven of my room barely in time to tidy up before Natasha Kosheleva, my former student and Eldar's former English teacher, was due to arrive. I had not seen her since the last time I was in Moscow, when we talked for hours and hours in my room in Moscow University as the samovar bubbled to provide tea and my sole source of hot water for a month. Natasha was, as always, on time and we were really happy to see each other again. She said we should go for a long walk and talk about "everything." Where we were headed I was not sure, but it was great just to talk to her.

Natasha Kosheleva translating in the middle of the very complicated discussions

As we ambled along, taking in great draughts of burned, leaded gasoline on an otherwise beautiful evening, she told me that she had left her doctoral studies at Moscow State University because of the serious downturn in her family's fortunes. Her father was a major-league nuclear research scientist in one of the (still) closed cities. His institute had long been unable to provide salaries and so he was provided with food and accommodation but nothing else. He had had no income for about a year. Meantime the grandmother had become incapacitated through illness, and so Natasha's sister had to stay home to look after her, abandoning her doctoral studies at Moscow State University. This placed the *entire* burden of supporting the family on Natasha. Meantime she had found a job with a Russian entrepreneur who traveled to Taiwan, Thailand, and other places buying items for sale back in Russia. She translated for him and was paid in hard currency, so this provided her with a good opportunity to make some real cash. On the other hand this was a waste of her considerable academic talents, and the university had been very upset that she left. In reality, she had no choice.

En route we passed a building called *The Museum of the Revolution*. I immediately thought of 1917, but I was confused by the fact that the museum had a modern-looking battered tram prominently placed in the forecourt. Then I realized that the "revolution" in this case was the one of August 1991, and the tram was one that had been used as a barrier in front of the Russian parliament and had been pushed aside by a tank. As we strolled through the evening sunshine she told me about the times of the coup:

"Yes, I remember that. I used to work in my laboratory each day, and to pass the time I always had my radio tuned to this new rock-music station. On that day there was *nothing*. Can you imagine? The station, and many others had disappeared. I mean that is really mysterious. Well, the government told us nothing either, and it was not until 4 in the afternoon that they even said that Gorbachev had been 'taken ill' in the Crimea where he had gone on holiday. Nobody knew what was happening. Then, when it was clear what was going on, my big field trip, for which I had been planning for months, was canceled. I was mad, I can tell you. But, whatever you see and hear, you must remember, there is no going back to the old ways. Now, I have to tell you, things are really terrible. We don't know what is happening or where we are going. I don't trust anyone at the top."

Echoing something that the Urumbaev family friend Misha said, Natasha maintained that there were too many people with powerful vested interests in the new business sector, and in politics, to allow the changes to slip away and the old system to come back.

After a walk of well over an hour we approached the point that Natasha had chosen for our destination—which turned out to be the Moscow Pizza Hut! Natasha told me that the Russian restaurants were so crowded and noisy that we would never have a chance to talk about anything. I cannot imagine why Pizza Hut would be any less noisy until I noticed the sign on the door that said that food inside was available for *hard currency only*. That would rule out most people, though the sign did mention that they had another location that accepted rubles.

The interior was sparsely populated and quiet. The menu looked vaguely familiar, but horribly out-of-place here. What was less familiar were the prices, indicating that a meal for two here was going to come to around $40. I wondered how a $20-per-person pizza dinner would go down at Pizza Hut's establishments in New York (or Bloomington)? But we did have a long talk, and it was clear that Natasha's main intention was to continue her studies, in the USA if possible. After we had finished our meal, we started to walk back, but eventually gave in and took a trolley. One extremely drunken man, with his severely sober wife, also tried to get in, but instead ended up performing a sort of spontaneous pirouette on the steps. That resulted, to his genuine astonishment, in his getting off the bus and ending up outside facing the opposite direction.

I bade farewell to the hotel on Thursday, and said good-bye also to my four very pleasant colleagues who were now going their various ways. Probably I should never see them again (though one of the resolutions of the conference was that they would do this each year). Misha collected me and my bags on time, and we loaded everything into his red *Zhighuli* station wagon so that I could move into the flat with Eldar's family.

At the Urumbaev flat, everyone was there to welcome me and we immediately proceeded to lunch, which was again already prepared and on the table. I took this opportunity to distribute the various gifts that Susan, Eldar and I had selected for the family. Definitely the prize for favorite went to a small stuffed penguin for Varya, Timur's 2½-year old daughter. Once more we all looked through the photos of Eldar that Susan and I had sent them over the last year, and I was impressed by how much he had grown, and by the number of times these photos had been looked at previously. Many of the best shots were not there because they had been sent to other family members, and so it was clear that we had to send multiple copies if we wished Ludmila to keep ones for herself. The family was delighted with Eldar's progress in school—he had finished the year with straight As— and since this seemed to be a recurring statement, it really did mean a lot to them that he had at last taken a serious interest in his education. They explained that previously Eldar had moved around a great deal, never able to settle into any situation for long before he was sent off again, and in Russian schools newcomers had a very hard time because there was a sort of culture against them. Since Russians customarily did not move around as much as Americans, there was less acceptance of new faces in a closed environment like a school class. Perhaps these were the reasons Eldar had disliked school in Moscow so much and had performed so poorly.

Lunch over, the family proposed a trip into the countryside around Moscow, for it was a truly beautiful day. Eventually we arrived at a point on the slopes overlooking the river where there was a fifteenth century monastery in which Peter the Great had spent part of his childhood, mainly organizing everyone into toy armies. It was a delightful setting with a fine vista across a broad bend of the river. The central building was fascinating, being, in essence, a gigantic white-painted brick tower with an encircling birch verandah and steps.

We had the chance to wander through this lovely, if rather wet, site down to the river and along wooded paths, up wooden staircases and over bridges. The site was pretty much our own that afternoon. Here and there were medieval wooden log buildings that had been brought from different parts of Russia and reconstructed. They included one that had been the home of Peter the Great at Archangel when he was there supervising the construction of his new fleet after his long stay in the Netherlands pretending to be a carpenter. It was remarkably modest for someone who was not only the Tsar autocrat but a physically enormous man as well.

Misha, the family friend and principal guide, was a great believer in conspiracy theory, which popped up regularly in our conversations. He saw the current situation in Russia as partly a result of the success of the CIA in overturning the old order and exploiting the weaknesses resulting from Gorbachev's political openness, and partly the total lack of an economic program. Misha certainly was no friend of the old order, and indeed had lost his job as a result of his refusal to join the Communist Party *twice* in his career. On the other hand, he felt absolutely no sympathy with the new order, which he saw as a group of "bandits and traitors." I was intrigued to know how the current political impasse would be resolved (though nobody anticipated the violent mayhem that followed in August 1993). He said that in his personal view there would be a civil war, but that the natural leaders of this country were the patriarch of the Orthodox Church, and the monarchy. That certainly caught me off-balance. He was quite convinced about this, and indeed he had a portrait of Nicholas II in his flat. I suspected that more people supported this point of view than we appreciated in the West.

Back at the house, more eating! Ludmila had made *manti*, a central Asian dish not unlike Polish *pirogis*, with meat in steamed dough, covered in melted butter. In fact, every meal had a central Asian twist to it, frequently featuring lamb, meat-based soup, and mixtures of meat and homemade pasta. Once again, the wine flowed, as did the ubiquitous cognac and vodka. Natasha, who had joined us for the evening, was clearly one of Ludmila's trusted friends. At one critical point Natasha turned to me and said, probably very wisely, "I think you should tell them we must talk about Eldar now!" That was the cue, and she steered the conversation into a very clear discussion of Eldar's different options. I gradually realized that, until now, these had not been clearly understood at all. Of course one of the problems had been that our communications—although made as precise as we could—were necessarily written in *English*, and had to be translated. We never had been sure exactly who was doing this task, and it turned out to be Timur's wife Tanya, whose knowledge of English was not comparable to Natasha's.

It became evident right away that they feared Eldar would forget his roots and perhaps his family too. That possibility, very obviously, troubled them a lot. I told them that, as I understood the situation, there was no necessity for him to assume US citizenship immediately, for once he got his resident alien or "green card," most of the current problems would be alleviated, if that was their central concern. However, not getting US citizenship would always leave him subject to the whim of the Russian government at any time he found himself visiting Russia (including being co-opted into the army). My most serious challenge was to convince everyone that we did not intend to take possession of Eldar, or "own" him in any sense that would estrange him from his family or his culture.

I now appreciated that I was in Moscow precisely at the most critical moment in this story, even though I had never planned to be here. During this discussion it became clear that many confusions and many reservations concerning our real reasons for wanting to look after Eldar were all being resolved.

After everyone else had gone, Natasha spent a long time talking very frankly to Ludmila about Eldar. It was long after midnight when Roman and I walked her to the nearest metro station, bade her farewell, and thanked her for all her help in clarifying so many issues.

While we were gone Roman Urumbaev rapidly converted the scene of the meal into my bedroom, draping a sheet over the double glass doors to protect my modesty. Timur and Tanya had left for their own apartment. I returned to find my bed made, and was able to sleep well, feeling a lot better after these ice-breaking discussions.

The next day, Eldar's brother Roman, who, I had learned, loved his sleep as much as Eldar, joined me for a huge breakfast of *blinis*[8], accompanied by a mixture of honey and nuts, wonderful gooseberry jam, tea, and coffee. He asked me to accompany him for a walk through the nearby birch woods so that he could show me all the places where Eldar had grown up, including the slide he slid down, the soccer field he played on, and even the school he hated! We photographed everything religiously to provide Eldar with some souvenirs of earlier times. This birchwood park was delightful and an unsuspected oasis amid the crush of high-rise apartments. Here, young women performed calisthenics, while others walked an amazing variety of exotic dogs, including some that must have occupied a good 10 percent of their owners' apartments. Roman also showed me his light-blue *Lada*, a Russian remake of a much earlier *Fiat* car, which was suffering from some brake malady at that time.

Back in the flat, Roman showed me his room in great detail, pointing out the ski rack he had made, and his vests from two competitions in France and

---

[8] Russian crepes

Canada in which he had participated. He then first showed me a video made by the ski championship organizers in which he was interviewed, followed by another video of his ascent to the top of Mount Elbrus. Like Eldar, Roman was clearly a remarkable skier. He had even brought back with him a clip of Russian and German cartridges that he had found while climbing in the Caucasus, mute testimony to the terrible fighting in those mountains during the last war.

Last in the video parade came a film of Timur's wedding. By a remarkable coincidence, Timur and Tanya were married on the same day in August 1990 as Susan and I. The film showed the whole family, including Nuris, approximately six weeks after I left him in Elbrus. I had no idea at that time that he had any other sons or that one of them was about to get married, even though we had talked about my own impending marriage. Timur clowned his way through most of the video, and at one point appeared standing in the pool in front of Moscow University with his trousers rolled up, threatening to pull Tanya in. At the end of the videos, I gave Roman my Indiana T-shirt to replace the Georgia Tech one he had been wearing since I arrived. I found myself liking Roman a lot, for he came across as a thoroughly sincere person, if imposingly reserved and deep. Since it was now lunchtime, he and Ludmila told me to fill up because we would be out all afternoon and there would be no chance for food.

Our plan for the rest of the day was to go to the outlying city of Zagorsk (now renamed to the original Sergei Pasad). Misha collected our group, consisting of myself, Roman, his diminutive ingénue girlfriend Sasha, who communicated using a little French, and—picked up en route—Timur in a handsome white suit. Meantime, even more threatening than the black sky was the traffic of downtown Moscow, which was logjammed (or "corked" as Misha called it). He had a method of driving that was based mainly on reckless and unheralded lane-switching. We made it through, but it left me in a state of nervous hypertension. Then the rain started to come down in great sheets, and the day looked hopeless as we fought to get out of Moscow's traffic into the storm-lashed countryside. Eventually we broke free and took off at high speed, slowing down only for the known traffic-police locations. All the time the rain was relentless.

We entered Zagorsk in a general feeling of hopelessness since it seemed we would barely be able to venture out of the car in this downpour. However, as we reached an overlook point for the old city, the rain stopped suddenly and the sun emerged, bouncing off the white walls of the ancient buildings and setting them in dramatic relief against the scudding blackness of the stormy sky. The city was truly one of the world's wonders, with brilliant blue onion domes speckled with gold stars rising over great white walls, lacing the sky with lustrous gilded triple crosses. Interestingly, because of its antiquity, nothing here was regular or vertical. All the lines were slightly out of true, giving the architecture a wonderful human quality. From our lookout point high on the walls we could see private houses of monumental proportions and surpassing pretentiousness built in red brick, but with galvanized iron roofs I associated with garden sheds. Who were the people with this sort of money?

We entered the monastery city, taking a detour to the equally medieval toilets where you had to perform without breathing, for the price of breathing was to lose your lunch instantly. Once beyond the miasma, however, the inside of the walled enclosure was absolutely charming and I felt like photographing everything over and over again. We entered one 15th-century church where a service was in progress. There, Timur and Roman bought candles to light in memory of their father. Then we ascended the great central bell tower by means of a wooden spiral staircase, which presented real problems for parties meeting midway who were headed in opposing directions. On the way in, Misha informed me furtively not to say anything, because the entry fee for foreigners was a lot higher than for locals. I, thus, dutifully nodded in mute compliance at everything the young woman cashier said. I found this place entrancing, and the monks in their medieval black robes and flowing beards gave everything an air of timelessness. But, times must have changed for them too, given the new tolerance of religion.

Eldar's brothers light candles in memory of Nuris

On exiting the compound we were greeted again by a roiling black sky, which lived up to its promise as soon as our visit was over, for as we reached the car the heavens opened and walls of water cascaded down again. We sat, perforce, in the increasingly steamy car where we discovered that Ludmila had provided heaps of food in the form of sandwiches, *blinis (crêpes)*, gallons of hot tea, etc., despite her admonishments that we fill up before we leave. We passed the time in conversation about the nature of the Welsh language, for which Misha harbored a strange fascination!

Back at Moscow we paid a short visit to Misha's flat. It was everything you would have expected. The main features included more stuff per m² than any place known to civilization and with dusty rocks on every surface. He had, for instance, installed a workshop *behind* the wardrobe in the bedroom, and had an entire bearskin on top of said wardrobe. Mineral specimens and fossils abounded on every surface. There was a photo lab in the tiny bathroom. His bed had five telephones on it. This was an extraordinary place, but he was clearly quite a craftsman, as well as being a photographer of considerable note, for some of his huge black-and-white enlargements were breathtaking. How could anyone live in this one room flat and tiny kitchen where there was no living space left? I just had to ask why he had *five* telephones, and the answer was intriguing and quite in keeping with the Rube Goldberg look of the place. It seemed that a friend of his had invented a circuit to go into a phone, so, when someone called the phone *told* you, (in a simulated voice in Russian), from where the caller was phoning. It also stored the last 50 numbers and would call any of them on demand: you simply spoke to it. He promised to adapt one for America, and give it to Ludmila to bring. I hoped the adaptation included teaching it to speak English! The other phones were ones with the same feature that he was hoping to sell.

At dinner, back at the Urumbaev home, Misha acted as translator. This turned out to be *the* really crucial conversation regarding Eldar because it seemed that by now trust had been established, and we did not need to equivocate any longer. I felt really comfortable by this time, and it was apparent that they were at ease with me. Misha, I fancy, had been urging caution upon Ludmila all along because he was a true Russian patriot and feared that Eldar would not only lose his identity and his fluency with Russian, but also the possibility to return to his native land. I explained that none of this need happen, and I would certainly not encourage it. I also went into great detail, again and again, to explain that this was not a "transfer of ownership," but instead a device to open options for Eldar without closing doors. This was, I sensed very strongly, the turning point and everyone was much more relaxed. Our discussions were characterized by total openness and honesty and we didn't seek a resolution that night, but instead made certain that everyone was clear on the facts and options.

The family helped me to understand the various dimensions of the problem as they saw it. Of course they loved Eldar completely; that was obvious. But, first and foremost was the fact that it had been Nuris' wish for Eldar to spend time in America, although, of course, he had never been thinking of anything more than a visit. The various members of the family around the table explained to me that if Eldar returned from America soon, he would face a very uncertain future in the Russia that seemed to be evolving dangerously around them. Misha spoke continually of criminals, bandits, and thugs when discussing politicians. This was a family of devoted patriots, and it pained them to see the rise of crime and the humiliation of a great power in these straitened times.

Someone remarked that even if Eldar came back from the USA with a good education there was a question about what future *anyone* had in Russia. The family had been severely hurt economically by the loss of the main breadwinner, for pensions had been beaten down by inflation. It also suffered from the previously unknown phenomenon of prices rising rapidly and, apparently, without any control. The last time I had been in Russia in 1990 it had cost me 50 kopeks to send a letter home. Now it cost 400 rubles. That was an 800-*times* increase in three years. To put it in perspective, this would have raised the price of a first-class letter in the United States at that moment to $256! Another problem that emerged was what sort of job could Eldar get in Russia? His brothers were adamant that he should stick with the American option. From the information given out at the conference earlier in the week I was able to understand their concerns much better, even to the extent that I wondered how long he might live if he returned home. What incentive, after all, was there for him to do well in the system as it was at this time? Furthermore, the family made it clear to me that, from his letters and calls to them, Eldar seemed happy about the idea of staying in the United States. The family painted a grim picture that evening, and I could see how humiliating and depressing it was for them and so many other Russians too.

The mood, consequently, had turned gloomy and despondent, though Timur made brave efforts to keep us going with an array of powerful spirits. It was well past one before I could reclaim my bedroom, which happened to be the same room where everyone was having dinner. I kept thinking how strange it was that Eldar grew up within these walls, and that I had never seen him in this setting. In an e-mail message he had sent to Roman Zlotin the day before, he remarked:

"It really is kind of strange to think of me here in your family while you are over there with my family." It was.

The final day, Saturday, was reserved for a visit to Ismailova Park, where the merchants and artists of the new Russia clustered to market their wares. We had arranged to meet Roman Zlotin in the corridor connecting the two lines beneath the University Metro Station. Roman Urumbaev and I sat there and watched the passing parade of the general public, which is always one of the best forms of entertainment anywhere. Almost everyone exited up the staircase marked "no exit." Roman Zlotin, fully clad in his uniform of denim, duly arrived, and we proceeded on a lengthy metro ride with a complex change somewhere in the middle. During the trip, brother Roman demonstrated his skiing prowess by the fact that even though everyone else in the train was hanging on for dear life, he went with the motion without once reaching up for support. This was most impressive.

At the park exit we proceeded to walk the wrong way, even though it seemed as if about one million people were headed in the opposite direction. There was a long pathway to the final selling ground, and this had been transformed into a sort of gauntlet of challenging hawkers. Among the interesting paraphernalia along that pathway, apart from the *matrioshki* salt, pepper, and mustard holders that Roman Zlotin bought for Susan, we saw a wooden trumpet. This was an instrument, seemingly from the medieval period, such as I had never seen. The gentleman selling it was a professional musician, and he demonstrated the quality of this instrument for us. The sound was astonishing in its penetration and volume, particularly from such a small artifact. I thought it would be ideal for starting large undergraduate classes at 8 a.m.

Along the way were people selling puppies and kittens. I saw these alfresco animal markets all over Moscow and there were obviously certain places where these pet exchanges were known to exist. And for the first time, I saw ordinary people selling their personal items—a shirt, some shoes, or whatever.

Most of what we saw was "souvenir" material: military badges, political pins, *matrioshki*, and every conceivable form of bric-a-brac. More unusual items included an old Estonian flag, a general's hat, a bronze bust of Nicholas II and another of Voltaire. Our selections were minimal and eventually we reached almost total saturation and decided to head for home. As we traversed a back way to avoid the crowds we came upon a solitary artist's stand. I must confess that the paintings were, according to my own unenlightened criteria, some of the only real art that I saw. The landscape watercolors were truly beautiful, and were the work of twin brothers. We talked and talked trying to decide which of these lovely items to buy. I eventually settled on one of Zagorsk, one of Suzdal, and one of who-knows-where for a total of $25. For me this was the best part of the morning.

Sudden Promotion

We then returned the way we had come, retracing our steps through the heaving throng in the metro back to Roman Zlotin's apartment for lunch. On the way to the door of his flat he paused to show Roman Urumbaev and myself his new car. It was a two-cylinder *Oka*, much like the smallest *Geo*. But by far the most interesting feature was not the car but the garage. It had been built out of the angle where two offset rows of garages came together. A triangular garage, in itself, was unusual, but this one had two trees growing through it and out through the roof. Only whimsical Roman could ever have dreamed up such a construction.

Indoors, Roman prepared a lunch of cabbage-in-batter and chicken along with wine and cola. After lunch Michael Kozeltsev, the conference organizer, stopped by unannounced (an endearing habit of the Russians long since rendered extinct in America). He wanted to talk over my impressions of the conference, and discuss how it might go the next time. While we were having an interesting chat the two Romans were talking in the next room. Roman Zlotin found out from Roman Urumbaev that the latter supported the idea of Eldar staying in the States one-hundred percent. Meantime the phone rang. It was my former student, Susan Cutting, calling from a village outside Moscow. She told me that she had seen me on a television program devoted to the recent conference. That was how she knew I was in the country and had guessed I might be visiting Roman Zlotin. There is no concealment in the information age. Up to that point I had no idea that I had been on the box!

The Family Decides

The final evening was a celebration. The family had also invited Natasha who was already there watching the news when we arrived. All the stops had been pulled out, and the champagne was flowing, with Timur, as always, opening the bottles with great flourishes. Toasts abounded faster than ever, and eventually each person spoke. Both brothers said that up to now they had been confused about the Eldar situation, not really understanding the possibilities, not knowing what to think. Now that they had met me and listened to the options—but most of all having translated a name into a real person—they both supported Eldar's staying in the States. Ludmila, her confidence much enhanced now, spoke at length, saying much the same thing, but adding that what Eldar was doing seemed to be a continuation of what Nuris would have wanted for him, and that everything seemed to be the result of the hand of God. This was a phrase that was to come up over and over.

Although this might seem to be a most unusual situation, in reality it was simple, normal, and straightforward because it concerned people, not countries or documents. Ludmila then told me that Timur had even spoken to Nuris' nonagenarian mother in Uzbekistan and she too had given her blessing to all this. Finally Ludmila said that she had decided, (and this clearly had not been easy up to now,) not only that Eldar *should stay in the USA*, but that she would like him to *become an American*. The brothers concurred. I had not expected the second point. At that moment Misha arrived and confirmed the general decision enthusiastically. I fancied this was something he would not have done at the beginning of the week. Most touching of all was the fact that Ludmila said that she felt truly, we had become not two families of Eldar, but *one* extended family, and that made it all so different. That, of course, was exactly how I felt about it. To emphasize this point I explained to the family that when a child was adopted in the US it normally takes the family name of the adoptive parents. Susan and I did not intend to do this: he would always remain Eldar Urumbaev. There was enough love to go round.

And so that was how this most important meal of my life ended: everyone concurring, everyone upbeat. On Ludmila's table were all the various papers that I was leaving for her to sign so that we could adopt Eldar. The last event was to walk Natasha Kosheleva to the metro once again at 12:30. Back in the apartment, I had to compress all my various gifts into my bulging suitcase. At that moment, deep in the recesses of the case, I found the watch I had "lost" at the airport, and felt guilt for all the suspicious thoughts I had harbored about someone having stolen it. I tried to sleep anticipating a 5:30 wakeup so I could get to the airport on time in the morning. Hundreds of mosquitoes ensured that sleep did not come, and I secured my most notable souvenir in the form of a body covered in bites.

And so, at 7:40 a.m. on Sunday, July 4, after a hurtling drive through the empty countryside with Eldar's brother Roman, his mother, and Roman's girlfriend Sasha (a remarkable act of friendship at this time of the morning), we reached the airport and said our good-byes at the end of a huge line—such an appropriate way to leave Russia. It was almost impossible to believe how much had happened in just one week. Thinking about it all, I soon left behind one of Eldar's worlds to return to him in his other world.

Chapter 14
Love's Young Dream

In early summer we planned to go to Canada to spend some time with Susan's parents near Toronto. Mr. Rund, who had replaced religion in our lives as the force instructing us what to do and not do, told us that it was fine for Eldar to go to the "contiguous states" since he would need no special documents to return to the United States. But we still needed to get him a Canadian visa, so we sent off for the visa application along with a yellowing copy of Eldar's newspaper interview, given soon after he arrived in America, to add a human face to the visa application. From the Canadian consul-general we received a charming letter remarking on what an interesting tale Eldar's was, and enclosing his passport with a visa valid for multiple entries for many years. I didn't think bureaucrats were supposed to behave like that.

We had to explain to Eldar that there was one small "complication" to our three-week holiday. Susan and I had invited the daughter of my oldest friend from Wales to come and stay with us for a month. Her visit coincided with the journey to Canada, so she would be traveling with us. Eldar's face lit up at this prospect until he thought to ask, "By the way, how old is she?"

"She is twelve, and her name is Mair [pronounced "My-er," with a rolled r], which is Welsh for Mary."

"*Twelve*! You mean we are going to be stuck with a *kid* for all that time?"

"She's almost as old as you are," responded Susan vigorously, thereby committing one of the greatest crimes against humanity known in the teen code of ethics. The difference between twelve and fourteen is a little more than 155 years, and several eons of maturity. It was foolish of us to forget that. We did not dare tell him that she had *just* turned twelve.

"I have an idea," Eldar retorted, having thought about the full horror of this situation. "When we travel, Susan, you could sit in the back with Mair, and I will sit in front with Randall. *You* can look after her. I would have nothing to say to anyone that age."

"No way kiddo," came back Susan's energetic response. "Adults sit in the front—kids in the back. You two will get on just fine."

It is amazing how all these tired parental clichés come out of your mouth when you have responsibility for a child. You never believed these things when you were that age, and now here *you* are using those same hoary old phrases.

Our plan was to collect Mair at Chicago's newly modernized O'Hare international terminal, and commence our holiday from there. Eldar sulked more or less for the duration of the five-hour journey through terrible traffic at the prospect of making conversation with, or even tolerating the presence of, a *girl*. At the airport we clustered around the exit from the customs area along with crowds of other expectant faces. Eldar, hands thrust deep into the pockets of his jeans, was staring at the floor and muttering, "Come on, come on, let's go, let's go. . . ." After an hour's wait the doors opened and through them passed a vision. She was about Eldar's height with long blond hair in the classic Lauren Bacall style flowing over her shoulders in waves. She had a near-perfect figure that no twelve-year-old should be allowed to possess outside a Nabukov novel. Her attire for the journey consisted of white bell-bottom jeans that she must have been sewn into lying down and a filmy, totally see-through lacy blouse over a black bra. Eldar reacted to this person immediately, much the same way a rabbit reacts to a rattlesnake, and when he realized that she was coming toward us he started to enter the early stages of cardiac arrest. He was frozen to the spot, and I thought he had forgotten to continue breathing.

"Hello Aunt Susan, I'm Mair," said the vision, removing her shades to reveal perfectly blue eyes.

I knew this blond/blue combination to be the apogee of excellence in Eldar's world. He was done for.

"This curious fellow with the choking expression is Eldar. Say hello, Eldar," Susan said with visible satisfaction, her tongue curled up the side of her upper lip, her eyebrow arched.

"I've been thinking," Susan whispered to Eldar as we left the airport arrival hall,

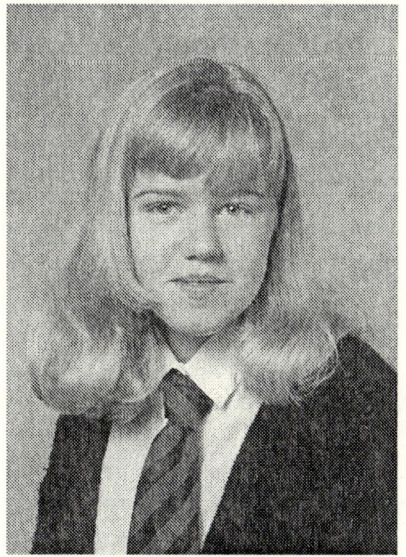

Mair, here even younger than twelve

"I think I was a little unfair to you earlier. You *can* sit up front with Randall, and I will share the back seat with *little* Mair."

"You try, you die," came the soft reply.

The first evening consisted of silent reverie. Eldar listened intently as Mair outlined some of the more curious and bizarre aspects of life back home in Central Wales. Interestingly she appeared to have a metabolism that functioned entirely without eating. Mair eschewed meal after meal, eventually revealing to us that she thought she was too fat. I should be so fat. But there was no real contact between the two teens at this early stage of mindless adoration. The first crisis occurred as we settled in for the night. Mair had lost the key for her suitcase. The hotel maintenance staff arrived with a tool I normally see used in films by people escaping from East Germany as they cut their way through steel mesh. The lock yielded like putty before such an onslaught. The case, however, had suffered from the fact that her shower gel had been liberated over the contents in transit.

North to Canada

We set off on our journey to Ontario, Canada, to stay with Susan's parents on the east side of Toronto, from where we would do some sightseeing further north. As we drove along the southern tip of Lake Michigan, we decided to stop at the sandy Indiana Dunes state park, which forms a passable, indeed very pleasant, surrogate for the major US holiday coasts from which the Hoosier state is equally remote. It was a gorgeous day. Below clear skies, in the hot embrace of the sun, we felt that the waters of the lake languidly lapping the sand were enticing beyond words. Unfortunately, our swimming gear was firmly trapped in the back of the car somewhere inside mounds of suitcases. That was really too bad. Mair and Eldar stood there looking yearningly at the water.

"Boy, doesn't that look good?" he said in a voice full of frustration, scuffing his foot back and forth in the sand.

"I'm going in!" exclaimed Mair.

"I wish we really could," responded Eldar dejectedly.

What happened next was what, I believe, is called a *defining moment* in life. After such a moment nothing is ever the same, like being shot, run over, or, as in this case, falling in adolescent love. Mair quietly and determinedly removed her shoes, and without a moment of hesitation, she rushed headlong into the waves fully clothed, disappearing completely. We were panic stricken and Susan's entire code of decorum and conduct had been torn up and thrown to the winds. Eldar was convinced he had just had a major religious experience.

A sudden inrush of breath from his direction was followed by, "She's totally crazy," as he stood there wide-eyed.

Then, two seconds later, completely upstaged and humiliated, and realizing that his entire future with this wonderwoman depended on what he did in the next five seconds, he broke away and dived in after her, and they threw themselves around with wild shouts of joy, screams, and laughter.

When they emerged we found that Mair still had her wallet in her jeans and was wearing her watch. So we spent some time laying out money in the sun to dry, and waiting until their clothes stopped dripping. After an eternity when they were both relatively dry again, Mair suddenly leapt to her feet and said:

"I can't stand it. I have to go again . . ." and she, hotly pursued by her worshiping acolyte, rushed into the waves once more.

"This trip is going to be *really* interesting," remarked Susan with the pursed lips, hooded eyes and worried brow that only mothers can achieve.

Once on the road again, it did not take too long for the back-seat pair to develop a curious form of rapport consisting of wild and frantic card games and attempts to teach Eldar to pronounce Welsh words (made up, to the untrained eye, almost entirely of endless, randomly placed consonants). They saw nothing, they heard nothing, they were, let's face it, not even there. For the remainder of the time in Canada they sat huddled together in the space behind the back seat of the hatchback. During these times they lapsed into a curious form of baby talk that they had evolved, or rather that Eldar had acquired when staying with Susan's young nephew and niece in Seattle for a week of skiing and sightseeing in March. One unfortunate side effect of this was that Susan's mother had to travel with a handkerchief rammed firmly into her mouth to prevent continual bouts of hysterical laughter at such remarks as, "I've bumped myself and I've got an owie," or "Look, it's a little goggie." Since Mair was profoundly into purple, Eldar suddenly acquired a fancy for a color he had never noticed before. They were totally inseparable, taking long walks up mosquito-infested lanes blissfully unaware of anything but each other. His admiration for Mair knew no bounds. When we eventually ended up at the giant theme park at Ontario Place, I tried to convince Mair to accompany me onto the roller coaster—a form of thrill for which I have a passion. No, that was "too scary." "Well, how about the Pirate Boat?" "That would make me sick," and so forth. Thus it was most of the afternoon, until she asked me:

"Uncle Randall, how much money do I have left in my holiday allowance?"

"Oh, you are pretty solvent, why do you ask?" I inquired.

"Well, I would like to go bungee jumping from that crane."

I could not believe what I was hearing. The Pirate Boat was too much for her, but hurling herself into space in high winds from the top of a construction crane, well, that was OK.

Eldar was, of course, suffused with admiration and was speechless. I agreed to her plan, but she came back very mad. She had been refused because of her age. She had been prepared to spend her entire holiday allowance right there on one mighty plunge. Eventually this duo was referred to by everyone in the party as LYD, or Love's Young Dream. We, of course, never used this expression in their presence.

At Gravenhurst, we ventured onto the lake in a rented motorboat of doubtful quality. Grandpa Peter had found a particularly "economical deal" as befits a Harvard MBA. He took off into the waves instantly at high speed, giving the people in the rear of the boat an experience much like that of an angry mob facing the firehoses in the Paris of 1968. That, plus the wind, reduced everyone to frozen jelly in no time. He could hear nothing we were saying, and had that disturbing Jerry Lewis look on his face. We eventually broke through Peter's manic glare behind the wheel, convincing him to head for more sheltered waters where the teens might swim and water ski, which had been the purpose of the expedition. Having found a suitable spot, and with the engine turned off, we watched Eldar descend into the water, lean back, raise his skis, holding the rope and bracing himself for the thrill to come. The thrill came in another, and unexpected, form. The boat would not start—the battery was stone dead. Yet another, and much bigger thrill was, however, in the making. Bearing down on us from opposing directions—but unmistakably headed *directly* for us were, on one side, the huge steamboat *Seguin*, giving us a live action replay of the last moments of the *African Queen* as the *Louisa* bore down on Bogart and Hepburn. Meanwhile, on the other side, the storm of the century was coming. We waved towels vigorously at passing craft until finally, we were rescued from the jaws of death by three women in a luxurious powerboat, who towed us home in a state of humiliation. Peter's manic glare had gone and he sat there staring at the over-groomed miniature poodles sitting on the stern of our rescuer's boat staring him in the eye.

Onwards now to Sudbury, with Grandma Verity's purse on the roof of their car the whole way. It had been put there while she rummaged for change at a gas station—and, amazingly, it remained there throughout the afternoon. When we stopped at an ice-cream parlor, Eldar's respect for his newly-acquired grandmother went up a quantum leap when she easily defeated him in a left-handed arm-wrestling match to the obvious displeasure of the rest of the clientele who were deeply displeased by the lack of decorum.

The journey home passed through Niagara Falls, but the magic was tempered by: i) some indefinable lover's tiff that provided a pouty foreground for all the standard holiday photographs; ii) an apocalyptic sky that brought down on us the entire Indian monsoon season in one day; iii) a near miss by a bolt of lightening that left the tang of ozone heavy in the air; and iv) huge lines of people for everything.

On our return to Bloomington, Voiko, our Bulgarian house sitter at that time, asked us whether we had been aware that there were 20,000 gallons of water in our crawl space. Frankly, we had not. Good soul that he was, he rented a pump and emptied out the lot.

Teen freeze-out at Sudbury, Ontario

Most of the time we were away, we had been thinking how good it was that Eldar had found a real friend (the Niagara crisis having since been resolved). The problem of course was that Mair was destined to leave very shortly. We didn't really see Eldar as the letter-writing type, but while she was there his devotion seemed boundless[9]. They never seemed to be in need of things to do. One time they rose at 3 a.m. to play monopoly. Fortunately, Mair's passion for reading encouraged Eldar to dip into books, which was something Susan and I had never succeeded in making him do. It was enough for them simply to enjoy each other's company for hour after hour. I pondered how many Russian/Kazakh/Welsh liaisons there had been before in history; not too many I imagined.

Eventually, after a four-week stay, Mair had to leave, requiring us to make another trip to Chicago. As always on these occasions there was time to kill, and the last thing in the world they probably wanted was a couple of oldies, (or *wrinklies*, as Mair told us we would be called in Britain), like us around, but that's life. As we strolled they always, somehow, managed to drop behind, holding hands, wordless, their presence revealed only by the

---

[9] Remember, we are in 1993 when the web was less than 6 months old, and virtually nobody had e-mail.

military clomp, clomp of Mair's purple Doc Martin boots. The hand holding was never to be seen if we turned around, but they forgot that shop windows reflect. We *really* felt like parents now. But, at the gate their teenage instincts reasserted themselves: they were too embarrassed to embrace at the moment of Mair's tearful departure.

For days afterwards, Eldar engaged himself in writing letters to Wales. I was sure the pace would soon slow. But even from the moment of her departure he had worked out the number of days until her school in Wales was out and she was free to come back next year. He seemed totally devoted to her, and to the best of our knowledge, no other girl was ever going to be allowed to occupy that sacred position in his life.

It lasted about three months.

Chapter 15
The Anniversary

On August 24, 1993 we celebrated the first anniversary of Eldar's coming to the United States. We prepared him a special "first birthday" card to commemorate the event. The exchanging of cards had always taken unpredictable turns with Eldar. Earlier in the year he had sent Susan a Valentine card showing, inexplicably, the *USS Enterprise* from *Star Trek*. The card bore the arcane message, "Happy Valentine from Space." But this was no less amusing than the birthday card Susan received from him the previous November. That had a printed message on it reading *To A Wonderful Boy*. The word *To* had been struck out, and the word *From* had been substituted!

The spirit of the first anniversary day was only slightly dampened by the fact that this was also the first day of the new school year, when Eldar would discover what lay in store for him during his first semester as a sophomore. It really did feel like a watershed since he now could look down on the younger freshmen in school, doing what he did last year. That step up the ladder gives high-school kids a real feeling of moving up and being veterans. The day was marked, as he came home that afternoon, by the discovery of his first letter from Mair in the mailbox. His excitement was palpable as he rushed into his room. His joy was unbounded, and he counted off another day until her return next year. Immediately he wrote back. Their exchange was not always by letter, and occasionally he was allowed to telephone. On one occasion this produced some excitement he had not anticipated, for instead of dialing the prefix 011 for international calls, he dialed 911, realized his error, put the phone down and called again. His conversation with Mair ended abruptly as a policewoman arrived at the door demanding to see an ID. This was a tricky situation for, of course, he had a completely different family name from ours. Eventually she was convinced when Eldar produced an ID document showing that he actually lived in our house, and had not simply broken in to make long-distance calls.

To round out the anniversary events, Roman Zlotin was due to arrive at Indianapolis airport to take up a teaching position at Indiana University for the fall. Susan and I went through one of those airport psychological warfare games, for the plane was not even listed on the arrivals board when we arrived there in the evening. Then we were informed that there was a delay, then another, and yet another. Eventually, by calling the airline direct, we discovered that the flight had been canceled long ago, and the rest was just public relations nonsense. I recalled it was not so far back that I had asked a desk clerk at Indianapolis about an overdue flight. He told me that he had just phoned Detroit and had been informed that the flight was taking off *as we spoke*, and would be here in about an hour. In fact, at that moment, the passengers had actually started disembarking from the jetway!

Since it was already 10:30 p.m., we were forced to stay overnight in Indianapolis without any of life's necessities, since we had never intended to be away from Bloomington. Early the next morning we were finally able to greet Roman, and his wife Sonja, as they stepped off the plane. The long wait, however, turned out to be worth every minute.

"For you. Most important documents," said Roman immediately, thrusting a large envelope into my hands.

Inside were all the documents necessary for Eldar's adoption, duly signed by Ludmila and properly authenticated and notarized by the United States embassy in Moscow. We were absolutely delighted to welcome both the Zlotins and their precious cargo.

As Eldar's second year in the United States began, it was astonishing to us how "normal" everything felt already. It was as though we had been parents forever—except for a bad case of total amnesia for everything that had happened before Eldar was 11. Susan no longer wrote his shower dates on the calendar, having successfully weaned him away from what she called "French levels of hygiene where they take a shower once a week whether they need it or not." There was also no longer any written record of how many days he had been wearing the same shirt, though she fought a losing battle with regard to the timely brushing of teeth. We presumed that you became accustomed to these things as children grew up. For us it was rather like acquiring an extremely complex gadget that had come without the instruction manual. Eldar was continuously astonished at the regulation and order in American life. Just as we had lost out on not raising a child the usual way, he (and I) had lost out on the process of growing up in America. So much was still strange (and sometimes ridiculous) to him, and as we started to see things through his eyes, we realized that we were all, in a sense, moving along a learning curve.

Most of all we remained concerned about the fact that he had so few friends, and almost none that we ever saw. This, I suppose, was typical "parent stuff." Our choice lay between feeling anxiety over the lack of friends, and worrying about the friends he might select. Yet, slowly he formed good relationships with some of the other international students at the school. The purchase of a bright red second-hand moped from his summer mowing money gave him new horizons, and he was able to go downtown, insofar as such a concept exists in a place like Bloomington. Mainly he cruised every backroad and subdivision, and ended each day by relieving the pressures of homework with a cruise in the dark (Indiana had never learned the benefits of having daylight-saving time, even though it manages to maintain three separate time zones within the state boundaries). Otherwise he often went for solitary walks at night. Though he seemed well able to cope with solitude, it was evident that he would much rather have had friends. Slowly, though, it was happening with a Nicaraguan here, a Venezuelan there, then a marvelously talented Chilean girl.

By now, Mair had, alas, faded with distance. The problem was that these people he met in Bloomington—the archetypical campus town—were transitory, often being the offspring of visiting faculty. So these friendships were painful in that they were destined to end quickly.

When the Chilean was first presented to us it looked as though he had crossed the Rubicon. Here was a beautiful, wonderfully talented young woman who clearly doted on him. At one point in the conversation I asked:

"So, Heather, how long are you and your mother going to spend in Bloomington?"

"Till Thursday," she said, and all options were off.

On the other hand, it seemed almost impossible for Eldar to break into the American circuit at school. Statements such as "Who is Elvis Presley?" could quickly isolate him from the mainstream of American culture. Furthermore, he had absolutely no interest in US league sports. For instance, he and Roman Zlotin attended an IU football game one afternoon: "part of studying for to become true Hoosier," claimed Roman. It was only at halftime that they discovered that Indiana was the team in red and white. They had been rooting for the other side right through the first half. They could possibly have survived that had not Roman asked his neighbor at half time, "Which one is Indiana, actually?" They escaped with their lives only because this was a football game. Had it been basketball in the Hoosier state....

Parents: To Be or Not To Be?

Now, with the arrival of Ludmila's consent, the matter of adoption was a reality and we had to move into high gear. So far, all our attention had been directed toward what Ludmila had to do, and when. The time had arrived for us to face the realities of the process of becoming adoptive parents. It was by no means an automatic thing that, his mother willing, Eldar would become our child. Just as one always seems to notice an account of an air disaster right before leaving on a flight, so it was now with adoption and us. Every newspaper we opened was full of horror stories of children being wrenched from weeping parents, children *divorcing* their parents, children being abused by their adoptive parents, and so forth. Aliens and Elvis had been replaced by child adoption dramas plastered all over the tabloids at the supermarket checkouts. Mr. Rund had already informed us that we would have to undergo a period of investigation involving a home study and interviews, as required by the State of Indiana, before we could petition for adoption. He had recommended to us an adoption agency in Indianapolis that had earned a good reputation in this field. We had to do this through the more expensive private route because time was short and we could not wait for an appointment with the relevant social services department.

The home for the Home Study

It was a bright sunny summer day as we arrived at the adoption agency, a modest private house on the north side of the city. Inside, the walls were covered with pictures of smiling and contented infants, but we searched in vain for pictures of anyone in their teens. Fairly quickly we came to realize that our case did not easily fit the typical mold. It seemed that this agency, apart from assessing our qualities as potential parents, acted as a middleground in the highly confidential negotiations between birth mother and intending adoptive parents, something irrelevant to our case. Our first task was to fill out an extensive form clearly designed with anybody but us in mind. The questions delved profoundly into fertility drugs, artificial insemination, and infertility (which we had never tested), into the "type" of child that you favored (a choice of one-out-of-one in our case), and into a welter of personal detail. The form also presented us with an estimate of the cost of adoption under "normal" US circumstances. By our estimation this was around $7,500 *more* than our Byzantine situation. If we were trying to adopt an infant from abroad, I worked out the calculations quickly, we would be looking at another $20,000 *more* than we should have to pay to accomplish Eldar's change of legal status.

A couple entered and sat on the sofa opposite us.

"You trying to adopt too?" they began, and then asked us, "How long were you trying before?"

Trying what? I wondered, and then it occurred to me, in a rush of embarrassment, what they had been asking.

"Ah well, we were never *actually* trying—we already had him, and he's 14. We are just here to adopt him,"

I explained the tale in as unconvoluted a way as possible, though I could see they were now terminally confused. Just then we, and they, were saved from recounting the entire Eldar story by being called into the interview.

The interview process was interesting because we were questioned separately, although we were together in the same room. The interviewer asked about our relations with our parents (in my case difficult, as they both passed on decades ago), siblings, and each other. All the time I was wondering, "What about relations with Eldar? Those must be important?" but we never got to that. I suppose the questioner never assumes that the potential adoptee is already living with you. This was a well-honed, "one size fits all" process, and I could see that we didn't fit into the system at all. I was defeated by a question about when I started dating. I think this was a matter of history rather than psychology in my case. We confused the issue a little further by explaining that *we* started dating (though I cannot see myself "dating" anyone at my age—in Britain this is a term strictly reserved for adolescent infatuation) in the Fiji Islands, which was where we met. We proceeded through religion, work, security, onwards and upwards. But no questions about us and Eldar. We found it all so very strange. He had been here for a year. When we asked, prior to the interview, whether we should bring him along we were told, "If you like, though it's not really necessary," so we left him in school. The interview over, we were informed that there would have to be a "home study," which would take place some time in the next week. But we must be prepared for that part of the investigation to be much longer—up to three hours.

On the appointed day the home study officer arrived, and very quickly we were into dating again, and most of the same questions, the idea being, we supposed, that the two interviews would compare our answers to the same questions to see if we were giving similar responses, a bit like grilling terrorists. Then we provided a quick tour of the house, which, that day looked a good deal more orderly than it had for a while, but I imagined they expected that. After something less than 40 minutes it appeared that the process was done.

"We just wondered," I mentioned, "whether you would like to ask Eldar anything? He is sitting in his room, and I am sure he would be happy to answer any questions you might have."

I could not believe that he was not going to be asked *anything*, until I realized that in 99 percent of the cases there was no child there to ask, and if there were it probably could not speak. And so, the interview process has, again, evolved to consider only the potential adoptive parents. It was also clear that the interviewer did not really have any prepared questions to ask in this situation and she looked distinctly uncomfortable. She entered Eldar's inner sanctum; they chatted; and eventually she said,

"Do you feel happy about this idea of being adopted?"

"Yes." And "Fine."

Now we would have to wait while the home study was evaluated and passed to the lawyer, to be added to the bundle of documents destined for the court. But Mr. Rund was ahead of us. On September 24, 1993, he faxed us with the following startling update:

> *During the past two days, I have had discussions with representatives of the Monroe Circuit Court, and I have been informed that because you and Randall already have legal guardianship of Eldar, and because of the freshness of the adoption home study, the Court will not require its typical or customary further investigation and supervision by the appointed adoption agency. Therefore, we will be able to get a final hearing on the same day that we file the petition. I recommend October 14 at 1:00 p.m. . . .*

We had a date.

Chapter 16
Our Son

Eldar did not put quite the spin on it that I would have liked. In order to present himself at the petition hearing on the afternoon of Thursday, October 14, 1993, he would have to miss some classes at school. Since he was not missing the whole day, he could explain this himself at the school's administration office without too much formality from us. He told them, "My name is Eldar Urumbaev, and I have to leave school early because I must appear in court." With a world weary look of resignation the school officer signed him out— no doubt having labeled him as just another hopeless juvenile delinquent.

We had arranged that Voiko, who played such an important part in making the first contact with Ludmila, would be present as our only guest at the ceremony. We had other motives too, for Voiko had been a photo-journalist with a Bulgarian paper in Moscow, and he was going to record the events for posterity. We were in a state of nervous expectation, though it was hard to see how anything could go wrong at this stage. We abandoned any thought of forcing Eldar into wearing a tie for the occasion, and he managed to look casual but respectable in a Waikiki sort of way. We collected him from outside the high school at the appointed hour, and withdrew to have lunch in town—his final meal before he became our son. Somehow there wasn't the sort of pregnant solemnity that accompanies the prisoner's last breakfast, or anything like that. He was taking it, like everything else, entirely in his stride. His principal emotion detectable to us was an element of joy at being out of school early.

It was a beautiful day; the weather had pulled out all the stops for the occasion. We made our way to Bloomington's new justice building, and there we found Mr. Rund, our indefatigable navigator through these tricky waters. However, he appeared to be as nervous as we were. That was, I thought, in a perverse sort of way, reassuring. Of course it would be impossible to get this far without a hitch, and Mr. Rund had noted that one accompanying court document approving the hearing of the petition was still mentioning a second home-study, despite what was said in the official letter fixing the date! Though he had tried to head off this problem, between the receipt of the document mentioning the second home-study, and our appointment for the petition hearing, he could not ask anyone about the matter because the intervening period was the Columbus Day holiday. Another cliffhanger. We made the sort of forced small talk that was common to all these occasions when one is in the presence of something intimidating and incomprehensible like the church, the criminal justice system, or media stars. Mr. Rund seemed to find our levity, as we remarked on our rather forbidding surroundings, reassuring. He had never, I thought, had a case quite like this, and I imagined there was quite a lot of legalistic finger crossing going on.

The information desk attendant directed us to the juvenile court. This was not exactly the atmosphere I had hoped for. It represented in its stark architecture the terrible power of justice, and it was impossible to believe that anything *good* ever happened to anyone in this room. Benches were lined along the walls, unlike the situation in every other court, including Judge Wapner's, which I had seen portrayed in the media. We made the best of it by joking, though it was hard to miss the fact that the door to the judge's quarters was quite evidently bulletproofed. One would never, I hope, get married in a place like this, or baptize a child in a room like this, so why adopt someone in here?

A court officer duly entered from behind the bulletproof door. "Hello. Is this the adoption party?"

I realized that we could be almost anything, including the parents of some teenage Dillinger. "That's us," we said, and the usher told us:

"Mrs. Taliaferro, the magistrate looking after this petition, would like to invite you to her chambers. It's a lot more cheerful than this place."

We poured out through the judge's last line of defense and continued on up the stairs. It was so strange to be doing this in a building that was a citadel of misery, failure, and calamity. Everyone seemed to be looking at us, no doubt wondering, "What did the kid do?"

Viola Taliaferro was the way all law should be; a strikingly elegant black woman, clad in pink and resplendent in pearls. She greeted us at her desk in the sort of elevated corner office for which junior executives kill each other. This was much better! Bright sunlight sparkling in a tastefully decorated room. Mrs. Taliaferro seated us in a semicircle and began by discussing a small piece of local scandal concerning the prosecutor's office, and then very successfully broke the ice by chatting about the background to Eldar's fascinating tale.

"You sure do all look happy anyway," she observed. "That is such a wonderful tale, and it is *such* a pleasure to be doing something positive, something really unreservedly happy in this place. That does not happen too often, and I am going to try to make the most of it."

The magistrate then proceeded to swear us on oath as to the truth of what we had submitted, and what we were about to say.

She leaned forward and said:

"So! Let's get on with it—are you the lawyer for this case?" she asked, turning toward a now even more nervous Mr. Rund.

"Ah, yes, that's me," he replied.

"That's good," she continued, "because I read this petition and I don't understand too much of what's going on—especially all those interesting bits in Russian. I never saw anything like it before. I am going to have to take your word, Mr. Rund, that what we have here is complete and correct. I can't even pronounce most of it." She turned and beamed at us.

First, Mr. Rund confirmed with her that we did not all need to go home and wait for another home study.

"Oh. We don't need that, I guess we have plenty of information here." Mrs. Taliaferro commented, waving the file. Mr. Rund, visibly relieved, assured her that everything was just as it should be. "Eldar's name is going to stay the same—is that correct?" she asked looking at the unfamiliar string of vowels, and we confirmed that was so.

"Eldar, because you are over 14, I'm going to have to ask you whether you understand what is happening here, and that you are willing to go through with this."

If anyone present should know of any reason why... started going through my mind. Eldar resisted the opportunity to say anything to our eternal detriment, and made do instead with a simple

"Yes, I am."

"That's fine then, because you do understand, don't you, that once this is done there's no going back on it? It's as big a step as you could take."

"Yes," he replied.

"Now, Mr. Rund, I see that Eldar does have a living parent in Russia, and I need to be sure that we have gone through the correct procedures for obtaining her consent and of making sure she understands the meaning of everything."

Here was a crucial point, for without all this being made clear, the way was left open for the case to be contested later. Mr. Rund assured the magistrate that Ludmila had seen all the documents in clear and accurate translations.

"You are absolutely sure about that?"

"Yes I am."

"Then, on that basis, I am prepared to go ahead and sign this document."

With that she put her signature on the paper before her, and called her assistant, who took the adoption decree to have the court seal applied to it.

"Now, you do know that this record will be sealed, because there is a considerable environment of secrecy around adoption to protect the adoptive parents from having the child accidentally discover his other identity. Of course, it doesn't make much sense in this case, but we have to do it anyway."

The clerk returned with the document. This whole time Voiko had been circling the room taking photographs of this most unusual event. Noticing him, the magistrate removed the three dead coffee cups from her desk. We were like a family at a wedding, feeling a great surge of relief and happiness and not a little surprise that we actually had done it. Eldar got hugs and handshakes from everyone. We posed for a family group photo; the first time, legally speaking, that we had been able to do this. It was a moment of unrelieved happiness. Mr. Rund was visibly as pleased as we. Possibly he was thinking: maybe some legal history in the making here.

A legal family at last

We proceeded through the marble corridors and halls until we came to the entrance to the justice building. Mr. Rund was already talking about the necessary steps for Eldar to become a US citizen!

"Thank you for all you've done. We still cannot get over how everything in Eldar's case just seemed to happen despite the hundreds of possibilities for things to go wrong," I remarked

"It's been interesting, and I'll send you those naturalization documents."

With that, after several false starts, he turned and left for Indianapolis. We were somewhat lost, standing on the sidewalk as a family. I didn't feel different, being a *legal* father that is. But most of all I was truly happy that Eldar wanted to live with us, and that we were able to do it without compromising his already strong bond with his *other* family as we had come to call it. The day ended over a huge steak—his unqualified favorite food—and an obscenely rich dessert.

"How would you rate this day on a scale of one to ten?" Susan asked him.

"Oh, I'd probably give it an eight," he replied.

"Eight!" she retorted startled, "Why only eight?"
"Well, I had to spend part the morning in school—remember?"
"Get out of here."

Marking the Passage

We had planned a celebratory party to be held on Saturday October 16, and had invited many friends, most of all those people whose lives had been touched by Eldar's story. There they all were: Emilia, who arrived the night before by bus from Pennsylvania despite a case of pneumonia, Roman and Sonja, Voiko and 45 others. For the occasion we sent out a card inviting everyone to "Eldar's Second Birthday." So many of our friends had had babies recently that we could not resist mimicking their cards. Inside our invitation the text read:

> *On October 14, 1993*
> *Eldar Nurisovich Urumbaev became the son of*
> *Susan and Randall Baker.*
> *Weight 135 lbs.,*
> *Time of Rebirth 1 p.m.,*
> *Eyes Brown,*
> *Hair Black,*
> *Moped Red.*

Someone, following the spirit of the invitation, presented us with a copy of Dr. Spock's classic work. Another gave us a bottle of wine, vintage 1979. We were confused by this because Eldar was born, first time, in 1978. "That was a bad year," we were informed. For our part we gave Eldar the brown leather bomber jacket he had coveted for so long. He adorned it with an American flag and a KGB pin!

We had also commissioned a cake, and atop it in colored frosting we had created a design to symbolize the day. It consists of a victory wreath, for this was a moment of triumph, encircling the letter "E" in both Russian and Latin alphabets. Curiously, one is almost a mirror image of the other, so the whole design had a splendid symmetry, and looked vaguely Napoleonic. Below the letters was the adoption date. Before we cut the cake, however, I wanted to say something to all those people who had agonized with us, encouraged us, helped us practically, or just lent a sympathetic ear.

"There is a remarkable theme to this story," I began, "...and that theme is that the hand of fate does seem to have guided this process. At every turn there seemed to be insurmountable problems and barriers. There were dozens of reasons why this or that would, or could, not happen. But the fact is that it always did. And, furthermore, Susan, above all, *never* for one moment doubted that it would. I must confess to being the voice for caution and concern. She was the voice of resolution and conviction. I just regret that Eldar's *other* mother could not be here. That was one barrier we could not overcome, and for that we must thank our own government who would not grant her a visa. Everything would have been complete if we could have made that happen. But we couldn't and that leaves a big gap in our celebrations because we are celebrating the considerable *expansion* of Eldar's family. And you are all his new aunts and uncles. I am so happy we came to see this day."

Then Eldar addressed everyone briefly and without notes. "I want to thank all of you for being here, and for making me feel welcome ever since I arrived. I am glad to be here with all of you. Thank you for everything."

We toasted the new family, and our new son, with champagne that had been pulled from that astonishing black bag in his closet. How appropriate.

"To Eldar: A fine Boy. Real Hoosier too!" said Uncle Roman. "Cheers!"

Settling back in

Soon after the adoption, on Susan's birthday in November, several things happened at once: i) Eldar decided to have his ear pierced; ii) He presented his new mother with a magnificent spray of dried flowers topped off with a peacock feather; iii) He made up his mind to take up Tae Kwan Do; iv) He started shaving; and v) we discovered that, after being firmly rejected for a visa *twice* by the US embassy, Ludmila went back once more and this time they simply granted her request with the minimum of formality. She was as astonished as we were, as nothing had changed. But this meant we could do the one thing we had wanted to do all along—bring both mothers together. For, astonishing though it seemed, they still had never met. Eldar had already sent over some money from his mowing profits to pay part of his mother's ticket.

Ludmila, naturally, wanted to come at the first available moment, probably at the end of December or in early January, for three weeks or so. There were problems with this because Eldar would still be in school, the weather almost certainly would be awful, and Susan and I would be working. For these reasons Eldar called and advised her to come in March when the weather would be better, he would have a week off from school, and we could all go off somewhere together. This was not a popular idea, understandably, because Ludmila had not seen Eldar for well over a year, ever since that day he left home on August 24, 1992, and she didn't want to wait another minute. We hoped she didn't think that we were putting her off, though it could easily look that way. On the other hand what would she do alone all day in the middle of winter in Bloomington, not speaking English and physically isolated in our subdivision on the east side of town? Fortunately, after Eldar's call, she agreed to a spring visit after a call from Eldar. Soon enough it came.

Ludmila's departure from Moscow was monitored for us by the daughter of the lady geologist from Tashkent who had attended Eldar's first birthday party. I had never met her, but we communicated regularly by e-mail, and she had a son about Eldar's age who was living with a family in Lincoln, Nebraska. She, like so many now, was drawn into the Eldar saga as a willing emissary, and she sent me a message to say, even *the day before* her scheduled departure, that Ludmila was still en route to Moscow from Tashkent in Uzbekistan. Apparently, Eldar's two brothers had purchased a white marble headstone for Nuris' grave, and she had been to visit the site. At the last moment an e-mail flashed onto my screen:

"Everything is fine, no reason for heart attack. Ludmila had arrived. She IS in Moscow and IS leaving tomorrow. Is everything and everybody ready to meet another mom?"

That was a good question. There were not too many precedents for two mothers of the same child to meet for the first time. How would they react to each other? How would they *speak* to each other? Through Eldar? Surely that would be a problem because most of what they would want to talk about concerned *him*. This could be very delicate—maybe even tense. Knowing them as I did, I was well aware that they were people of strongly held convictions, compounded by an age difference of almost twenty years. But, I kept my concern to myself, especially as the night before his mother's anticipated arrival, Eldar was hyped up to the limit with excitement and anticipation.

On the day of Ludmila's expected arrival, March 4, we readied ourselves for the four-hour drive to Chicago. As usual I checked the e-mail, and there was a note from Moscow telling us that Eldar's mother had successfully departed Moscow airport and was in the air on her way to Chicago.

After an easy drive, we arrived just in time at O'Hare International Airport. At least we did not have to stand around watching the arrival board, for it showed that the plane had already landed early. It was a fascinating, unique, moment. Eldar was alert and chewing his lip, eyes glued on the exit door. Susan was running on almost pure adrenaline. Through the door came an entire adolescent Russian basketball team, then a trickle of men; and then, there was Ludmila. Susan spotted her first, recognizing her from photographs taken during my Moscow visit. Now the circle was complete. Eldar rushed forward and they embraced in a true Russian bear hug. She laughed, eyes wide, hand over wide-open mouth in astonishment to see how much he had grown, for he had long since passed her by. He had been well below Susan's height when he first arrived, but he had soon grown taller than her too (as he liked to remind her frequently). Then came the moment when the two mothers met. It was clear from Ludmila's letters that she respected Susan as the driving force behind Eldar's schoolwork and character development. All formality was abandoned and they greeted each other with hugs. I did not know who was more nervous, but I am sure they had gone over this moment repeatedly in their minds. If only they could talk to each other. For the last ten minutes Susan had been repeating a phrase Eldar had taught her, and she delivered it handily. Ludmila had no idea what she was saying, but repeated "thank you, thank you . . ." and continued staring at Eldar and laughing in astonishment.

Eldar greets his mother for the first time since coming to the United States

We had decided it was unrealistic to make the four-hour plus drive back to Bloomington that night, so we had reserved two rooms in a motel in northern Indiana. Ludmila talked incessantly to Eldar in the back seat of the car, recapturing for him all the events of his family since he had been away. We all indulged in a good Mexican meal. Mexican cuisine was a first for Ludmila, who was astonished more by the amount of food that appeared than by its content. After that she always greeted each restaurant meal with the same surprised laugh and look of astonishment with which she had greeted Eldar.

The long drive home next day was dedicated to an intense back-seat debriefing between Ludmila and Eldar, which was encouraged by the fact that we had to drive through hour after hour of impenetrable fog. (Although, it is always a matter of debate how much there is to see in northern Indiana *without* the fog). The day started with a gargantuan breakfast, during which Eldar had the daunting task of attempting to translate the entire menu to his mother. This must have used up a great deal of energy, for he avidly consumed not only his own vast meal, but everyone else's leftovers as well.

En route to our house we stopped at the supermarket to pick up some essentials. Ludmila was so transfixed by the scene of endless choice that she stood and stared in confusion. But, at last, we arrived at Eldar's new American home, and welcomed Ludmila, telling her—with real sincerity—that it was hers too. We then took her on a short tour that ended up in Eldar's room, where she was clearly reassured to see photographs displayed of Nuris, herself, Timur, Roman, and the rest of the family back in Moscow. She was pleased also by the fact that we had similar pictures elsewhere in the house, and not just in Eldar's room. This made her feel comfortable in a strange environment. She ended the day by sitting quietly and talking with Eldar in his room. If only, we said to each other that night, we could talk in a common language, the next few weeks would be so much easier for us all. But we also wanted her to have all the private time with Eldar that she would like. We had determined that there was to be no competition for affection here.

Eldar still had one week of school. Each morning before he scrambled out of the door, Ludmila quietly came downstairs, sat in his room, and chatted with him until he left. Each evening she sat with him, even when he was doing his homework or just preparing to go to sleep. These were private and precious moments, and we never asked about them or intruded on them. We were contented seeing that she appeared happy with what she saw and heard, and that she evidently did not carry remorse or regret about the changed circumstances. It was also clear from the start that Eldar was happy being

The Extended Family

with us, and he took Ludmila on a tour of his school, speaking highly of some of his teachers. Because Ludmila and Eldar were comfortable together with the situation, we felt comfortable too.

The problem of communication was solved some of the time through the services of a charming and talented Russian student from Ukraine named Tamara Vishkina. She was someone to whom everyone quickly warmed, and she gained Ludmila's confidence, perhaps due to the fact that Tamara was studying in the United States while her husband and children remained in Donetsk. Through Tamara, we were able to obtain, from Ludmila, a much better idea of how things had been in Moscow during the last months. We also found out that Ludmila preferred to be called *Lusya*. Also, for part of the first week, Roman and Sonja Zlotin were in Bloomington, though both would be returning to Moscow in a few days. Sonja was able to take Ludmila around to KMart and the local shops, both of which were within walking distance of the house. At first Lusya asked us why Americans could possibly need so many shops, but it was not long before she was in practically all of them most of the day. She delighted in the fact that it was all right to try things on before purchasing them, and was astonished by the idea that customers could return something if they didn't like it.

With each passing day Lusya became visibly more relaxed. "I simply cannot imagine how Eldar ever adapted so well to these enormous changes," She told us one day. For his part, throughout his mother's visit, Eldar acted the devoted son, tirelessly following her around the fashion stores and translating for her. Even though we knew for a fact that this was not his favorite pursuit, at the end of one tiring day he turned to Susan and said, quite sincerely, "This has been a *great* day." For her side, Lusya exclaimed to Sonja, at the end of a mammoth shopping session, "This is like paradise here." Ludmila also got swept up in Eldar's recent preoccupation with Tae Kwon Do, attended his class, and watched the video of his test for the purple belt, in which he broke pine boards with his hands and feet.

In the middle of Ludmila's stay we decided to spend one week visiting Susan's brother, Michael, and his family in Seattle. Since Eldar's family was all dedicated to skiing, we felt we needed to get into some more elevated topography than the Hoosier state could provide. Also, Eldar had fallen hopelessly in love with Seattle the first time he had visited it a year ago. This time we found out how unusual our domestic situation really was when we called to make reservations at a bed-and-breakfast in Bellevue, Washington.

Susan:
"I just wanted to check with you about the sleeping arrangements. can you tell me what rooms you have available?"

Reply:

"Well, I have two rooms: one with a double, the other with two singles."

Susan:

"Oh, that's fine. My husband and I will take the double, and our son and his mother will take the two singles."

"Pardon?"

"Do you mind if I cook something?" Lusya asked one day, telling us that she had never had an experience in her life where she went on vacation and did *nothing*. That was the beginning of a cooking storm. Eldar was in seventh heaven, as he was now able to have all the things he remembered and loved as a child. Susan was not about to stop this indulgence, though she worried about the radical change of diet. And indulgence it was, for Lusya prepared every item by the gross. Many of the ingredients had a Central Asian origin, some were more plainly Russian, and *all* were deep fried, soaked in butter, or covered in syrup, or all three of the above.

After a week of this, we discovered that Eldar was spending his pocket money on skin treatments for acne. This gave rise to the following bathroom conversation I had with him as he stood before the mirror applying various gels to his face

"So, what is all this skin treatment?" I inquired.

"Oh, my face is breaking out."

"Do you think that could have anything, possibly, to do with the fifteen crepes you ate for breakfast? All this oil is bound to be bad for you."

"No, it has nothing to do with that. It is all connected with my age. All kids go through this."

"Really? And it always comes on this fast. You don't think it has anything to do with diet, like the fact that we have used up two bottles of oil in only nine days?"

"Nah."

"Are you willing to join me in a small bet that your skin trouble mysteriously clears up when your mom goes home?"

"Hey, I ate this stuff for years and never had a problem. It's just a thing that all kids go through. I thought parents were supposed to know these things."

"Oh we know. Be sure, we know."

I leave it to your imagination what happened when his mother left, though of course, it was not one of those things about which it was wise to speak.

Just as happened with Eldar after he arrived, Lusya continually produced gifts for us from a huge bag. One evening we were excluded from the living room and asked to busy ourselves in the kitchen. We had no idea what was going on, but there was a considerable delay. Eventually we were asked to return, and there, set out on the table, was an exquisite tea service from Uzbekistan in dark blue and gold with floral designs. In place of cups, the tea service had bowls, which were set on a matching ceramic plate around a large teapot. We thought the most astonishing thing about this was that it survived being carried in a soft case all the way from Moscow, or Tashkent as it turned out. But our surprise was even greater when we realized that Lusya had actually brought *two* of these services—the other for Eldar! And so it went on with paintings, a lazy Susan, cognac from Armenia, black caviar, and powerful green tea from Central Asia.

The night before we left for Seattle, Eldar had to deal with a sudden, unique, personal problem. We had recently acquired a recorking device for wine bottles based on a vacuum pump that extracted the air from bottles after they had been recorked. Eldar discovered that if he put the device on his skin and worked the pump, then the pump was held there on his body by the vacuum. Unfortunately he chose to amuse us all by applying the pump to his cheek. What he had failed to notice was that it left a mark very much like a gigantic hickey. So he had to travel with this unmistakable, huge sign of affection stamped into the middle of his face for several days.

The week in Seattle was an unqualified success, finally consolidating the growing friendship among Lusya and ourselves around our common love of Eldar. Susan's brother turned out to be her complete antithesis, invalidating all theories of genetics. With beard, pony tail and ultimately informal style of dressing, he worshiped at the shrine of bird watching. His house also had what you might term an "informal look": Susan's *Home and Gardens* approach was clearly not manifested there. Yet, despite outward differences, they were obviously the very best of friends.

We spent the time skiing, touring the Olympic peninsula, taking in the spectacular mountain views from Hurricane Ridge—a sight that clearly made Lusya homesick for her time with Nuris in the Caucasus—and eating, eating, eating: Thai, seafood, Chinese, Italian, and a first sight of broccoli for Lusya.

On a walk around Seattle in uncharacteristic sunshine, she told us that, at first, she had felt intimidated by skyscrapers, associating them with criminal elements. But now she liked them and she wandered around with her eyes fixed on the heavens. She also became a very willing surrogate aunt to Susan's nephew, Tim, and niece, Cassidy.

On one occasion, as we were making our way back from a day of skiing in the Cascades, Tim, aged three, told us, after noticing Eldar's earring, "My daughter has an earring." This, of course, was news to us.

"Oh, I didn't know you had a daughter. What's her name?" Susan asked.
"Her name is Jasmine," he informed us immediately.
"Oh, really. And how old is she?"
"Ah, she is 48."
"48. Hmmm. And how old are you?"
"49."
"And who is Jasmine's mommy?"
"Daddy."

In this relaxed atmosphere we came to learn all sorts of new things. Lusya amazed us by saying that she had taken her degree in aerodynamics, going on to work on medium-range missiles! Later she had put her mathematical skills to use when working with Nuris on avalanche research, and had gone with him to Afghanistan. Clearly, from everything she said, Nuris' death had left an enormous hole in her life at a time of chaos and terrible uncertainty in Russia. She also revealed to us more of the problems surrounding the decision to agree to Eldar's adoption. In central Asia, tradition did not easily encompass the idea of a child being raised outside the extended family. Beside this, there were more difficulties than we had imagined over the possible loss of Eldar's cultural identity. Clearly, she had undergone many struggles beyond the obvious major one of being Eldar's mother and allowing him to go off to start a new life thousands of miles away in an alien, and previously hostile, society. She told us that even her own father had said initially, "You wouldn't really send Eldar there, would you?" But she had become convinced that Eldar's lifestyle in Moscow, following the death of his father, was destructive to his nature, and she appreciated that he felt this way too. This had helped form her idea that it would be good for Eldar to get away, at least, for a time.

Tim discussing his daughter Jasmine aged 48

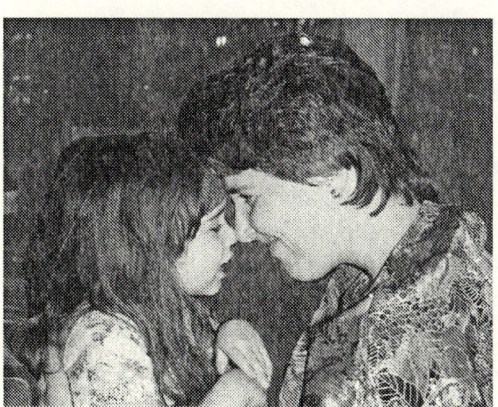
Susan and Tim's sister Cassidy

As one more indicator of Eldar's changing status, his new birth certificate arrived. This was a curious document indeed. Since he was adopted he would need in future to produce a birth certificate for various purposes. Obviously adopted children would not use their *original* birth certificates, for that would reveal both that they were adopted, and who their birth parents were. Such a revelation would break the essential secrecy surrounding the adoption process. For these reasons, in Eldar's case, a "new" birth certificate was issued with the names of the adoptive parents (us), and the place of birth given as Russia (even though I was in Paris, and Susan in Williams College at the time!).

In different circumstances a sharp child would quickly deduce that the situation looked suspicious if he worked out that his parents were not in Russia in 1978, and were not married at that time. And this was to say nothing of the fact that he appeared to have a totally different family name from his parents. Apart from all this, almost every part of the certificate had been transcribed wrongly—nobody in North America seemed able to copy the word *Urumbaev*—and so it had to go back more than once.

Eventually the time came to prepare for Lusya's return to Moscow. But we felt we could cope with her departure more comfortably now, for we knew that this coming separation of Eldar and Lusya would not be so full of uncertainty. It would be difficult, as it always is, to leave a close family member for an extended time. But now there was the real sense that we were all one family. As the days of the last week passed by, Lusya went into high gear in terms of both cooking and shopping. She ventured out alone confidently now, and returned with straining plastic bags. We settled down to the inevitable gargantuan meals each night. Her suitcases bulged with plastic wrap, a potato peeler, chocolate mints, gifts for the entire family in Russia, and every spare photograph of Eldar we could produce.

The last evening followed an Olympic-class shopping day. We noticed that Lusya always shopped for others, but almost never for herself. This day had produced a new ski jacket for Eldar, shoes for his brother, and many other things. Lusya was using English phrases more frequently now; she had learned quite a few basic words during the three weeks. We used this opportunity to document all the various members of Eldar's family so we could construct his family tree. Although we had a computer program to do the work, it collapsed at the idea of a child with two living mothers! So we then constructed two trees and tried to fix them somehow with adhesive tape.

At dinner, the genealogy over, we gave Lusya a tiger's eye necklace and matching earrings as a farewell gift, along with a watch, for we had noticed that she had been wearing Eldar's watch. In return, Lusya insisted that

Susan have the Afghan garnet necklace and earrings that Susan had silently admired throughout the visit. At first Susan was reluctant to take so precious a gift, since Lusya had had them for many years. But, it soon became clear that the gift was sincere and genuine, and that Lusya truly wanted Susan to have them. Susan was moved beyond words by this gesture, and they hugged each other over and over: a rare event for Susan. Lusya spent the end of the evening sitting with Eldar in his room in quiet contemplation.

The next morning, with Lusya's bags packed to capacity and almost too heavy to lift, we loaded the car. Eldar, now armed with his learner's permit, was going to drive us part of the way—something surprising to his mother who remembered the skinny thirteen-year-old lad who had left home for America. She told us what a relaxing time this had been, and how happy she now felt about everything. It was obvious that Eldar had loved having her here, for he had been the devoted son throughout her visit. Her presence, anyway, had eradicated the tortuous problem he had previously endured of "choosing" one family over the other, as was evident from the comfortable way we all now interacted without formality or reserve.

As I took over driving from Eldar, he opened the laptop computer in the back of the car and began on the document that would form part of this book—his personal perspective on what he called his "two lives." During the journey his "real" mother helped him with questions of detail. For the first time, she also asked us whether Eldar had ever been any trouble to us. This was an interesting situation, since *he* had to translate both the question and the answer. Fortunately for him, or us, the answer was an unqualified "no."

Inevitably the time came for the two mothers to say farewell, and for Eldar and I to say our good-byes to her as well. The drive had been much faster than we could have anticipated, and so we ended up at the airport in Chicago with that awful situation of lots of time to fill and nothing adequate to say. Lusya, bless her, seized the moment and said that she would make her way through to the departure lounge. Some hugs, kisses, handshakes, and she was through. Her yellow jacket was visible until she turned the corner and was lost to sight. No wrenching farewells, because now we knew that this was just *adieu*, and before long our family would come together again—the next time in Moscow in the summer of 1995, by which time, bureaucracy willing, Eldar would have his US citizenship. The Aeroflot jet thundered off on its journey to Moscow, and with our son firmly in control at the wheel, he and his doting parents made their way home.

The future seemed set.

Eldar's diary 1994

In Moscow when I was about 12, I started doing Karate, then I had to quit after one year, because I had to go to Terskol, and then after my father's death and everything I couldn't do it again. So when I arrived here I thought maybe they have Karate school here. Now I'm going to Monroe County Martial Arts, I learn Tae Kwon Do. I really like it; it's good exercise, it's a lot of fun, and I meet a lot of people. It teaches me respect for people, discipline and lots of other things.

I was adopted on 14th of October, 1993. It was hard for me and my mom to decide, but we both thought that it would be the best thing to do. I was very nervous about this because I thought it would be very hard for my mom. Whenever she asked me about it I would say: "I don't know, I'm not sure," though I knew that it would be the best thing to do, because if I go back it would be very hard to catch up with school, and everything else, also I thought that with the things happening in Russia I would not be able to get a good education. It was my only way I could stay here. Besides, I am happy here.

In March of 1994, my mom came to Bloomington. It was a great experience for her, me, Susan, and Randall. I was really happy to see her after a year and a half. I have probably changed a lot since I last saw her, for one thing I have grown two inches. She definitely never heard me speaking English, plus it was her first time abroad. We decided to go to Seattle to visit Susan's brother. It would be good for her to see more of the US, not just Bloomington. We went skiing, even my mom who hasn't skied for about five years, and wasn't intending to try to get back on skis. She really liked Seattle. This visit was a very good break for her from all the hell that is going on in Moscow. It was the first time she didn't have to worry about anything in her life. It was very hard for me to see her leave.

And so here I am; I changed my language, my country, my family, my culture, everything. Is that an interesting life or what?

The Americanization of Eldar

Susan in the Office

Chapter 17
The Cold Hand of Fear

Lusya left on the 29th of March, just before Easter 1994. It seemed that so many good things had happened to us: all of them unexpected. Our lives had more meaning and purpose, and we both felt we had a new perspective on what is, and is not, important in the great scheme of things. We could now set our sights on a visit for all of us to Russia when Susan could meet all the relatives and see something of Eldar's home country for the first time. That was in the future, but right now, immediately after Lusya's departure, Susan's enjoyment of the holiday was marred by a persistent and inexplicable pressure she felt in her head and stomach. Bloomington has the reputation of being the allergy capital of the United States, and so we thought her symptoms were probably related to that annual tribulation in some obscure way. But when the pressure increased. resulting in severe headaches and the sound of her heart beating inside her brain, which prevented her from sleeping, Susan reluctantly took her problems to the doctor.

"I think it is probably sinusitis, Susan," Dr. Sharp observed, "But let me look in your ear. Put your head on one side."

Dr. Sharp had that variety of sixth sense that distinguishes the best of the general practitioners. As Susan tilted her head, Dr. Sharp's keen glance took in something else. As he put it later, "My hair literally tingled and stood on end." Then without losing a beat, or changing his tone, he continued to look in the ear, and asked tangentially

"How long has this vein been so prominent on the left side of your neck?"

"Oh, that's recent. I noticed it the other day. Do you think it has something to do with the headaches?"

"It probably does. I would like you to have a chest X-ray. I will book it right now for tomorrow morning."

It was hard for Susan to understand what a chest X-ray had to do with either sinusitis or prominent veins. However, Dr. Sharp's sixth sense had served him remarkably well. At the end of the following day he was on the phone.

"Susan, I've got the report back on those X-rays and they show a slight abnormality in that there is some enlargement of the lymph nodes near the lung. This would press on the blood supply returning to the heart from the brain, and this obstruction would account for the pounding in your head, as well as the distention of your neck vein. I have made an appointment for you to have a CT scan tomorrow, and I have asked them to biopsy that mass. I just want to be on the safe side. Just don't eat anything after you go to bed tonight, and come and pick up some barium that will be your breakfast. It is quite disgusting."

This was only the third time Susan had been within the walls of a hospital. The previous occasion was when she had visited the husband of a colleague. He had returned from a period at the National Science Foundation in Washington DC, only to be diagnosed with stomach cancer that had metastasized. His case had proven to be hopeless and his terrible decline had thrown Susan into a truly depressed state, for she had become involved in visiting him and preparing food for his wife. Because she was well aware that he was my age, she became concerned that the same thing could happen to me, and arranged for our insurance agent to call, so that I could complete the paperwork involved in taking out a large policy on my life. This made sense. I was significantly older than she, we now had a child, and she had seen at first hand what could happen, and it had shaken her badly. The insurance agent, while writing out the policy, remarked to Susan:

"And how about you? It would cost very little to add your name."

"Henry, I exercise regularly, I eat sensibly, I have never smoked, and in four hundred years nobody in my family ever died of cancer."

"In this business, my experience tells me you just never know. But I understand. We will keep it just to Randall's life. This new cover should make you feel more comfortable."

"Sure does. I could never keep Eldar and the house on what I earn."

The CT scan went off without incident, and we were asked to go to the offices of a surgeon in one of the town's older houses on Friday for an interpretation of the result. I collected Susan from work and we entered the world of Norman Rockwell. It looked as though everyone in the room and the room itself had been commissioned for the cover of the *Saturday Evening Post* round about the time the Japanese were bombing Pearl Harbor. In truth, neither of us knew the significance of any of the medical phenomena that were being checked out.

The surgeon was a straightforward and compassionate man. He had clearly inherited his father's practice and preserved it as a monument to him, for his equipment belonged in the Smithsonian. But he knew his stuff:

"All right Susan, I don't have the actual CT scans, but I do have the report that has been faxed to me." He paused to speed read the document. "Well, you have a tumor about 11 x 4 centimeters just here," he said pointing to a position on his upper right chest. "You can't feel it because it is *inside* the chest cavity, and does not protrude onto the surface of your body. There is no way to tell whether it is malignant or not from this information. It could have been growing for some time."

It was only with the use of the word *malignant* that either of us became aware that we were in fact talking about *cancer*. I had heard the expression "your blood turns to ice," but had no idea what it meant until then.

"You mean it's cancer?" said Susan, suddenly alarmed.

"Absolutely. That's what it looks like. But we have to run some tests and I don't want you becoming unnecessarily worried."

I later read, in a pamphlet on cancer I was browsing through in a doctor's office, something that was absolutely on the mark. It said, "Once the doctor utters the word *cancer* the patient retains very little of what follows." How true. The word continued on and on like a Tchaikovsky symphonic ending in my brain. I had called the Eldar fax "one of those moments that change your life forever." Now I was sitting through another. Even though the words were not addressed to me, the shock wave encompassed both of us. I realized, at one point, that my jaw had dropped, and that, for a moment, I had actually stopped breathing.

"I am having you admitted to Bloomington Hospital on the eleventh [this was Friday the eighth] for a needle biopsy that I shall perform on you. Then we will have a better idea."

He really belonged in this Rockwell landscape, for although Susan bombarded him with questions, he was patient and profoundly understanding. In spite of my own sudden paralysis, I was waiting for him to pull out a pocket watch at any moment. Susan, for her part, demonstrated the controlled, positive attitude that characterized her reaction to all situations. But, that evening she wrote in her diary: *This is scary stuff to contend with. Statistically I think there's a good chance that it is benign, and my instincts tell me it is too.*

We decided not to tell Eldar anything at this stage. He had already had a hard time getting over the death of his father without worrying now unnecessarily about Susan in the absence of some hard facts. A week ago we had been a family with nothing worse than a bad headache to concern us.

Now we were fixated on the most frightening word in the English language. Since surgery was involved, Susan went into work on Sunday and cleared the decks in anticipation of a possible absence of two weeks. The whole situation had a sense of complete unreality—even the ridiculous—about it.

On Monday Susan was established in a bed on the fourth floor—the cancer ward—of the Bloomington Hospital. Now it all seemed even more impossibly fantastic, but there we were. After a short time during my visit, Susan realized that she knew the voice of the person in the room's other, screened, bed who was being visited by her husband: a woman working at the university with whom she had communicated over the telephone and by letter, but had never actually met.

"Connie, is that you?" she asked tentatively

"Certainly is. Who is that?"'

And so a sense of something familiar helped her to counter the terrible, undeniable reality of what this place is about, in spite of its disguise of reassuring pastels. The bond of collegiality was immediately tested as the roommate's oncologist arrived, sat on the edge of Connie's bed, and in a sad but businesslike way, told her that the cancer had progressed to her brain, and that at best she was looking at four to eight weeks more of life. This terrifying news, almost the first thing we heard during my first hospital visit, was like being struck dumb. Apart from the fact that this was clearly the worst moment in her friend's entire life, and we were intruding on it, it was the last thing Susan wanted to hear in her situation. There was no way to ignore that distressing conversation, even though it was not intended for us, being conducted behind drawn curtains.

The silence after the doctor had spoken filled the room palpably and killed everything else. I felt like the worst possible form of eavesdropper, wrongly privy to this most intensely personal and tragic of moments. I can only speculate on what effect it had on Susan, but she and I found ourselves exchanging a look of terror and disbelief. Susan was quite literally stunned by this situation. This was a young woman to whom the doctor was talking, just like Susan. I wanted out of that building right away. Susan remained as stoic as ever but she was coping with the awful news about her friend, and the obvious icy thought "Am I next?" I was thinking the same thing too because Connie's husband was sitting on the bed shattered and trying to hold on to reality. But reality was not the place to be right now. Sadness, terror, depression, despair; I don't know which was holding the winning hand, but they were all putting their cards on the table. I had to be strong for Susan, and yet not look like I was indifferent to what was happening in the room. Once the doctor had left, it was Susan who broke the silence, because silence is the most intimidating thing of all.

"Who's your doctor?" she asked Connie.

"His name, believe it or not, is Fritz Tai. Susan, he is truly wonderful and you could not be in better hands."

"I will ask for him," Susan replied.

This businesslike air, though entirely contrived by Susan, broke the curse, and a slight gleam of what might pass for normality crept into the room.

Her choice of oncologist was an excellent one, as the coming months were to show. Connie seemed to take the news astoundingly well. But maybe I was taken in by the extraordinary front she put on, for by now, after only an hour of my visit had passed, I was finding it hard to cope with what was happening in this place, and *I* was not the one who was sick. I was ashamed of my reaction. I began to feel like I was watching all this from a distance, maybe as a way to preserve me from the horror of reality. After all, that was my wife, aged only 34, in that bed. Was she going to get the same message as Connie any time soon?

Later that day, after Susan's surgery was over, and she had partly recovered from the effects of the anesthetic, she called me from her bedside phone. As I said earlier, in common, I believe, with most Europeans of my generation, I tend to think that the telephone was invented solely to convey disastrous news, like its partner the telegram. Nonetheless, I had to listen:

"The surgeon said the results were what they had suspected—lymphoma. But this is a very treatable form of cancer. He said it could be much worse, but it is shocking to think I have cancer, especially as there is no history of it in my family. First, they will have to do a CT scan to make sure it hasn't gotten into my abdomen. You know the lymph glands are part of the immune system, and so anything residing there can travel all over the body in a short time. They will also have to test my bone marrow. Then they will start chemotherapy, which means filling me with lots of toxic chemicals. It also means hair loss, yikes. Let's hope, since I am so fit, that my body will resist well and conquer the cancer completely."

It was typical of Susan, though, that she determined to make an appointment to have her hair cut off rather than wait for it to fall out in clumps. This was all part of remaining in control.

That night I had to tell Eldar because there was no longer any doubt about what we were facing. I found him in his room sitting at his desk.

"Look, I don't know any easy way to say this, but Susan has cancer. Right now we don't know how bad, or treatable, it is. But she is going to be in hospital for a while, and things will get clearer as we go along. She thinks it may not be all that serious, but she will have a lot of problems. This is really tough on you, bearing in mind what happened to your dad. I just wanted you to know and understand. It is very serious."

At this point I found that I could not continue because I was so choked up. He had looked up suddenly when I mentioned the word *cancer*, but from then on he stared at his desktop, which was his usual way of dealing with emotional crises. I knew immediately that this was going to be hard because he always buried his feelings way down deep where nobody could find them. I put my arm round him, and said we would have to support her in whatever way we could.

"That really sucks," he said, and closed down.

I went to my desk and sat there, lost and weepy. Then I thought, "I'm damned if this thing is going to turn me into an agonized wreck. There has to be something I can do." I started right away to write a large-format book for Susan to keep beside her in hospital and out, like a friend. It would contain a calendar, note pages, places for her guests to sign, lots of room for her favorite lists, etc. But it would be an absurd kind of book that would laugh at the whole situation. When I had finished, I christened it *Susan's Big Yellow Lymphoma Fun Book*. Her calendar entry for that day, for instance, read: *Catscan fails to locate cats*. This book was to become a sheet anchor for what was to follow.

The hospital room soon filled with hoards of visitors, plants and flowers, and also the files from her office that Susan insisted on having sent in regularly to allow her to keep on top of things. By Wednesday the doctors had reached an impasse. They could not determine the type of lymphoma she had from the needle biopsy, and more radical forms of biopsy failed to obtain any usable samples.

"Diagnosis, Susan, is everything in this business" the surgeon informed her. "I have never seen anything like this fibrous mass in twenty-five years here. So I am sending you to the Indiana University Medical Center in Indianapolis. They are the experts. Let them work it out. You will be in excellent hands. Best of luck. You're one of the toughest nuts I've run across."

He shook her hand and left.

We were now initiates into the grim world of terrifying *uncertainty* in which all cancer sufferers dwell. They are, for instance, never cured but, instead, go into *remission*, which is a condition in which you are waiting for the other shoe to drop: a sort of medical purgatory. The spectral incubus of this monstrous disease occupied center stage henceforth, and dominated every thought and action unless we kept it firmly at bay. We were both entering fear's own awful domain, but our methods of combating this evil homunculus were different. Susan applied an iron will and a steely determination to succeed, while I treated the situation as absurd because

I can deal with bad things only when I can laugh at them. Our journey to Indianapolis provided fodder for both approaches.

Susan was interred in an ambulance with two young women straight out of a sitcom. I was to trail them in my car. All the way up Susan plied them with her determined words and good humor. When we reached Indianapolis we seemed to wind around the most tortuous route possible, until I realized we were going along one particular street for the third time. Suddenly the ambulance pulled over and parked in a bus stop. In the middle of this incomprehensible situation, one of the women ran back and, totally embarrassed, said:

"Hey, we're lost. Do you know how to get into the Medical Center?"

I had not the faintest idea. With that a police car pulled in, having been summoned by the ambulance on their radio, and we had to fall in line behind him the short distance to the hospital entrance. I promised the two ambulance women faithfully never to tell a soul about what had happened. I remembered the words of my mother who used to say, "Listen carefully, I can tell you this only *once*, as I promised never to repeat it."

"What next?" not "Why Me?"

A hospital represents, if you let it, the ultimate example of loss of control over life. Others regulate what, and when, you eat, and must assist in most bodily functions. The upper echelons muse over your damaged body, and exchange incomprehensible polysyllabic incantations. In spite of all this, Susan was determined to retain control. When her temperature or blood pressure were checked, as they were incessantly, the nurse's common practice was to write down the figures and, without a word, slip away. But Susan demanded to know every figure, and its significance. She also insisted on keeping in shape, even if it meant trundling the IV around the ward. She read everything, blue pencil in hand, and had sheaves of questions ready for every unsuspecting operative who put his or her head around the door. Laughing at the *Fun Book* with each new entry we invented gave her a sense of perspective and us a concrete demonstration of our unwillingness to be intimidated or cowed by this awful thing. She was due to go to a conference in Miami just after the scheduled end of the Indianapolis internment, and she was *determined* to go. Every aspect of the treatment was recorded in her files, and her bedside was littered with editing work from her job at the Office of Publications at the university. But deep down, although she did her best to hide it just like me, she was scared. Really scared.

Around this time I had my own minor scare with prostate cancer, and went to have an ultrasound, which has to be one of life's greatest indignities.

I was terrified, and too fearful to ask all those bold questions that Susan would have fired off without hesitation. Instead, like a typical male, I lay there while the nurse maneuvered the probe and periodically went "hmmm." This went on for an hour, and four agonizing days later I learned it was a false alarm, and the nurse had been going "hmmmm" because she couldn't find what she was looking for.

If only I had Susan's will, for part of being in control, also, is never asking "why me?" I think that there is, honestly, no answer to that question unless you believe in some sort of idle deity with nothing better to do than to pick people out of space for pain and suffering. Indeed, from a fortune cookie, one lunchtime, came an excellent piece of wisdom: *In life there are no rewards and no punishments; merely consequences.* Susan never once voiced the "why me?" argument during these early days of terror. However, I was reading at her bedside one afternoon, and to my horror I discovered that my old friend Murray Cox, who had edited an article I published in *Omni* magazine, had died of AIDS. He was, like her, young, smart, personable, and a true friend. I hesitated, but then showed Susan the article since she had quite clearly seen the expression on my face. She read it, and was devastated that so kind and gentle a person should have died:

"Why *him*?" she cried. "He was such a perfect human being."

I agreed, but at the same time, my mind was asking—ridiculously I know— "why *you*?"

At Indianapolis the diagnosis was swift and terrible. Susan had a diffused, large-cell, non-Hodgkin's Lymphoma: a particularly aggressive and frightening form of cancer. This piece of bad news was given to both of us as we sat in the hospital room on April 15th. We determined that each step of the way would be revealed to both of us together so that Susan should not have to be alone when the next frightening revelation came. On the other hand, I could not be in the room 24 hours a day.

"It figures," I remarked. "This is the day the *Titanic* sank, and also the day the IRS tries to sink the rest of us who leave posting our tax returns till the last minute. I won't have any difficulty remembering *this* anniversary."

Susan was immediately attached to a team of doctors, with one of whom she immediately established a rapport in Hindi, which she had learned in her Peace Corps days.

"Let me explain the situation to you," said the head of the team. "This is a very determined and aggressive form of cancer: a bit like you, actually!" he laughed. "We have a protocol, along with the University of Nebraska, which offers real hope in your case. Basically, we will harvest some of your stem cells: the ones that make the white blood cells. We will freeze them, and then we will subject you to a dose of chemotherapy that would, otherwise, kill you because it will destroy your immune system. But this heavy a dose should kill the cancer cells, you understand? Then we put the extracted stem cells back, where they will multiply in your bone marrow. This should give you a better than 75 percent chance, and we have been getting good results. You will have to spend time in strict isolation because you will have no immune system. But then the stem cells will take up residence in your bone marrow, and spontaneously rebuild the system, so you should recover quickly and be able to leave. I am going to go through the protocol with you, and then I want you to think about it, and let me know later whether you want to participate."

"As I understand it, this form of cancer is so aggressive that it will spread and grow rapidly if we do not hit it with the bone marrow transplant. Is that right?" asked Susan.

"Probably, well, yes."

"Then, since the alternative is to die, I think I would like to go with the protocol. Where do I sign?"

She proceeded to initial every page, but only after she had made sure that I clearly understood each part too, because this was to be an experience we would have to share intimately for months. Now that she was headed somewhere, and there was a clear, if alarming, path to follow, Susan's spirits lifted visibly. "Let's do it." Right away, almost before the ink was dry, she had an ultrasound, a spinal tap, a catheter insertion in her side to allow the free flow of drugs, and she started chemotherapy. All before dinner arrived. She was exhausted, but determined. The worst part of the ordeal for her was another cancer patient in the next bed. This woman was a determined smoker—nothing to lose now, I supposed—whose life was a total mess, and whose husband called after she was admitted for cancer treatment, to let her know that he was divorcing her. She was also addicted to television, even when asleep. Her anarchic life was anathema to Susan, who eventually engineered a move to a silent, sunlit corner of the ward. From here she continued to run her home, family and work. In her diary, however, she confessed:

> *I feel so fortunate to be in such good hands. Randall has gone home each evening with long lists of things to do, people to contact, items to bring, tasks to complete. He must get hardly any sleep, poor guy. He seems to be in a dreamworld and all this is unreal. Plus he has a full-time job, and Eldar. I have never felt so loved in all my life, and I am so grateful to all my dear, dear friends.*

Of course, what about Eldar? One of the main reasons he had come to us was to recover from his father's sudden and violent death. In less than two years he had made a remarkable adjustment, only to be confronted with this new emotional roller-coaster. Susan's feeling was that he should focus on his daily routine or, "keeping everything normal," as she called it. Everyone was now trying to support everyone else to such an extent that *all* emotion was becoming dangerously bottled up. Stoicism, reserve, fear, whatever the cause, we were not facing the emotional trauma as reality. We all knew it, but we didn't know how to get out of it. In the pretend world, Eldar went to school, paid quiet and respectful visits to Susan in her room, wrote pieces for the *Fun Book* and so on. But he, and we, kept reality firmly at arm's length.

To our mutual great relief, Susan's stay was successful beyond expectations, and very soon she was packing to make the 50-mile journey back home. She would have to undergo chemotherapy until the tumor had shrunk by 50 percent before she would be eligible to proceed to the bone-marrow transplant. This was a condition of the Protocol she had signed. The chemotherapy, on the other hand, could be administered on an out-patient basis anywhere.

Living with cancer

Back home Susan hugged the cat and rejoiced in being in her own surroundings again. Then, exhausted, she crashed on the couch. Eldar, clearly uncomfortable, asked cautiously:

"How are you feeling?"

"Pretty rotten kiddo. But so happy to be back home."

"You look good."

"Thanks. Hey, do you want to see the staples in my neck. Look!"

"Cool. I've got Frankenstein's monster for a mother."

We had to get used to a strict regime. She had to wear a mask until her white blood cell count climbed back up. Otherwise, life was passably normal, except she could not eat salads, or raw anything, in that state of reduced immunity. And she had to stay away from crowds, or anyone with the slightest sort of illness.

Each day the catheter had to be cleaned and sterilized. Back at the hospital the nurse had given me a quick run-through of the procedure, but I knew I was uncertain. The first time I tried, I compromised the sterility, and for the first time in my life I lost it completely. I had no idea how frightened I had been even though—for Heaven's sake—it was Susan who had the cancer. I became stupidly hysterical and instead of comforting my wife, I was calmed down and comforted by *her*. I was humiliated, and felt both stupid and shamed. I felt as if, with all she had to go through, I had failed her in this one simple thing. Susan, however, remained totally calm.

"Let's go over to Dr. Sharp. He, or his nurse, will show you. Don't panic."

They did, and I never got it wrong after that. Plus the doctor did not make me feel like a fool. However, in that childish display earlier in the morning, I did get a small peek through the window of terror that I was trying to keep firmly shut. Life, I had to face it, was not in any way normal.

Later that day I went to teach. When I came out I remembered I had many prescriptions to fill for Susan, but for the first time in my life I could not find my car. My mind would not function and it had blocked out this one simple detail. One of my faculty colleagues stopped me:

"What on earth are you doing?" she asked, reading my look of total anguish.

"I've totally lost my car, I just can't think, I just can't think . . ." I said over and over.

"Get in," she said, pointing to her car. "I'm either going to drive round till I find your car, or take you wherever the devil it is you're all steamed up to go."

With this total no-nonsense attitude, she restored my sense of equilibrium for the second time that day. After that I never panicked again. But I knew now what real fear was, and how much I valued what I could lose. I was also aware of the black pit that lurked just beneath the surface, and how close to the edge of it we all were. I also now knew without any doubt how very much I loved Susan. Indeed, I knew this in a way that few are privileged to appreciate. I resolved to serve that love, and found myself writing my feelings down at my desk in the form of a poem that would let Susan know how I really felt, whatever lay ahead. In a way I was almost grateful to this illness for opening my eyes to the immensity of real love, and the foolishness of hiding that strength away. Perhaps my words look rather adolescent now, but this is what I gave her, and at the time it said exactly what I felt. It still does. Later I would come to know how important this act of revelation was:

Reflections on a brush with the sleeve of the Dark Angel
There are things we take for granted
While our lives become routine
Trivia commands the day
So the meaning is not seen
And many people live like that
While the magic fades away
And so, this terrifying shock
Has caused us both to say:

"What if the worst had happened
When we stared Death in the face?

What would our union have counted for
Had he extended his embrace?"
And so, when terror comes to stalk
And do its ghastly worst
We can smile, grasp hands and cite
This reversal of its curse . . .
"While we do not thank you
For the cruel game you played
If we are really frank, you
Restored our love this way."

    Life was different in other ways than simply living with the regimen of coping with cancer. Up until the diagnosis, there was no doubt that Eldar had held the center stage. We reverted to the parent norm, subjecting everyone to each nuance of his progress, the latest photographs etc. He enjoyed this attention, and it spurred him on to ever greater progress in school and at home. But now the limelight moved decisively toward Susan. "How's Eldar doing?" was replaced at once by "What's the news of Susan?" There was no other topic of conversation. Flowers poured in, the telephone rang off the hook, and visitors lined up for an audience. At the same time, the "hopeless male element" was kept well supplied with food that arrived daily, or simply appeared outside the door. That is, until Susan had recovered much of her strength and she took over the role of cook once more.

    But, these changes were hard on Eldar in several ways. First of all, I believe he was frightened because he had already known tragedy first hand, and had become so comfortable in his life with us that to see it threatened again so soon was a terrible blow. Next, he liked being the focal point of our lives, even though he was shy, and strove hard to make us proud of his more visible achievements. Despite the problems he remained "full of

Eldar works off frustrations with Tai Kwan Do

beans," as Susan liked to remind him. He rapidly rose through the belts at *Tai Kwan Do* developing wonderful flexibility and control. Susan, watching him, recorded: *he works himself up into a frenzy of raw energy, perhaps to deal with depression.* It was true that a real transformation took place on the martial arts floor where his face showed a degree of concentration I had rarely seen in him. Sweat poured off him in streams. I also tried to keep him focused on this book (initially designed to end with the departure of his mother). He became very much more involved in the autobiography, originally entitled *My Two Lives*. It provided him with a creative task and an outlet for whatever was brewing inside:

Keeping in shape in the Hoosier National Forest

"Hey, you could become famous," Susan joked. "Would you want that?"

"Of course dude (!)" he responded. "I want to be a teen idol."

His circle of friends was consolidating, even if it was not growing much. It consisted of a hard nucleus of a Venezuelan, a Nicaraguan, and an Indonesian, with others on the periphery. We wanted him to have a real alternative to thinking all the time about the possibilities that lurked in the future.

"I really envy Johnny," he told me one evening. "He can wow the girls and do the Lambada."

"At the same time?" I inquired.

Throughout these months, (April through June), Susan had been going through round after round of out-patient chemotherapy, during which time the tumor shrank most satisfactorily. Our optimism grew. By June the growth was down from 11 centimeters to four. The smaller tumors in the abdominal area (for the cancer had, indeed, spread) had shrunk, or disappeared. Most important, Susan was back to her old self again most of the time.

One Saturday afternoon she stood up, and said "I'm going to a movie. I'm not a prisoner."

So in her mask, which she had to wear to reduce the risk of infection, we made our way to the local bar that doubled as a cinema where they were showing *The Remains of the Day*. This turned out to be one of the most uncomfortable experiences of my life as we watched unfold the story of a British academic (played by fellow Welshman Anthony Hopkins), who loved a much younger strong-willed American who *dies of cancer*. I did not know where to turn.

"Wow, that was *great*." said Susan, still streaming with tears from the wrenching death scene.

"Did you know what this film was about before we came?" I inquired.

"No, but what a great story."

I marveled at her detachment. I also felt uncomfortable in May when I saw Susan reading everything there was to read about Jacqueline Kennedy Onassis, who had just died of the same form of lymphatic cancer.

Still, everything was on course for the bone-marrow treatment. The tumor was shrinking to well below the Protocol's required level of 50 percent of its original size. The time was set for the period of incarceration, and Susan's parents were driving down from Toronto to hold the fort during the anticipated time of sterile isolation. Plans were made for a return visit by the lovely Mair, and for she and Eldar to stay with relatives and friends in New York, thus getting Eldar out of the high-pressure zone. Everything seemed to be lining up like ducks in a row. Tests confirmed Susan's bone marrow was clean, and the collection of stem cells was scheduled for Monday July, 11.

On Thursday July 7, we awaited the arrival of Susan's parents. When I returned from work I was surprised not to find them already at our home. A scrawled note from Eldar said that they had phoned, but nothing else. This was his normal message. They should have arrived hours ago. Around five in the afternoon Peter Hobbs, my father-in-law, called. The news startled us. They had turned the wrong way onto a one-way system in Indianapolis and wrecked the car. Susan's mother had been injured by her seat belt. The plans now were that they would rent a car in Indianapolis, and drive down once they had made arrangements for their own car to be rebuilt. But, they said, the whole thing would take "many weeks." Susan was stunned, not by the injuries, but because she had given them specific route information that ensured they would avoid going through Indianapolis. The old Susan reasserted herself rapidly: They had *disobeyed orders* and she was very mad. But, at least it meant they would be here for several weeks while Susan went through her bone marrow transplant.

Then another phone call revealed that Mair would not be coming because her parents felt, at the eleventh hour, that they could not afford it. Eldar was devastated as this was the one positive thing he had been hanging onto all this time. He decided he would go to New York alone. Things were, all of sudden, becoming unglued.

Most of the next week was consumed by daily round-trip journeys of one hundred miles to Indianapolis, where Susan's stem cells were collected by centrifuge. This procedure involved lying down for hours in a position that made reading, or anything else, more or less impossible, and she was not one to sit, or lie, still even at the best of times. Tubes came from both her arms because the machine drew the blood from one, extracted the stem cells, and then put the blood back through the other. Slowly, the pale yellow fluid collected. We looked at the process in fascination because we were watching something that, very soon, could mean the difference between her life and death, once the heavy-dose chemotherapy was delivered.[10]

"Do you keep those very safe?" Susan inquired of the nurse-technician.

"We sure do," came the reply.

"But what happens if the building burns down before you can put them back?"

"You'd better be sure to burn down with it, Honey," came the reply.

We learned that there was an opening in the bone-marrow transplant isolation ward on Friday.

"Do you want it?" the orderly asked.

"Just try keeping me out."

Everything was set. The family, now including Susan's battered parents, gathered for a stupendous Moroccan meal at a new restaurant in Bloomington. We toasted our heroine, and everyone felt the same profound sense of purpose and optimism that Susan exuded.

"God bless you, Susan," said Mohammed the bearded Moroccan restaurant owner, his head cocked to one side, his arms extended. "I will be praying for you."

Mohammed and Susan hugged, both crying. The evening ended in mint tea poured with considerable accuracy from a great height.[11] Just one more day of stem-cell collection, and then the *cure*.

What happened next Susan recorded in her diary entry for July 14 (the following day):

---

[10] Basically, what the bone-marrow transplant does is that it allows you to receive higher doses of chemotherapy than would otherwise be tolerable because they would kill the bone-marrow cells as well. By removing them, and then replacing them the patient is enabled to survive the chemical bombardment.

[11] I met Mohamed El Bekty again in 2004 at his new restaurant in Indianapolis, and I asked him if he remembered those dinners. Not only did he remember them, but he remembered what she had ordered, and how she wanted it cooked ten years before.

> <u>Not</u> a good day for me. I had noticed last night in bed the pounding of my heart which I feel in my head. This was one of the original symptoms of the illness. I mentioned it to Elaine, the nurse, collecting the stem cells as she was hooking me up to the machine.

I remember that incident with the pure clarity of white light. I had suspected nothing of this, and was sitting by the bedside reading while the machine hummed and whirred. The moment she made the actual comment to the nurse my entire being was suffused by a gripping chill, and I *knew* instantly the meaning of what Susan had just said. It was impossible! Everything was going perfectly. She was responding like a model patient, and we had come all this way since April 15—three months! Nothing could go wrong *now*: not on the *last day*.

> *The doctor ordered a blood test and a CT scan. I had a bad feeling about it, and my fears were confirmed. The tumor had gotten bigger....This means I cannot go ahead with the transplant tomorrow. Instead, they recommend two to four rounds of chemotherapy separated by three-week intervals, using different drugs. This also means that they can't use the stem cells they collected. This is <u>very</u> discouraging news and I could not help but cry over it. Everything had been going so well. It's hard for me to stay positive <u>all the time</u>. Still, I've talked it over with people who have survived much worse odds, and I must take courage from their accounts. Susan wrote in her diary.*

We were right back in the pit of uncertainty.

Chapter 18
The Way Back

The implication of the renewed tumor growth was that Susan would have to go back onto several more rounds of conventional chemotherapy. However, as the previous ones had not been able to hold their effect long enough, she would need stronger doses now, and this meant they could not be given on an out-patient basis. Here, perhaps, was the worst news of all, for Susan came to hate hospital life with a vengeance—the loss of privacy, the dreary food, the inevitably periodic awful roommates that fate threw her way (tragically, the admirable Connie died almost eight weeks to the day, just as Dr. Tai had indicated, after that fateful first meeting with Susan). Without a doubt the prize for "Room mate from Hell" went to the woman who complained day and night to Susan about the pain and suffering she bore as a result of her illness. She went on endlessly and self-indulgently about it. Only on the third day did Susan discover that the woman had *hemorrhoids*, and was in oncology due to a shortage of beds. The woman received a short lecture on the relative merits of the two illnesses, but she was not deterred, and the wailing went on. However, there was no alternative to this hospitalization regime. Everyone shared Susan's real sense of disappointment, and her spirit of onward and upward—regardless.

Eldar had taken the news very badly. He had imagined, as had we all, that he would take off for Brighton Beach, where Russian is the first language, and come home to a magically restored normality. Although Eldar felt frustrated, and overwhelmed and confused by everything that was happening in his new world, he tried to carry on as though nothing was happening. He had intimated that he felt he was like a lightning rod for disaster, and I hoped he was not assuming any "blame" for what was happening. Though I think he was. On the other hand, he seemed to be home from school "sick" with greater frequency, something we had never observed before. He never mentioned Susan's illness at any level. It would have been so easy to read this as indifference, and here the cultural gap between us raised significant problems. I was never sure what was "appropriate behavior" in these circumstances for someone half Kazakh, half-Russian. Meantime, his mother expressed her deep feelings in letters in Russian that were powerful even in translation. For her, a major part of the reason for the change of life for Eldar, was to overcome the tragedy that had occurred in his life—and here he was facing it again, so soon. Lusya and Susan had become very close, language notwithstanding, and Lusya was feeling this very badly—and not just for Eldar's sake.

Susan's life had resolved itself into a mixture of relentless hope, the search for small victories, and of drawing strength from an astonishing circle of devoted friends and colleagues. Once everyone had heard about her setback, and the need to get back on track for a possible second try at the bone-marrow transplant in the early fall, they all responded wonderfully. In a few short weeks, the mail and faxes flowing into the house told of:

I. Prayers offered by the Tibetan community around the Dalai Lama in India initiated by some of my former graduate students

II. Candles lit in Notre Dame (Paris), Barcelona (Spain), Sofia (Bulgaria), and Moscow.

III. Prayers offered by the Serbs in Vukovar in occupied Croatia in a roofless church that had been mined by the departing Croat army. The letter said: *You know, in my country when we wish somebody good health we light a candle. Our church had been mined and destroyed by fire, but the walls are still there, and the roof is the sky above, so we have never been so close to God, and I hope he will see our candle and help your wife and you.*

IV. 600 folded paper cranes made by the fifth-graders at a local school when they learned that the crane is the Chinese symbol of long life. The cranes were suspended from the ceiling, and eventually our group family photograph for the year's Christmas cards was taken under this protective umbrella.

Perhaps the most intriguing of these many letters of support came from a former student, Kadidiatou Ly, who originated in Mali, West Africa. She wrote to say that her mother, back in Africa, had sacrificed a goat, some kola nuts, and several meters of cloth with a local *shaman* who had prepared a mixture of herbs wrapped in a cloth that was to be worn next to the body at all times. This talisman was called a *Grigri* and would arrive soon, along with some protective powder to be put in the bathwater. Lastly, Susan was to heat up seven coals, drop them into water, and hurl them into the distance. This she did after Eldar had finished barbecuing one evening, much to his total astonishment.

"What the heck are you doing?" he asked as the coals sizzled in the coffee can full of water.

"It's just an old African remedy," she replied, and threw the contents of the can into the garden.

"I see," responded Eldar, knowing better than to delve further into the actions of his deranged mother. He hadn't yet gotten over her habit of demonstrating how her regenerating hair could be pulled out in clumps.

Susan, Randall, and Eldar 1994

Christmas with Cranes

"That is so gross," he observed, "but being bald is cool. You could take up rock."

"You know, I was thinking," I overheard her say to him, "I have this client at my job who is a real pain in the neck. Next time he comes in and complains, I am going to grab chunks of my hair and rip it right out in front of him and tell him what I think. What a chance! What do you think?"

"I think you need help because you are crazy. But that's a really cool idea."

Susan was rapidly moving back into control, concentrating now on visualization. Using her intensely focused mental powers she concentrated on seeing her tumors shrink within her. Eventually she settled on Pacman charging around inside gobbling up evil growths as the agent of her visualization, but for gender-sensitive reasons the job was allocated to Ms. Pacman. The real problem now was that her desire for control of her situation was compromised, quite unintentionally, by the lingering presence of her parents. They were still trapped by the inevitable delay in rebuilding their car in Indianapolis, and the weeks dragged by. Of course, the original plan had been that Susan would be locked away in isolation all this time. Instead, because she was responding really well to chemotherapy, she was back at work, definitely wanting to be "in charge." It was the atmosphere at home, instead, that was becoming charged. This was no reflection on her two devoted parents; it was just that there are times when Susan needed to be alone, or at least try to feel she was back in a sane, normal environment.

Their car having been repaired, Susan's parents left on August 3rd. The next day was our fourth wedding anniversary. This was a very precious time with our happy marriage challenged by the ever-present monster, and we chose to celebrate it in the Moroccan restaurant. It was to become our inevitable venue before all big medical events. The following day Susan was due to enter Bloomington hospital for her final round of chemotherapy before the next— and probably only remaining—chance at the bone-marrow transplant, and a real hope for life. As always, the chemotherapy went remarkably well, and she suffered little in the way of reaction, going straight back to work. But, the question remained: "Would the chemotherapy hold until the bone-marrow operation?"

To help ensure this, Susan initiated a world-wide round of visualization. By e-mail, and in over one hundred letters, she sent out a plea to all our friends to concentrate hard on shrinking this tumor by August 23, which was the day of the CT scan that would determine her eligibility. From all over the world came the enthusiastic replies, including some asking how they could best do this? Susan described the tumor, and its dimensions. "Now, get to it! I want global convergence!" she exhorted. All the external indicators were good, and Susan's inner feelings, too, were all positive: *I slept nicely and dreamt that the tumor is only 2 centimeters long now*, she recorded in her diary on August 13.

Meantime, in other parts of the universe, events were shifting. Mr. Rund re-entered our lives by reminding us that the time had come to move Eldar in the direction of obtaining his "green card," for permanent-residence status in the USA. Two days before the CT scan was due we mailed off a package containing birth certificates, tax records, fingerprints, guardianship and adoption papers, etc. Once Eldar had his "green card" we would be on the way to his eventually gaining citizenship and a passport, so it would be much safer for him to travel. Until then, although he could travel and return on his "green card," his passport would be Russian[12], which meant the Russian officials could do whatever they wished with him if we went there next summer—including draft him. Certainly, his "green card" would ensure his re-entry into the USA, but it afforded him no protection overseas by US diplomatic representatives since he remained a Russian citizen. But, once Susan was recovered, we did so much want to go together to Russia to unite the two families for the first time, and at least the process was moving. The risk of going on a "green card" was still considerable, however.

On the evening of August 22 every ounce of energy the family commanded was directed at the CT scan the next day. Eldar would start school as a junior that day too, though his triumph was again overshadowed by the enormity of what would be happening in Indianapolis while he was in class meeting his new teachers. That day Susan could only pick at her food:

I didn't have much appetite for dinner—it's hard for me not to be nervous about the CT scan tomorrow. This will be a defining moment. People all round the world will be thinking of me.

Tuesday arrived, and Eldar paused before bolting for the door. "Good luck. I hope you get the answer you want." He looked like he wanted to say much more but couldn't.

"So do I kiddo, so do I."

As always in these tormenting situations there was a long, unanticipated wait in X-ray at Indianapolis. Susan settled down to work on some files she had brought along, but the atmosphere was wrong even for a workaholic such as she. Instead she started in on a book of short stories by Barbara Kingsolver, and was done with two-and-a-half when the call came.

I tried not to get too nervous—I felt pretty confident, and the signs seemed good to me; no more pounding in the head, shortness of breath like last time. The scan was uneventful and I was left with Barbara Kingsolver. Before long the nurse came back in, gave me a long look, and then threw her arms around me. "It's smaller, smaller, smaller," she said, and we cried and cried. Stem cell collection can start right away as the tumor is 50 percent gone.

---

[12] Actually, of course, it was still a Soviet passport, as Russia had still not printed replacements.

Home again we went crazy with the news. But our joy was tempered. We remembered that it was at the end of the stem cell collection that things had gone wrong last time. They must not go wrong now. The stem cell harvest was scheduled immediately so no time would be wasted during which the tumor might start to grow again. To reduce the stress Susan decided to stay with a friend in Indianapolis.

> *They also told me that as a result of all these treatments, I might be experiencing early menopause. Imagine. I got married only four years ago, I became the mother of a fifteen year old last year, and now the hot flashes. Life sure whizzes by, She wrote.*

We prepared for Susan's departure. It was likely that at the end of the week of stem-cell collection she would be admitted for the bone-marrow transplant, so she was going to be away from home for a long time. Everything went like clockwork during cell harvesting, and as they completed the last day the orderly asked,

Susan before the bone marrow transplant

"Now you don't have any pounding in the head, shortness of breath, anything like that?"

"I sure don't."

"That's good because a room has opened up, and you may be admitted right away. There is no point in hanging around. Let's get on with it. I will see you back here tomorrow."

I was thrilled, and we went back to Bloomington in the highest of spirits. Susan did a hot-water laundry of things to take into isolation. We celebrated the second anniversary of Eldar's coming to the USA by satisfying his passion for huge steaks. Then, the now-traditional dinner at the Moroccan restaurant, which was an emotional scene for everyone knew exactly *how* important this next phase really was. And then, on the second day of September Susan wrote:

I said farewell to Eldar, Dolli and the house, since it will be a while before I'm back. We got to Indianapolis, and they were not quite ready for me, so Randall and I went out into the glorious sunshine and just walked around. It will be a long time before I can do that again. We stood at the roadside, held hands, and looked up at the black windows on the sixth floor—the bone-marrow transplant isolation ward that will be my home for, who knows how many, weeks. I felt like some junk food. Then I entered my new kingdom. I had a window, thank Heavens, with a sunny view. There is a reclining chair, an exercise bike, and the whole room is screened off with plastic. Air moves out from the room under pressure preventing infection from entering the room in the air stream. I unpacked, and Randall put up some family photographs. I put up some of our hundreds of paper cranes. I had to go for an X-ray, and the technician asked me whether I had any metal "such as hair pins." I took off my turban and showed him my head." Where would I put them?" I asked. "Good response," he replied. After Randall left, I asked if I could have a last walk. They agreed, and I took a last stroll in the cool night air. Then chemo and dinner. I threw up the lot. But I am on track now.

For 25 days Susan remained in her plastic kingdom suffering nausea, turning lobster red in response to one of the chemicals and smelling strongly of garlic from another. But each day she increased her distance on the exercise bike, and built up her spirit and body. Meanwhile, back home, Eldar and I were the target of an army of frenzied cooks. We were too polite and disorganized to say no to anything, and soon the refrigerator was packed. Our opening words to anyone who came to the door were always "Would you like some lasagna?" It was an interesting change for a while, but we missed Susan desperately and my fear was compounded by loneliness of the worst possible sort, even though we drove to see her as often as we could. In isolation she had a strict visitor regime. One person per day could cross the "plastic curtain" but only after scrubbing up, and putting on mask and rubber gloves. A large chart showed the progress of all the many blood elements, and until one of them climbed substantially she would have to remain in strict isolation. After that she would graduate to modified isolation, which meant she could walk the halls of the isolation unit dragging her IV. Mostly she was her resilient self and kept going on a steady diet of Wimbledon. But sometimes the strain would show.

> *For some reason I started crying and just could not stop. Randall had been just about to leave, and somehow I just felt bad and needed him to stay until I felt better, which he did. I can think of no reason why this happened at this moment. But I suddenly realized how much I love and miss him. Later the hospital put me in touch with a woman who had survived the same illness I have six years ago. She gave me a lot of reassurance. Her name—Susan Baker!*

On September 23, exactly three weeks after entering the bone-marrow unit, Susan was moved onto modified isolation. As she walked the corridors she started reading the plaques on the wall given by relatives. This stopped when she realized that all of them were for former inmates who had *died*. "Does nobody leave here vertical?" she asked. It seemed such a damaging thing psychologically for patients trapped in these corridors with nowhere else to go. Are these what you would want to read walking the corridor? To take her mind off these depressing memorials I told her that, as a prelude to his upcoming sixteenth birthday in four days, Eldar wanted to have a party at home. Psychologically, we had never grown up with this concept, and physically we had no basement in which to hold it. Someone once remarked to us,

"You don't have children, do you?"

"No, how do you know?"

"The number of breakable objects below one meter."

Eldar's invitation to the party, to which I had agreed, contained the intriguing phrase *Positively No Parents!* I talked to him about that, and said I would stay out of the way upstairs to prevent the eternal embarrassment of his having to reveal that he was not the product of immaculate conception. We eventually "agreed." I closeted myself in my bedroom and waited for the worst. Soon the "dudes" arrived—all greeted by the universal "Hey. What's happening dude?" This was followed by *great* music, and the sound of pizza deliveries. After an unknown period of time, the music stopped and a total silence fell upon the house. I intoned a prayer and made my way to see the damage. But, at the doorway to the huge lounge I stood transfixed. Nothing could have prepared me for what I saw. Nothing. The place was immaculate, there was not a plate in sight, nor was there a plastic fork, food on the floor, or stains on the furniture. Indeed I could not find any trash at all. Even the housekeeper never did such a job. Only parents know the meaning of guilt.

On September 25th I recounted this wondrous tale to Susan at her bedside. She had been for her stroll along death row (as she called the corridor of memorial plaques), and was looking radiant. She had established a tremendous rapport with the nurses because of her fighting spirit. "You are one spunky woman with true grit, but an occasional pain in the rear," was the classic comment I caught once. Susan and the nurse immediately hugged, as Susan looked at me over her shoulder and said: "They ain't seen nothin' yet!"

The nurse, who had been out of the room to answer a call, returned. entered the room, put her hands on her hips and gave Susan a knowing look with her head cocked on one side.

"Woman, that call said that you're out of here tomorrow. God bless us all." We both looked up shocked.

"Really?"

"Good Lord, you're fitter than we are. You've already been home and back a couple of times on that exercise bike. Get packing," the nurse said firmly.

"Yeah!"

Susan cried and tried to do the high fives, which brought the IV hurtling down on my head. She cried and clutched the stuffed copy of Dolli that one of the nurses had given her, and which was never to leave her side. Everyone had to sign the now much-fattened and dog-eared *Lymphoma Fun Book*. Then we departed.

"I want to stop and buy Eldar some earrings on the way," said Susan, who had paid for him to have his ears pierced on his previous birthday. His big day was September 27—the next day.

After many emotional reunions, Susan decided to cook

The two Dollis

an Indian curry for Eldar's sixteenth birthday. I could not credit that she had just left the isolation ward. Of course, once again, she had to wear a mask everywhere because her immune system was still non-existent, but she was behaving as though she had had nothing worse than the flu. The contrast with just a few months earlier was amazing. Everyone had told us that this illness was like a roller-coaster ride, and it certainly was. Then a large box appeared in the garage, which I assumed it must be a welcome-home present for Susan, but when we opened it we found it filled with copies of the book *Summer in the Balkans* that I had written, and in which Susan featured prominently. Now, with the published copies right there, we really felt good—just like we had had another child. Our first child, meantime, had gone to the mall to get a haircut. He returned shorn of his thick long mat of glorious Central Asian hair, and with a much more conventional layered high school style in its stead. It looked good, and was certainly more manageable than the flowing locks he had worn before. We celebrated his reaching "carhood" as he called it. He had been scouring the used-car advertisements for weeks.

"You have also reached 'workhood,' Eldar," Susan reminded him. "That way you could *pay* for a car."

Susan had already realized that the alternative to helping Eldar find a car was that she would constantly be locked into an ongoing crisis with him over borrowing our own vehicle. He had a driver's test scheduled for November 22 and then the crisis would really break. Each night Eldar had been going to sleep counting off the number of days until he got his driver's permit.

The check-ups continued to look fine. All trace of the tumor had now gone, and it really seemed that life at last could begin again. A final routine follow-up visit to the Medical Center in Indianapolis produced hugs and tears all round. They were happy to see Susan well, as she was happy to be well. They see altogether too much misery on that ward. But life had yet another surprise in store for us. On the way back home we were rear ended by a lady who was window shopping and driving at the same time. Susan immediately *leapt* out of the car, and gave vent to months of pent-up fear and fury yelling at the already startled woman in the middle of the road. Eventually discovering that Susan was a cancer patient, the woman was so guilt-ridden and Susan so overwhelmed by her reaction, that they ended up in the parking lot hugging and crying. Before this I had called 911, and a police cruiser pulled in:

"I did it. It's all my fault," the woman said through her tears.

"Well, that simplifies things a lot," replied the officer.

"Oh it is entirely my fault, everything officer," the woman repeated.

"Yes Ma'am, I got it the first time."

In the midst of all this confession, grief, and compassion, and incidentally, the highway, came a call to my mobile phone. It was from Mr. Rund:

"I'm afraid there may be some problem with Eldar's permanent residency situation. It seems that the INS may not count the first year he was here as *full* guardianship. They will count only from the time you adopted him. I don't know where they get this definition of different types of guardianship; it doesn't exist in the law. Anyway, I am working with them, and will see what I can do. But I am not hopeful. It just means that we shall have to wait another year. Sorry."

This was bad news because it meant that we could not go to Russia next summer without the change of status. We decided to drive to the west and down the California coast instead. But then, no sooner had Mr. Rund's augury been given to us, than we received a printed notice from the INS in Indianapolis requiring Eldar to attend an interview to review his status. What was going on?

The Interview

"Oh," said Mr. Rund in answer to our confusion, "*that* is not significant in itself. They interview everyone. But I will use the occasion to see if I can't press the case that you were full guardians. Bring along any evidence of support you gave him, insurance, you know, that sort of thing. I think we might have a chance."

"You know this is my birthday[13]," said Susan. "I feel lucky about this."

"Ok. Let's meet in my office early, then we shall go to the INS for the 9:30 appointment."

Indeed it was Susan's 35th birthday, and a time for celebration. Nonetheless, the day did not start well as the power went off and I could not open the garage door. So, I walked to work, arriving just as two cars collided and one burst into flames. Definitely bad vibes day for some people. I tried to set these bad omens aside. During the afternoon Eldar presented Susan with a set of wine glasses, we were a family again, the news was good, and we were determined to turn this interview to advantage.

Susan then said:

"When we are up in Indianapolis, I have decided to have this catheter removed. I have had it for months, and I don't need it any more. Let's kill two birds."

We had no idea how important the congruence of these two events was to be.

At 7.30 a.m. we departed for Indianapolis. Our champion, who had just gained his red belt at Tai Kwon Do, was horizontal on the back seat all the way to Mr. Rund's office. He was unrecognizable in shirt, tie, and jacket for the occasion, though his cataplexy was familiar enough. Mr. Rund, cheerful and distracted as ever, went concisely over the brief he had written based on the minimal number of precedents he was able to locate. He was prepared to give it a try, and we had reams of documents with us to show how totally Eldar had been in our care that first year. Then, like a sound lawyer fellow, Mr. Rund ran through the various attributes of the individuals who might review the case that morning. The bad news was that the person with whom Mr. Rund had discussed the arcane nature of Eldar's case, and who had proved understanding, was not available on this day. Gloom was writ large on Mr. Rund's expression. Last on the list of possibles was a lady, formerly a nun, who Mr. Rund assured us to be "of the sweetest disposition, but, I fear,

---

[13] November 6, 1994

unlikely to dive into these dark waters at short notice, and we do so want a result as soon as we may get one, don't we? All told, we must hope fate does not put us in her direction."

We proceeded, I with Mr. Rund in his improbably old and modest car, Eldar and Susan in our large black saloon (what Eldar referred to as the *Politburo* car). I pondered the meaning of Mr. Rund's car. I found the unpretentious antiquity of it strangely reassuring. His fees were modest, and his record excellent. As anticipated, the time given on our appointment, rather like airline schedules, was more of a rough approximation than anything based on precision—and so a long wait ensued, and I drifted off into woolgathering among the indeterminate gathering of nationalities yearning to breath free.

I recalled the time when I had gone through this same process myself in 1990; my own naturalization interview. My application forms had been mailed in with a check. That had posed a problem as the requested sum was stated differently on each of the three forms, depending on the date when they had been printed. Playing safe I sent a check for the highest figure, only to have the entire correspondence returned because the correct sum was not stated anywhere. The papers then sat back in Indianapolis unacknowledged for eight months. There was no perceptible way to contact a living person over the telephone. Eventually, one of my well-connected friends asked me how the process was going. When I told him, he was shocked and said he would speak to the senator's office. Coincidentally, I was informed the very next morning that the paperwork had been completed, and that I was due for my interview. When I arrived the room was packed with people from south of the Rio Grande and west of the China Sea. Eventually my name was called and I was ushered through the portals into a cubicle where a woman, still processing a file, pointed, without looking up, in the general direction of the chair, and very carefully, and slowly, in what the Voice of America used to call *special English* enunciated

"s-i-t d-o-w-n."

"Why thank you, I certainly will," I replied, causing her to look up in shock. We progressed through the interview to the questions about the American constitution and the like,

"Mr. Baker, can you name the two senators from Indiana?"

"Certainly. I would look like an imbecile being a professor of public affairs if I couldn't do that, eh? Well, there's Dan Coates and . . . ."

My mind went absolutely blank. I described the other incumbent (who was to run on the Republican ticket for president in 1996), his military record, his time as a Rhodes Scholar, his special Congressional interests, his height—everything but his name.

The silence was embarrassing, and the interviewer feigned to write important things while I scrabbled around in my brain. I looked down. My file was open on the desk. Pinned to the front was a small memo that read *Why has nothing happened to this case in 8 months?* and at the top it said *From the Office of Senator Richard S. Lugar.* It also spelled facsimile incorrectly. But . . .

"Dick Lugar. That's the guy," I said and beamed.

Uncle Sam welcomed me to the fold.

I was roused from this reverie by an announcement over the public address system:

"Eldar Uru...um...Urumbeef," came the call,

and we were in. Mr. Rund failed to disguise via some morose facial gestures that our case had, indeed, fallen into the lap of the former lady of the veil. Worryingly, he suddenly seemed less confident than he had been. Our entire party, feeling extremely nervous, was compressed into a broom-cupboard room, and then compacted even more so that we, the principal villains, could be encompassed in the view of the video camera during "processing." First of all I was asked to tell the story of Eldar and how he came to be here. I had this down to a practiced and polished art form, and the lady became clearly charmed by so curious a tale.

"That's delightful, and most unusual." She smiled.

"Now, I do have one question, and that is about the first year he stayed with you. There is some doubt as to whether that would count as full guardianship . . ." The Rund eyes rolled upwards.

"Ah, I have here insurance documents showing he was added to my policy in my capacity as his guardian, and all bills and receipts relating to his schooling, clothing and many other things. Also he became the sole beneficiary of our wills."

"Good, good. That will all help."

"Ummm," from Mr. Rund, who was pressed against to wall next to the door. "I have prepared a brief that shows, most convincingly I believe, and in the light of all the precedents I could find, that the period most certainly counts in the sense interpreted by the INS."

"Have you? Oh, that will be most useful," the lady said, laying it gently on the file and tapping it sensitively and reassuringly with her fingers.

"I will read it most carefully, and get back to you *later*," she said, still smiling. Mr. Rund changed posture and switched gears simultaneously. This was *not* the answer we wanted. This meant the paper was going to be reviewed—who knows?— possibly in New York, Mongolia? We would never get an answer now.

"I wonder if I could prevail on you to read it now," said Mr. Rund as earnestly as he could, trying to avoid sounding either overbearing or groveling, with almost zero expectation of changing the situation.

"Well, I am very busy now, and I have lots of appointments, and we do not open in the afternoon."

I could feel our chance slipping through our fingers and into the black chasm of bureaucracy from which there is no return. Was there nothing we could do?

"Excuse me," I ventured timorously. "My wife is being treated for cancer, and indeed is here for treatment at the Medical Center this afternoon following bone-marrow surgery. It is a great burden for us to make these journeys, and in view of all the uncertainty about her future that swirls around our heads, the resolution of this matter would be such a *blessing*. I fully understand your tough schedule, but . . ."

The effect was electric and absolute.

"Oh, I am so sorry. That is terrible. Look, why don't you wait outside and let me give this some thought right away. And, I will need some more photographs. There's a place that does it down the hall. Let me work on this."

We left the cubicle, and I turned to Susan apologetically, "I'm sorry if I appeared to be trading on your cancer like that, but the lady was a nun, and I am sure has a good heart."

"Smart move," said Susan.

"I hope you didn't think that was just a ploy?" I asked

"Smart move," she winked.

"I wonder why she needs photographs?" observed Mr. Rund with a curious look.

We sat there, photos in hand, until the next attempt to pronounce Eldar's poor mangled name. Once more into the cubicle. Nothing could possibly have prepared me for what I saw the moment I walked in. Mr. Rund was similarly astonished, but the effect was lost on those who have not been through this process. Lying on the officer's desk was a *Certificate of Naturalization*. Now we know what the photographs were for. Eldar was about to become a *US citizen*. We had been nervously maneuvering toward the possibility of a Green Card: No more thought of green cards—this was *it*! He swore to renounce all foreign potentates, and then signed—and got his name wrong! Her started crossing it out.

"What a scuzzy mess, Eldar, and now that will be with you forever," I said.

"Don't worry," said the lady from the INS, and proceeded to hand him another engraved certificate. This one he filled out correctly, and it was taken away, embossed, and we were, well, done.

Eldar was an American. I was astounded. Mr. Rund looked jubilant and, to be blunt, rather post-traumatic. Susan said, of course, "I knew this was going to happen, *really*."

We left the building and realized we had nothing arranged to commemorate this enormous moment in Eldar's life because none of us had anticipated it in any of our plans. We invited Mr. Rund into a nearby church basement cafe and celebrated with sound vegetarian fare. We were ecstatic. It is not often that something goes so unexpectedly, and, with due deference, when there is a lawyer present. We had come to appreciate that Mr. Rund always told it as it was, if anything a bit heavy on the negatives, so we did not build up unreasonable expectations. We toasted the former lady of the veil, and Eldar remarked, "The Hand of God again? Could it be?" As we left the lunch, Mr. Rund remarked:

"Well, that was a good lunch and a good day's work. See you again soon."

"No," said Susan, rather stopping us in our tracks.

"But you won't. This is *it* Mr. Rund. You've done it all. We're home and dry."

"Oh my goodness," he said dropping into the guise of Bert Lahr as the timorous lion, "I believe you are right. Oh my goodness yes. Well, congratulations."

And off he went. And off we went to the hospital to have Susan's catheter removed. It was a symbolic moment, for its presence symbolized a continuing link with that miserable disease. Her recovery after the bone marrow transplant obviated its necessity any longer. Now at the Medical Center we could indulge in true happiness, real joy, hugs, kisses, tears, and much waving of the Certificate of Naturalization. How truly wonderfully *everything* had resolved itself. Susan wrote that night:

Welcome home from the cancer ward

November 17, 1994. At 3.30 p.m. we were allowed to leave the Medical Center, my body whole and unencumbered once more. We went back to Bloomington to resume a normal life. Eldar will phone Moscow tomorrow, and he will apply for his passport too. Now we will <u>all</u> be able to go there; I am well, and he is free to travel. "The Hand of God again, yep, yep", said Eldar on the way back. I think he may be right.

Chapter 19
Life begins again

Few of us have the opportunity to rediscover life quite the way that recovering cancer patients do, having stared down death for so long. But our lives had turned a corner, and I was sure we would see everything differently. That may have been true for a day or two, but for Susan, the prospect of going *back* to our former normality had been, and remained, *everything*. She was not looking for new levels of consciousness, transcendent religious experiences etc., she wanted it *the way it used to be*, all too briefly. This was, of course, something of a disappointment for Eldar who had envisaged Susan morphing into some sort of gentle flower child surrounded by a perpetual warm fuzzy glow of reassuring happiness and inner joy. This would have relieved him of some of the pressure that resulted from Susan's capacity to monitor and micromanage his life—especially his personal hygiene. ("What, only two pairs of underpants *again* this week?" "Your hair looks like it's time for an oil change.") But, his New Age vision was not to be.

As rapidly as possible Susan started working, cooking, shopping, and all the other things she had done with the same determination as before. I had imagined she would have focused on the "big picture," and talked about grand holidays, metaphysics, new approaches to life. Instead she berated me about the state of the refrigerator, the unbelievable quantity of food sitting inside it, and so forth. Even Eldar was mystified by this, and he mentioned it at dinner:

"I thought people who had these life-threatening experiences were supposed to be changed, you know, all mystical and things. They would discover what is important in life. So how come you still worry about all the little things? Where is this new perspective?"

"How long have you been wearing that shirt?"

"I guess you are recovered ok."

In short order Susan re-established the orderly household she had left. Lists proliferated at terrifying speed, and the usual domestic crises came back to center stage:

> *Eldar thought we had gone for the afternoon, but Randall and I had merely walked to the store, and came back by a rather different route. We were surprised to see him sitting on the porch—though I realize now that it commands the best view of the approaches to the house! We thought at first that he had locked himself out. . . . As we came up the drive he suddenly took off, alarmed and much shaken, on his bike, and it suddenly dawned on me—he was having a smoke. Sure enough as I approached the front porch I smelled cigarette smoke, which was coming from a half-smoked, still-lit cigarette that he'd left lying there on the wooden steps—great fire hazard! Looking through the cracks between the steps onto the ground below I saw dozens, no scores, of butts. The smoking gun literally. At dinner we raised the subject. After all I had been through with cancer, how could he want to give himself the same illness. I felt terrible. He told us he had started about a year ago. Most of his friends are from countries where smoking is common, and though he would deny this to his dying day, he is very influenced by peer pressure and the need to be accepted by some group. I think he is a lonely and shy person. I told him we were making no demands on him to stop. Just be up front about it, and try to stop. He is an outstanding sportsman—why would he do this to himself? I don't think we really understand how much Eldar has been through, and he never gives us the slightest indication.*

One emotional change had occurred, however. Susan was now captivated by the idea of a Grand Family Christmas reunion. I realized that this was one area where she had rediscovered the importance of something that for so long had been taken for granted. Writing up a storm, she pressured everyone to gather at the family home in Garden City, Long Island, to re-establish a tradition that had lapsed. It was, of course, difficult to say "no" to someone who had been through what Susan had lately experienced, and so affirmative replies came in from Seattle, England, Toronto, and many other places. She wanted old animosities set aside, and a return to what a family should be. Just before going to New York, we would travel to Boston to see Susan's 89-year-old grandmother who lived in a home there. All this represented *life* to her now, and what life should be about.

She became the patron saint of kindred matters, and we her faithful acolytes. For Thanksgiving while Eldar rode the bus for some obscene number of hours to visit Martina in Pennsylvania, we joined our neighbors, only to find that Dolli the cat had walked over with us, entered ahead of us, and proceeded to take over the entire evening. I felt so relieved that I did not any longer have to juggle every day to manage teaching, Eldar, and the many unpredictable demands of medical treatment. Most of all I was happy to be free of those endless journeys back and forth to Indianapolis, and the uncertainty and fear that had made them necessary. We were quickly falling back into our old, and very comfortable, ways.

To the abyss

It was two months, to the day, on November 26 when Susan made the following small entry in her diary,

My stomach felt bad all day. It's felt bad for some time now, so I didn't go with Randall to collect Eldar off the bus from Pennsylvania.

We had expected there would be some after-effects of all the battering that Susan's body had endured over the past seven months. But the next day she wrote,

I awoke in pain after a night of continuous horrible anguish. I was actually moaning out loud, and I tried to sleep propped up. It was the same at work. I went to see Dr. Sharp, and he thinks I now have ulcers. Great!

Susan was placed on a corrective diet. As the days went by the situation, if anything, got worse. At one point she had to leave work and go home to bed with severe back pains. An X-ray confirmed the presence of several ulcers. Dr. Sharp was, as ever, ahead of the game and told Susan he wanted her to have a scope test in which they would enter the stomach, look around, and if possible take samples of what was going on there. The ulcers had become associated with a tenacious itching, and that did not seem to make sense.

December 6 was not a good day. I had an ultrasound done of my gallbladder and kidneys to see if there are any stones there. But the technician spent most of the time probing the liver. I asked if she could see anything there, and she said "yes." She took the film for the doctor to look at, and he agreed it looked like lymphoma. The cancer is back. Not news that I wanted to hear. I threw up dinner. A blood exam showed that my liver enzymes, markers for lymphoma, are shooting up too.

The news could *not* have been worse. Susan and I went back to see her oncologist, Dr. Tai. His expression as he spoke was more eloquent than his words. He tried desperately to be encouraging, but without being unrealistic.

"Yes, it's back."

"So, what do we do now," came Susan's immediate and characteristic response.

I found myself, instead, staring back into that black, yawning chasm in which the insatiable monster lived who was trying, once more, to devour our lives and happiness.

"Susan, you have to understand that the bone-marrow represents the heavy artillery. If that fails there is not much we can do. I spoke with the Medical Center in Indianapolis, and they believe that another bone-marrow program will not work. We have to fall back on chemotherapy, but if you have relapsed from huge doses, it is unlikely that smaller doses will do much. But we can try different combinations. Then, of course, there are the experimental options, and we could look into those."

"I will look into everything and anything. I am not giving up now, believe me."

"I understand. I just want you to know what position we are in."

In my anguish, I felt that the world had just gone unspeakably mad and was falling apart around us. We had thought all this was over, but now we were right back in the maelstrom with time very much against us. I took my cue from Susan. If she wanted brave, then brave she would get. If she wanted to let it all out, I was certainly ready to join her in that, there and then in Dr. Tai's back office. She chose stoicism, and continued with many, many questions. So, now the immediate future was to be a crazy race against death, and in the short run, rounds of continuous chemotherapy in the hospital she hated so much. I had to give her all the support I could muster.

Randall has been so wonderful all day, so loving and supportive. I now know I love him more than I can say.

Somehow, I had to tell Eldar. Once again I found him in his room. This time it was infinitely more difficult. Slowly I worked my way through the explanation until I reached "It looks very bad, Eldar, very bad." And that was it. One more word and I would burst into tears there and then. Eldar was devastated, and this time there was nothing he could say. Was his life destined to be dictated only by grief and tragedy? Here, in Bloomington he seemed to have found stability and direction, and now, after a seeming reprieve it was all being blown to pieces. Maybe I should have tried to say more, and then perhaps some stupid male barriers would have been cast aside to our lasting benefit. But, embarrassment defeated honesty once again. I told myself that if Susan was holding together, and concentrating on the fight ahead, I was damned if I was going to let her down.

And then, by an act of supreme irony, Eldar's new US passport arrived that very day. What chance of using it for us all to go to Russia now? At that moment I reached the lowest point of my life so far, though surely nothing compared to the depths there Susan must have plunged. I was sick with anger and frustration. At my desk the next day, I found myself writing to purge my anger and despair:

For the first time in my life I simply do not know how to cope. That's it—pure and simple. Even typing this is almost impossible because the screen swims through a distorting cloud of tears. And I thought that was something I never did.

Right up to this point, (December 9), there was a sense of manageability about Susan's lymphoma. It was hard to be anything other than optimistic as she had beaten back the monster until now through treatment and sheer strength of will. But this cancer is like Victor Frankenstein's monster for it is stronger than its creator in its determination and hideous destructive strength.

The actual discussion we had held with Dr. Tai had been grotesquely civilized as we went through the prospects, such as they now were. I just don't know how anyone can make a profession of seeing people with awful illnesses, constantly having to cope with the delivery of terrifying information to frightened souls. We took it all in a resolute sort of way, I think because such awesome news takes time to work its way through the shock barriers. I can hardly believe now the way we sat there and discussed the circumstances in such a coldly clinical way. God alone knows what Susan was feeling. She was then, and always will be the very definition of courage in my eyes. As a way to release these emotions I wrote:

I am now given to crying—privately of course—most of the time. This is awful because I want to be as strong as she, and I couldn't even talk most of the time today because I am so choked up. What use is that to her? We said that everything would be as "normal" as possible—but what household "normally" spends its time weeping and unable to speak?

The next few weeks were filled with a tumult of activity as Susan phoned around the nation seeking possible alternatives for her treatment. At the same time she was, despite brief respites from chemotherapy, clearly going downhill as other symptoms set in including an even more ferocious unrelenting itching and a persistent cough. Both of these started to sap her energy, erode her spirit and make things just that much more difficult. Each CT showed lymphoma spreading to different organs, and growing. Each chemotherapy would push it back dramatically, but not enough to stabilize. The pills multiplied, the diet became more complicated, and the normality of life yielded, a little more each day, to the intrusive demands of treatment to control her illness. In spite of it all, Susan fought on with everything she had, regularly returned to her office at IU Publications at every opportunity, continued to run the house, and maintained a very passable imitation of how our lives had once been.

Holding On—the family under siege

This left me in a total dilemma—one faced, I am sure, by all spouses in this situation. Of course, I had to be as supportive as I could. On the other hand, I wanted to keep a sense of normality too. My colleagues at the university broke all records for understanding. The dean had made it absolutely clear that my time was my own, and the school was ready to back me at all times with any option I needed. Five faculty members were always ready to step into my classes without notice. However, the need for this arose only once. Now, looking back, I think I was wrong to be "so normal," even though it gave me something familiar and reassuring to hang on to. My time should have been spent elsewhere. But I did not understand that clearly at the time. The old cliché "Business as usual" seemed the only way to, perhaps, pretend that a normal life could go on.

More and more often I had to wage an internal war with mean-spirited anger and frustration. When a family member has cancer it amounts to what I thought of as a crisis "trump card." There was absolutely nothing I could say about myself, or my own condition, that had the slightest weight or significance in the context of Susan's cancer. Even to speak of stress, anger, or the physical pain associated with continuous indigestion, seemed absurd, small-minded and inconsequential. Accordingly, I could never speak of my feelings, for I would be letting the side down. Every conversation outside the home began with "And how is Susan today?" I can't excuse or justify it, but I began to feel resentful, and even kept my office door closed specifically so people would *not* ask me this. My assistant, Maggie, the only person who understood talked to me instead about my own condition. Apart from her, only once was I asked, by a colleague I barely knew:

"How is your health?"

"Pardon? It's my wife who is sick."

"I know all about that. But I am asking about you. I bet nobody asks *you* how you are getting through?"

"How on earth did you know that?"

"My wife went through cancer last year. She's fine now. But I remember how it was only too well. Come to lunch and I'll talk to you. I know what is going on."

I felt like a door had opened. Just to talk about it was such a relief. At least I would not feel contemptible and treacherous talking to this man. He agreed with me that the only way to survive was "day-by-day." "Don't anticipate worries. Handle only the ones you have." My main concern was never to be anything but a total support to my wife's demonstrable personal courage and determination. I was the "supporting cast."

Lost in all this turmoil of emotions was Eldar. We blessed the day that Susan had encouraged him to take up Tai Kwon Do. I am convinced that the companionship of that disciplined sport, the opportunity to let off profoundly suppressed emotions, and the personal leadership of his teacher, whom he worshiped, saw him through this terrible time. Indeed, with that, and the prospect of a Christmas trip to Boston and New York, he had enough to anticipate that he could divert his thoughts away from the crisis building at home.

The reunion at Christmas now assumed a position of enormous importance in Susan's mind, and she made it quite clear that she expected everyone to come. In truth they had little chance of making an excuse when she herself, with all her problems, was going to be there. They all agreed, happily, to be in Garden City and in good spirits. Dr. Tai had concocted some chemotherapy that could be delivered on an out-patient basis, and that so lifted Susan's spirits that she entered the Christmas aura a few days early. Furthermore, in her enormous web of telephoning, she had discovered from the National Institutes of Health three experimental programs for "lapsed bone-marrow" patients, as she was now known. She would use the visit to New York to have an appointment with the Sloan Kettering Memorial Hospital, and discuss the possibilities of getting on a trial they were just about to start. For this we had to assemble over 20 pounds of medical records and X-rays that would accompany us. Ever looking forward, Susan wrote:

> *I spent 5 hours on the phone tracking experimental treatments. The University of California at Davis says they have been conducting trials*

since 1985, and one third of their people go into remission—though they always relapse. They breed antibodies to your own cancer, and then they irradiate them and release them into your body so they seek out the cancer cells, attach to them and then zap them through radiation. To get onto these trials I have to be off chemotherapy for four weeks and pass certain tests, including one showing that my liver can take the shock. My liver seems to be where the trouble is focused, so I'm not sure about that. At any rate, I have new avenues to explore. Then there's the spiritual avenue through mind-body control, which may be my best hope of all. I think I must try fundamentally to change my outlook and become more loving, caring and giving, and less critical, anal-retentive and domineering. If I can make peace with the mind, the body will follow.

The Reunion

At Indianapolis we boarded the plane with chiller boxes containing $2,500-worth of blood supplements, and the huge bag of medical records. Susan had just come out of chemotherapy, and for her this meant she was at her peak. She was positively excited that this huge family gathering was coming together finally. She was wearing her mask the whole time because of the deadly danger of infection. Apart from the mask, however, it was difficult to imagine how ill this woman was from the tremendous happiness and strength she radiated. She had slowed down, that was for sure, but she was definitely the Susan we knew and loved (and feared a bit occasionally!)

In Boston we had been put up in the home of our host's aged mother who was in the Carolinas. This house was a perfect time capsule. I don't think the lady had purchased anything after Ed Sullivan passed away. Everything worked, but it was like being locked overnight in the Smithsonian. Indeed, Eldar and I took off to see the Children's Museum in Boston, and walked into an exhibit called *How Grandma Lived*. It was a carbon copy of where we were staying. The venerable charm of this old home was now violated by the depredations of Eldar's early Christmas present—a radio-controlled Porsche that ran every moment we were at home. The weather was a succession of those perfect brilliantly clear sharp days made for walking. Slowly Susan and I made our way around the charming gentility of the area, savoring every second that we could be free of pills, injections, IVs, and all the paraphernalia that marked the passage of our daily lives.

Christmas passed with a disarming sense of normality—precisely the effect that Susan unreservedly wanted more than anything. By now her energy levels were low, and normality was purchased at the price of constant rests and naps. In between, however, she was suffused with the spirit of the season, and made everyone feel comfortable and profoundly happy. It was a somewhat strange Christmas as we were spending it at the home of friends of Susan's family, rather than with the family itself. But it was no less a family Christmas for that. What greater act of kindness than to open their hearts and home to someone so much in need of love?

In true Christmas fashion we gathered around the table. "Cousin" Chris, back from the Peace Corps in Kenya, met Susan again for the first time in many years, and they were clearly overjoyed to see each other. As our host was a devoted hunter we feasted not on turkey but on elk; a good strong, lean meat unfamiliar to me. Tradition was restored by the entry of the flaming plum pudding, exciting to Eldar who stared in wonder at this pyrotechnic offering. How often during that day we escaped the clammy hands of mortality, and only once did Susan let go and cry. That was when she was holding a card from Eldar, which said, quite simply: "Merry Christmas! I hope that this Christmas is the best Christmas you ever had in your life. I also hope that you get better very soon. (Like tomorrow!) Love, Eldar." It may not have been the most fun-filled and carefree, but it definitely *was* the best Christmas, and we understood oh so well what the season was all about.

As I said earlier, our visit to Boston had been arranged to give Susan a chance to visit her grandmother, Peter's mother, Viola Hobbs, who was then a resident in a charming institution in Newton Upper Falls. Viola's mind was no longer sharp, and there was some question whether she would even remember Susan. Susan, however, wanted to see her.

"This may be the last chance," she said.

I, at first, understood that comment to refer to Grandma's 89 years, but with a chill I realized it had a terrible double meaning.

Fortunately, Grandma knew full well who Susan was, though she did ask her over a dozen times, "Well, where are you living now my dear?"

She also recalled who I was, but the presence of Eldar was a bit of a mystery. The sudden appearance of an unheralded adolescent son required some explaining at the best of times.

Susan and Grandma Hobbs

Still she was happy that he was Eldar, whatever that meant. I watched this vignette of the devoted granddaughter and the adoring grandmother, and suddenly I was overcome in a way I had not experienced up to this point.

Grandma had clung onto life through nine decades, and now drifted in her mind quite randomly through the years. Next to her, attentive to her every wish, was Susan: young, alive and starting out on life's journey. But which one of these two persons would depart life's embrace first? God forbid that I should share such thoughts or sentiments with anyone, but they were there inside me and they would not go away. I had to leave the room briefly for I came within an ace of losing control completely. Grandma of course, was not aware of Susan's condition, and if I burst into tears, that would require some difficult explanation. Eldar, with extraordinary understanding, told Grandma once more where we lived, and played well the role of the ever-dutiful grandson. She, of course, until now had no idea that this grandson ever existed. It was also strange for Eldar to meet his grandmother for the first time at age sixteen, and then have to ask her name.

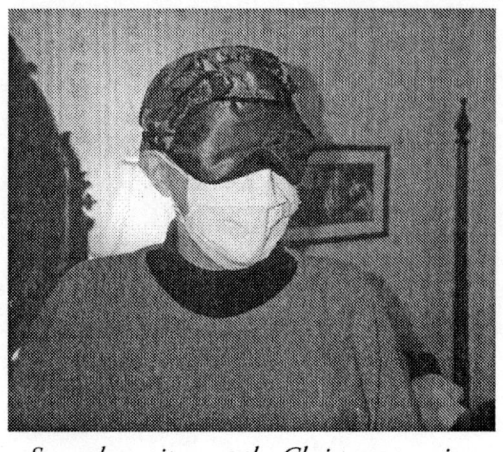

Susan hams it up at the Christmas reunion

We disembarked the Boston-New York shuttle at La Guardia into the waiting arms of the reunion vanguard, complete with van. They, like everyone so far, were astonished at how healthy Susan looked—for she did, though at some considerable cost. This was the first meeting with Eldar for some of his new family, but the novelty was overshadowed by the great concern for Susan. I felt so bad for Eldar that this was how he made his first appearance before so many members of his new family. Normally, he would have been the center-stage attraction. But he took it well, and was fastidiously polite and correct.

During the next few days Susan developed a highly-regulated regime of sleep and reappearance, so she always looked at her best. She astonished me, for I knew what a toll these attempts to look natural were extracting, but I neither hovered over her, nor acted the ever-solicitous husband, because "normal" was what she wanted, and normal she would get. Eldar and I meanwhile spent time walking Broadway. He wanted so much to have a "real" New York pizza and so I ordered one. Unfortunately I ordered an entire one with 22 slices. It was too good to leave behind, and so we carried the wretched thing the entire length of Broadway from the Custom's House to the Empire State building. Eventually the box disintegrated, so Eldar went into a Russian shop and asked them in Russian for a bag. They were so astonished that his wish was granted immediately.

Susan and I had scheduled another day for the interview at the Sloan Kettering Memorial Hospital, one of the most famous cancer centers in the world. But despite her hopes it became clear rather quickly, even with our pounds of X-Rays and documents, that their experimental protocol was at too early a stage to help. They were working out doses, and Susan's case was rather too far along for that level of preliminary investigation. It was disappointing, but they suggested the work at Davis as more appropriate.

The Great Reunion

Strangely enough, even after another setback in our relentless search, Susan did not seem unduly depressed or downhearted. The situation anyway was instantly improved by the discovery of a good Indian restaurant (our passion) on 69th and 1st. While we ate there was no unnatural or forced conversation between us, we just discussed what to do with the rest of the day. I never did understand how she could carry the burden of these accumulating disappointments without any observable sign of distress, and I told her that:

"I never lose hope. That's how," she told me over lamb curry.

"And I never lose hope in you either," I reassured her.

"I know," she replied.

We spent the afternoon wandering happily through Central Park, despite the crippling weight of the X-rays and medical reports, and the biting winter wind charging up Fifth Avenue. Susan walked slowly but purposefully. She knew she had to save her energy, for that night would be the reunion dinner: the focal point of the whole trip.

That evening twenty-three people gathered in Port Washington, all in awe of our central figure. Everyone was determined that nothing would spoil this most wonderful moment. Who knows what we ate, or what we said. We were there, and she was there, and we all posed, quite automatically, around *her* for the reunion photograph, and she looked radiantly happy, and that is all there is to say. I not only loved her more than I could say, but I was prouder than I had ever been. How ironic that it took something like this to highlight something so obvious. I was overjoyed that she had seen, in this evening, her dream come true.

I was also scared to death.

The reunion took a great toll on Susan, and she had to spend a substantial part of the remaining time of our stay in bed. Furthermore, everyone seemed to be developing colds, which were very threatening for her. Nonetheless, she let young nephew Tim come to see her armed with some paintings for her to see:

"Hello Tim. Can you explain some of these to me?"

"Yes. This one shows jelly from a jellyfish. That one is the insides of a rabbit, and the third one is a carrot out for a sail."

"Oh yes, I can see it all now. How kind of you."

Chapter 20
Shortening odds

When we arrived back in Bloomington, Susan was exhausted, but not too tired to stay up and see in the New Year with Soviet champagne—yes, things were *still* emerging from the copious black bag that had accompanied Eldar more than two years ago. (Was it really only two years from that high to this low?) As we greeted the New Year, it afforded us an opportunity to say a few honest words about the period that lay ahead. I had a real concern because the reunion that had occupied Susan's mind so completely over the past few months, and provided her with a target and a mission was over, despite its enormous success. Now I was desperately anxious that only her illness would be there to occupy center stage. Worse, the Sloan Kettering visit had not produced any of the new avenues for which we had hoped, and upon which she could have focused her attention. In fact, the doctor with whom we had spoken had astonished us by commenting:

"You know, if I am honest with you, the treatment of cancer has barely advanced at all in twenty years. We do the same brutal things, but now we have discovered ways of giving patients bigger and bigger doses. Deep down we still don't know what this thing is, why it happens, or any solid way of preventing it."

It didn't help that on two occasions during that period in Long Island I read substantial pieces in the *New York Times* on what appeared to be radical new approaches to cancer. Yet, on our journey home, rather than be angered or frustrated by these announcements at this late stage in her illness, Susan turned to me on the plane, tapped the paper and said. "You see, there is always reason to hope. Remember what the specialist said in Indianapolis. He told us that the attitude of the patient is the best predictor of response to treatment. No, I have a very good feeling about the Davis study. I talked to them, and they were wonderful. Even though they had never met me, they spent ages explaining everything. I will have to have a large biopsy taken of the tumor from the liver, and they will study it, and use it to breed the antibodies that will carry the radioactivity to the cancer cells. Problem is you have to be off chemotherapy for four weeks to have the healthiest possible liver. We'll see. I feel much better now because the game plan is shaping up."

On January 6, Susan had a CT scan to monitor progress in the two-and-a-half weeks since she had received the last chemotherapy. In the evening, in his office, we found Dr. Tai reading through the report. As usual, he started straight in on the facts. There really is no other way, I realized, to handle these situations. There is only one thing the patient wants to know, and they don't want it gift wrapped.

"It looks bad, Susan, I have to tell you. There has been a real proliferation of the tumors, and in a shorter time. The out-patient chemotherapy is not holding them, so I want you in for continuous treatment. I have called the hospital and you will be admitted tomorrow."

The double blow of the proliferating cancer, and a return to the place she hated most on earth, hit Susan hard. I didn't know how many more of these terrifying disappointments I could stand.

"But what about the biopsy to get on the Davis study?"

"Oh, we will go ahead with that."

This was vital because it kept the avenue of hope open. Susan immediately launched into all sorts of questions about Davis, and they discussed the Protocol for over an hour.

"You don't think I could, maybe, wait, because I have to be off chemo for four weeks?"

"Susan, you would not last four weeks. We have to move *now*."

Dr. Tai had researched this thoroughly himself, and devoted endless amounts of time and patience to Susan. He never tried to patronize her, but was as businesslike as she. I never understood when this man slept for I found him at work or in the hospital at all hours of the day or night. Furthermore, he always called back to answer Susan's alarms. They made a perfectly compatible pair and she formed an unrelenting respect and care for him.

But, in this particular case, once we were out of the medical building and in the car Susan cried. Scared she might be at breaking point, I reminded her that today was the Orthodox Christmas and that we had been invited by a group of Ukrainian students to dinner. I said:

"Let me give them a call. They will understand."

"No. I am going. I will give them a call and tell them that."

The students were astonished, and a little unnerved hearing that Susan was about to re-enter the hospital. When we arrived the spread, as is usual in Eastern Europe, was already set on the table, and everyone hovered solicitously around Susan, delighted that she had come. We started the meal with sardines, at which point Susan left the table hurriedly, rushed to the bathroom and threw up. The students were now feeling extremely awkward, though they wanted to do anything possible to help. Walking very slowly, Susan returned:

"Right, now let's try again."

She proceeded to eat like a horse, and stayed until well after eleven, though she spoke to us after dinner from a recumbent position on the couch.

Control or support?

We were now entering a very difficult phase. More and more time was taken up simply with the endless round of chemotherapy, X rays, allergists, and the entire phalanx of support services. And yet Susan worked on shopping lists, and continued to go to her office at the university at every opportunity. I knew that this continuing "normality" meant so much to her. But she simply could not go on doing all these things. Friends offered to come from North Carolina to stay and help. The husband, Westy, was someone that Susan met at a conference some years back and befriended because he seemed "older, and left out of things." The couple had since retired, and willingly dropped everything at Susan's request. More than anyone in the world she wanted them, and she cried and cried when they said they would come. Truly, I did not know how to react to the conflict between the reality of what Susan could do, and what she appeared to want to do. I ran whatever chores I could.

First, however, Susan had to spend several days in hospital, but her joy was unbounded when she found out that because of her condition, her terrible, persistent cough, and other factors, Dr. Tai had ordered her into a single room. She raced her wheelchair round in circles and gave high fives to everyone, and then shot off through the door into the room, as though Dr. Tai might change his mind if she did not immediately stake out her territory. As usual she reorganized the microgeography of the room, which she had down to a fine art. Woe betide anyone who moved anything.

Once in bed, she was immobilized fairly quickly by the insertion of IVS in both hands. Then she had the liver biopsy and which left her with a surgical scar and the most intense pain she had ever known each time she coughed—which she did often. It was getting harder and harder, "But, it is necessary if I am to get on that Davis study. I cannot lose sight of that."

Once, during a conversation with a nurse, Susan was asked why she was always accompanied by the stuffed calico cat.

"What is the significance of that? Is it like a lucky charm?"

"No, it is just that this is the best I can do in the absence of the real thing."

"Why don't you just bring the real thing?"

"You're kidding!?"

"No, cats are allowed to visit."

And so it was that Dolli became a faithful visitor to the fourth floor, and was the excuse for innumerable contrived appearances by orderlies and nurses. These small victories meant so much to Susan who regularly needed something positive to counter the eternal presence of negative signs. Dolli, too, took it all in her stride, and as long as she could find the most painful post-operative location on which to lie, she was blissful.

Susan was released, (she always used that word advisedly), seven days later. My colleague Maureen, who was around Susan's age, accompanied me to the hospital. We packed everything on a cart and went down ahead to get the car. Susan was wheeled by an orderly to meet us. On the way down the orderly remarked:

"Susan, you are so lucky. You have a beautiful cat, and such great parents."

"When did you ever meet my parents?"

"Just before they went to get the car."

She greeted us at the car with "Hi Mom, Hi Dad," but I believe Maureen did not catch that. The orderly would have been admitted to her own hospital if she had.

The family and stress

During the time since the reunion Eldar had had a number of triumphs. He had landed a job at McDonalds. Susan asked him when he came in, still dressed in his burger uniform:

"Well, how was the first day on the job?"

"It went quite well. Most of the time I had to watch an instructional video on buns."

"You seem a bit young for that."

The Rubicon had also been crossed and Eldar now had a car, since he had a job to pay for it. All his collected lawn-mowing money went toward its purchase, and I loaned him the rest. A detailed schedule of payments was signed, and the struggle began in the eternal competition for his wages between me and the manufacturers of the world's largest sound systems for cars. Money was not Eldar's strong suit. But, from our point of view he had become invisible. Susan wrote:

He is working himself too hard, we never see him, and he is not happy. He was always cheerful and positive. Now he seems detached and solitary.

He seemed either to have, or more likely, simply did less and less homework. He always maintained it was done in school, or there wasn't any. I was reluctant to press him on this because he was clearly under stress, and was working it off in his own way, but he was becoming depressed. He began coming home from school and sleeping—sometimes seventeen hours at a stretch. Then he started skipping martial arts classes, especially the ones that were routine, but required, in favor of the ones he enjoyed. The signs were all there, but I was too obsessed with circling the wagons around Susan against ever-shorter and more vicious odds to pick up on them.

Then, one Saturday evening, Eldar walked into my study.

"You're back early."

"Well, I couldn't find my friends. But here you are. This is the answer we are looking for."

I had no idea what he was talking about, but he handed me a sheaf of photocopies.

"I went to the local library, and I went on the Internet, and found this stuff. Susan needs this. The other stuff is not working."

What he had was a description of a herbal tea based on a Canadian Native-American formula that was claimed to have extraordinary powers in combating "terminal" cases of cancer: though, of course, nobody used that expression round our house. I studied it.

"Eldar, this looks great. I'll show it to Susan tomorrow when I visit her. Thanks a lot, she will really appreciate this. This will give her new hope"

He clearly felt so good at being able to do something in this environment of clearly deteriorating prospects that I ordered the substance from Pittsburgh immediately. Susan was enthralled, both at a new avenue of optimism, and that Eldar would have done this for her. The truth is they had never achieved what you might call an "intimate" relationship—they were both too strong-willed and control minded for that. This was so tragic because they both could have been so much closer in many ways. But, once more, this illness had opened doors to a young heart that might otherwise have remained closed.

On Valentine's Day, for instance, she found a card at her place at the table. The writing was unmistakable. The card said:

I know this is very hard time for you, and that's why I want you to know that I am always with you, and I'll do my best to make you happy.

I could not have conceived of Eldar writing such an openly emotional statement before this. Susan was moved beyond tears, and it never left her collection of precious items that made the trek to the hospital and back. Eldar could put none of what he was feeling into the spoken word. Where Susan was concerned he didn't need to now. Nevertheless, his own depression symptoms quickly multiplied.

I was in the middle of the "control" dilemma at this time. When Susan came home from the first spell of chemotherapy for 1995, she tried to resume her old ways immediately, and this produced a crisis. She wrote:

The sheer quantity of donated food in the refrigerator—some of it quite old—put me in a real state, and this was almost the first thing I did on getting home. There are containers there to be returned to so many people, and absurd amounts of food for people to eat. Finally, after getting myself into a cataclysmic coughing fit I calmed down. This is just silly. I need to concentrate on important things, not stupid tasks. I'll try to keep a positive state of mind, since stress and worry will not help me heal.

When the herbal tea arrived, it came without instructions and this was the straw that set me off. I became absurdly uncontrollable, ranting and raving. My rage at this miserable situation over the last few months had always been simmering just below the surface, desperate to be released on an unsuspecting world. Both my mental and digestive system would have benefited, I am sure, from the occasional screaming session. Now, suddenly it seemed we were all heading rapidly toward chaos. Several more visitors began coming to take the pressure off us and look after the household, but they were always waiting to take their cue from Susan: "What would you like me to cook?" "What can I do now?"

One day as I was helping her through the daily ritual of covering herself with cream to stop the nightmare itching caused by the decline in liver function, Susan indicated I should sit by her on the bed:

"I want you to understand something. I am desperately lonely. Right now I am unhappy most of the time. I want to see my friends. I don't *want to be in control.* I don't want to make decisions. I want other people to make decisions for me. Do you understand? I need more fun and laughter and things to look forward to. It's so hard for me to keep my spirits up. Nothing seems to go right anymore. Why can't I get some breaks? I've always been a lucky person, but not now it seems. I'm not afraid of dying, Randall, really I am not. But I do not *want* to die—not now."

This was crossing a watershed for Susan, for she had hoped that I would realize this was a time to hand over the reins, without having to put it in words to me, since that was like an admission of defeat. But, I had been less than adequate in picking up on this, and now felt more awful than ever that her life had been even more stressful than it needed to be. I, too, had failed to open up as much as I should have to both her *and* Eldar. Even so, I continued to work, and I fear I shall always carry a sense of guilt about that.

Her parents came back again and life changed now that we understood much better what she wanted. Many months earlier Susan had bought tickets for *La Bohème*. Her cough was too bad to sit in an auditorium, so she stayed home, but insisted that I go. I admit I felt relieved that she did not come, for I had been dreading this occasion. After all, we were living that opera's plot on a daily basis—and I couldn't help remembering what happened to Mimi in the end.

The month ended with my birthday. Susan sat me down at the dining table and told me to close my eyes. Then she handed me a totally remade album of our wedding photographs. The old one had been damaged by humidity, and she had taken it apart and lovingly remounted these mementoes of the happiest day of our lives. I felt moved beyond words looking at those frozen memories of boundless bliss we had shared, unbelievably only four years before. There she was on every page like some Nordic spirit with a wreath of leaves and floating white gown. I did not know what to say. I do now. But that knowledge doesn't help. Now I cannot look at that album at all.

Life in the Shadows

The liver biopsy that had been extracted with so much pain was ruined. We never determined how it happened, but it was unusable. The shorter and shorter time between the chemotherapy and the breakdown of the liver function meant that it would not be possible to repeat this operation. When we heard that news, Susan was hurled into the pit of despair and anger beyond words. But, by the end of the day she was back discussing options with Dr. Tai. They decided to try and enter the Dana Farber trials in Boston, because that linked the Davis treatment with chemotherapy, and Susan always responded well to the latter—in the short run at least. Hope centered on this now, plus the herbal tea, and there was no doubt that Susan looked and sounded better since she had been taking it, whether or not it was doing anything clinical. Lusya sent an amber ring and necklace to bring Susan some cheer. One evening she called, and though they didn't have enough of a common language (and Eldar was out), they talked and talked, and cried and cried. I think it was one of the most important conversations of the entire ordeal.

Susan's parents had to return, briefly, to Toronto leaving just the three of us again. Her father left behind a computer chart of the more than twenty different medicines that Susan was a required to take daily. Medical care now occupied most of our lives. Susan, at this point, tried to increase the hope factor by looking for a support circle of fellow patients:

> *I didn't think I needed such a group, but now I do. I think I may need professional help to boost and strengthen my spirits, and morale, since I feel depressed too much. Everyone says how strong I am, but right now I don't feel strong; I'm just going through the motions each day. I explained it as best I can to Randall. I don't like to be alone. I miss not having my parents here. They were able to take charge. The cold weather does not help. If only spring were here I would feel better just seeing things growing and enjoying the warmth.*

Her friends at work were still her principal circle of support, and there was more love in that office than any place on earth. Susan continued to try to maintain a routine of work there. I made myself available for everything I could think of that she needed. What I stupidly did not realize was that she needed *me*, not my services. But, the work I did was my anchor, too.

On March 3 another blood test revealed a spread of awful figures. Susan wrote:

> *I was devastated. Nothing could raise my spirits.*

This was followed by the night from Hell. Her accursed cough had reached terrifying proportions, and I felt more and more that it was this cough was sapping all the energy she needed to fight the disease. I felt that the doctors just regarded this perpetual irritation as a sideshow to the more "serious" matter of cancer: all except the allergist who did everything he could, but to no avail. Dr. Ruff was a curious and eccentric figure who had appeared on the scene late, but he became desperately concerned about Susan, and was clearly upset in a way that years of professional practice failed to conceal. I felt that if we could conquer the cough, Susan's chances would improve, if for no other reason than that she would get some sleep. But, sleep was almost impossible now, no matter what chair, sofa or bed we tried. All I could do was sit by her and help her move during the increasingly miserable nights.

Another terrible night. Randall was with me through all this agony. I am definitely getting worse by the day.

On Sunday March 5 Susan was advised to go to the hospital to get a blood transfusion as she was very weak. As she sat there with the blood dripping into her, periodically coughing outrageously, I made a desperate plea to the doctor:

"There must be *something* we can do about this cough. It is killing her."

"I think she may have pneumonia; there is fluid in the lungs. I am going to put her on antibiotics, and also oxygen to help her breathing, but I will need her to move in now as these will have to be delivered continuously."

This seemed like the best news I had heard in weeks. If they could *just* tackle that cough. Susan had made every effort to conquer it. She had been in work on Friday, and went out to lunch with two friends on Saturday even though it had been hard. But now I felt we were getting somewhere. I felt elated.

"I think we are on the up-and-up Susan."

"I hope so. There are lots of things I shall need. But right now, I would really like to try and sleep. Why don't you come back tomorrow after lunch? They are always doing things in the morning, and if I can sleep I would like to."

"Sure. I'll come and sit with you tomorrow."

I went back home to the house in which Eldar was "parked" while all this chaos swirled around his head. He went to school each day. I gave him as much time as I could, but he was getting very short-changed, and was now sick more than he was in class.

The Parting.

The next day was one of my teaching days, a Monday. I actually felt much better because I was convinced that Susan was at last getting attention for something that should have been tackled weeks, or even months before. At lunch I met with my co-professor from the Physics department. He, as always, was very solicitous about Susan, and frankly could not comprehend how I was teaching a course with him in the shadow of this hideous thing. I gave him my encouraging news. We had to finalize some grades, which we usually did at a local restaurant. My lecture with him was set for four.

"I'll see you at four for class Bob, I'm going to take some things to Susan, and then I'll spend the evening with her. See you in about two hours."

And I left for the hospital.

Nothing could have prepared me for what I saw when I entered the room. Susan looked *awful* and was clearly having terrible difficulty breathing at all. Her lungs were congested, and the cough was there worse than ever. But the moment that defined it all was when I noticed that she was coughing blood.

"Look at this. I never did that before."

Right there, in an instant, Life went completely out of control, over the edge. I froze, helpless, horrified and furious beyond belief. Even now I can barely write about this moment without falling apart:

"Look. Here are your things. I am going to leave for just a moment, but I will be back *just as soon as I possibly can*. Hold on. I love you."

"I love you too," came the feeble voice.

I somehow drove, streaming tears, in an uncontrollable state to Susan's office. I don't know why I went there, but I knew I had to make some telephone calls immediately. Her friends gathered round me, sensing right away that I was in a hopeless condition, and that things with Susan must be very, *very* bad. First I asked Professor Bent, whom I had just left at lunch, if he would stand in for me at short notice. He readily agreed, and cycled over to get the lecture notes. Then I felt I could not go on with all these people comforting me—it was simply making the emotions harder to control, and I was collapsing rapidly. And so I went home. There I called both Susan's parents, not long back in Toronto from Bloomington, and her brother in Seattle.

"I think you should come immediately. Immediately. It looks very bad" was about all I could manage, but the tone must have been sufficient, for they were in the air within hours. Eldar was home from school sick again, and I told him how things looked. He was deeply upset, and said he would try to join us later at the hospital, but he was concerned because his heavy cold could be infectious. At this point, I told him, it probably does not matter. Lastly, I asked my assistant, Maggie, to inform people that I was unlikely to be around, and just how serious the situation looked.

That done I rushed back to Susan's bedside. The transformation in so vibrant a person was astonishing. I held her hand and we talked. She was drifting slowly in and out of awareness. I looked up, and there was Maggie, standing behind me having appeared silently from nowhere. She had arrived to take charge of my life, and God knows how I would have made it through without her. Streams of visitors poured in, and tried to keep Susan cheerful, but the shock was written large on every face. This was it.

In this way we passed the long afternoon, and as Susan weakened, a bright cheerful late-winter day yielded to a penetrating thick swirling ground fog of a sort I had rarely seen in Bloomington before. That was joined by a persistent rain, and outside, darkness came about two hours ahead of time. Out of this mist came a sick Eldar:

"Hi Kiddo. Are you feeling better?" Susan asked.

"I suppose. But I had better wear a mask and stay over here."

Much of the time they just looked at each other. Susan was having difficulty holding focus or attention, but Eldar just crouched against the wall not knowing how to handle this catastrophic change. This was awful for him and it was obvious he had a bad feeling about what was happening. He stayed a long time, but eventually Susan said:

"You had better go home now. Maybe you will be better for school in the morning."

"Ok. I hope you get better too." He tried a sort of hug, but she was so festooned with tubes that he was afraid of causing havoc.

He resisted his habitual ending of "Have fun." She watched him go, and smiled at his departing figure.

It was her last sight of the new son that she loved beyond words.

Around eight in the evening Dr. Tai arrived. Susan sat upright in bed immediately as he came in, though she did not open her eyes.

"Hi Dr. Tai."

"The situation is this, Susan. The lung problem is due to the spread of the lymphoma after all. The cancer has spread through the kidneys and liver extensively. I don't know what good it would do to have another round of chemotherapy, but if that is what you want, be sure I will do that for you. I know this news is hard, but I also know you like it straight."

Throughout this delivery Susan did not move, and continued to sit bolt upright.

As her eyes were closed, it was impossible for me to tell whether she was comprehending this or not. I looked at Dr. Tai indicating this worry. He seemed perfectly confident that she knew exactly what he was saying.

"Anyway, Susan, I'll leave it with you to think about. I'll be out by my desk. Just let me know."

As soon as he left the room Susan said, without changing her attitude:

"You know I don't want more chemotherapy."

"Shall I tell Dr. Tai?"

"Please."

This was her final control decision in a short but determined existence. Her life was to be hers to decide upon. With that she indicated to me that she would like to dictate her journal entry for the day. I was astonished to see that it was complete up to this lunchtime. However, the previous entry was written in a spidery hand quite different from Susan's regular style that had held up right to that point. She dictated, slowly, and with great difficulty, precisely what had just passed with Dr. Tai. It ended:

He left the decision to me. I told Randall to tell him I did not want more."

And there, after 63 volumes that began when she was seven, her diary ended for ever.

I found Dr. Tai at his desk, though I was certain he knew what the answer was going to be. Susan was sleeping now, so I joined Maggie in the waiting room, periodically returning to sit with Susan. Maggie was a lifesaver, marshaling the people flying in, calling, taking calls, and keeping spirits up. The succession of visitors was relentless, and the hospital allowed free movement. Periodically Susan awoke to see a circle of friends. She recognized them, but said to nearly all of them

"Go home, you must be tired. It is so late."

Of course they would not leave.

Outside the weather was taking on Shakespearean proportions. The rain was lashing down from a sky rent apart by mighty flashes of lightning. Through this extraordinary storm and floods Susan's parents drove from Indianapolis airport. I could not imagine what condition they were in, after learning of Susan's critical condition having to catch a plane immediately, and now trying to drive through this typhoon at close to midnight. But in the early hours they arrived and camped out at Susan's bedside. The sight of their first born was the final hideous shock of a terrible day for them.

At four in the morning I prevailed upon Maggie to leave. She had her own family, and she couldn't go on like this indefinitely. I bunked down at five beside Susan's bed, and gained an hour of sleep. Then I went home to make sure Eldar woke up to find someone in the house. He had refused to sleep at the home of friends, but I did not want him to be alone on that morning. I drove home through darkness and flooded streets to find that Eldar was sufficiently recovered to go to school, as Susan had wished, and I took some time to send out a an e-mail message to let all our friends know what was happening. From all around the world, including the Antarctic, the replies began pouring in.

When I returned to the hospital around eight it had started to snow, completing the cycle of horrible weather that had started the previous afternoon. Maggie was already back! Susan was sitting up in a chair, occasionally making contact with her visitors, whose numbers had swelled to include Voiko (who was in a worse condition than anyone), her best friend Nan, and a few others. She had been told that her brother, Michael, was coming from Seattle, and he was due to arrive at around 11 that morning.

From time to time she checked the clock. Then Susan asked me about some small medical bills.

"Oh, don't worry about those. They were nothing. I paid them."

"No, I pay my own way. Give me my check book."

"Here it is, but you don't have any more checks left. Don't worry, it was only $8!"

"At home you will find a new check book in my desk."

This seemed ridiculous, but she was insistent, and so I left once again. On the way home my car phone rang. It was brother Michael, who had become hopelessly lost and was telephoning from the local mall. I raced to the mall, collected him, and then fulfilled my duty with regard to the check book. As Michael came through the door to Susan's room she looked up immediately, checked the clock as if to say "what kept you?" and smiled. They embraced, and at that he burst into tears. She was losing consciousness fast now, but not before she asked me for the check. She tried so hard to write her signature, but it was unrecognizable, taking off diagonally across the face of the document.

While she and her brother spoke, Maggie and I took a break in the corridor. There we were approached by a young nurse who tried to get me to confirm that Susan had a living will on file, because the end was now inevitable. Because Susan was her own age I suppose, and because of the tremendous spirit to survive that Susan had exuded, the nurse became so choked with tears she simply could not get the words out at all. I understood what she was trying to ask, and reassured her that Susan would never have left so important a decision to fate. Indeed, she had only recently revised her living will.

The nurses moved her from the chair and placed her on the bed, and Dr. Tai appeared.

"I will give her something to relax her," he said, and she was given several injections.

After these she deteriorated very quickly before our eyes, and soon was no longer among us in any conscious sense. There was a horrible inevitability about everything now.

Time was short, but Susan still fought hard. Her father begged her to "let go," telling her that though we all loved her and would miss her more than we could say, this was what she had to do. It was time to end the battle. I held her hand, but there was no response to my pressure. I watched her face the entire time. Should she recover consciousness, even for a second I vowed, she should see me, and I her. For a moment her eyes opened wide, but I saw no spark of recognition. She fought for every breath, her brother telling her all the messages that her nephew and niece had sent until, too distraught, he could speak no more. Her friends stood around the wall like a Greek frieze frozen in incomprehension and total helplessness.

At 1:35 on March 7, she stopped breathing: paused, started again, and then stopped with a clear sense of finality. The hand in mine relaxed and was still forever. It was over. Until the very end she had remained in charge of her life.

We left the room almost immediately, for Susan, as we knew and loved her, was not there any more, and we all sensed that. I realized suddenly that Eldar would soon be home from school, and sent Voiko—who had first spoken to his family—immediately to break the news so that Eldar would hear it face to face when he came home. Twice in his life, in quick succession, Eldar would come home from school to find someone he loved taken from him. This tragic assignment made a terrible day a thousand times worse for Voiko who, months later, was unable to speak of any of these events.

People dispersed and I made arrangements to meet up later. I had no idea what was expected of me now, and I looked around. There was a gentleman standing next to me who, I realized, had been there for a while, saying nothing. I had no idea who he was, but clearly he was not one of the medical staff, as I had assumed he was. He had been waiting until I was alone, and then he said,

"Is there anything I can do to help?"

"I'm sorry?"

I responded feeling embarrassed that I did not recognize him, and so his question just added to the complete disorientation and confusion that was my mind at this moment.

"Oh no, I apologize, I somehow thought you had realized who I was. I am the chaplain."

He could have said he was the captain of a whaling fleet at that moment; it would not have registered on my mind. He understood that, and very softly said, "Would you like me to say a prayer or two? It's just the three of us now, and this is a very terrible, but important moment." I returned from wherever I had been mentally lodged as he said that.

I will confess that neither Susan nor I were particularly religious, and so this could simply have been an embarrassing moment: I not knowing what to respond, and not wanting to hurt the feelings of someone who had taken this trouble. I had absolutely no idea how he had got there, or why. He was just standing there when the crowd had gone. But, then I realized that I was neither embarrassed; nor fumbling for a polite rejection. Suddenly, this was *very important*. I have no idea why, and I am sure this would not have occurred had the spectral chaplain not manifested himself in the corridor.

"Please. I really would like that," I said as I opened the door on the mortal remains of what had been, until twenty minutes ago, Susan, my wife. She looked, well, *empty*. Of course she looked sick, and frail, and all the other things that go with a miserable terminal illness. In age she looked indeterminate, but the strength and vigor, the energy and the spirit were quite clearly, gone, and without that whatever was there could never be Susan. It was not a part of anyone I knew, but it *symbolized* who had been here until less than an hour ago, when she had taken her life, bag and baggage, with her. Except that is, of course, for our memories. Somehow it felt inappropriate to be praying over the *body* in bowed reverence, for it was not Susan. On the other hand, it was the last, ephemeral connection with the corporeal being who, this very morning, had sent me scurrying for her checkbook.

The Chaplain, I suddenly realized, had stopped speaking, but was not going to make any move until I did. Ask me now, and I could no more tell you what he said than I could have brought her back to life. Some day, I am quite sure, probably by virtue of quantum physics, that we shall learn of, and prove, the existence of many more dimensions to physical space and time than we can presently perceive. Current thinking suggests somewhere between 9 and twelve dimensions during the fraction of a second that constituted the "Big Bang" which brought us all here. I have long believed that one of these dimensions will be the line between life and death, the body and the soul. Religion and Science, I believe, are on a path of convergence. So, as I stood there, I was imagining her making that passage into another totally different, but somehow connected, state. So, this was passing through my mind as he had been speaking. I needed to be present at that changeover, believing as I do that it is not instantaneous, but is indeed a transition. I was extremely grateful to the Chaplain for bringing me back; he for *his* reasons, and me for mine, but quite possibly both of us sharing in the same experience. A common element in all the "near-death" experiences I had read over the years, was the fact that the departed was above their own body for some moments, having recollections of things that occurred *after they died* but from a perspective about ten feet up. For this reason, at the precise moment she died, I broke away from looking at her face, and looked directly up, and smiled. Who knows? But I would like her to have that last memory.

Anyway, he brought me down to earth very gently by saying, "Is there something, perhaps, *you* would like to say?" I was about to share the most intimate moment of my life with a total stranger. Indeed, I never did discover his name, though he had told me what it was when he had introduced himself, and I never saw him again. Nevertheless, it seemed very appropriate and I am so glad he brought me back for this last parting.

"I can only say now that in death, lying here like this, she is demonstrating how *fantastically alive* she was. I know what the spirit means now that she is gone."

"She may be gone, as you say," he responded, "but dead? No, whatever made her Susan is still alive."

"Well," I said, thinking as a scientist now, "you can neither make nor destroy energy, so I guess you have to be right!"

With that, we left, and he quietly melted away into the corridor. And now, I thought, I must turn my thoughts to the living, and Eldar, who had now to go through losing a second parent in four years. Even so, I thought, in tribute to this very complicated life of ours, he still has two left. And with that I went home to start an entirely new life.

Later that day I tried to capture my feelings in a letter I sent to our friends all over the world. I cannot do better than to reproduce that here:

> On March 7th at 1:35 in the afternoon, a group of family and friends gathered around her bed at Bloomington hospital said a final farewell to Susan. Despite having one of the most miserable illnesses known to humanity, by sheer power of will she had contained most of the pain, and had squeezed from the eleven months of illness a truly remarkable quality of life. Indeed she had worked until the previous weekend, and entertained two of her friends to lunch just three days ago. When her oncologist told her on Monday night that the war was lost, she took the news with typical courage, and refused more treatment. She chose, in death as in her life, to take control and let courage be her guide. Indeed, I would say that courage alone had held back this illness, and once *she chose* to accept the inevitable, the disease consumed her quickly and totally—but at least sparing her the pain and misery that commonly accompanies cancer.
>
> When she went, she went quietly. She had waited for her brother to fly in from Seattle. She kept glancing at the clock while struggling for breath. He arrived. She recognized him, smiled, and after that took her departure from us. As her husband I learned everything from her, including the courage to face her death with her strength and visions. Our spirit is one of optimism. We have all shared in the appreciation of her short life, lived to the full. A life that touched the hearts of so many.
>
> Randall and Eldar.

Epilogue

It took two years, following Susan's death, for me to put this account together. For quite some time, emotions were too raw and overwhelming, the future seemed incomprehensible, and the two survivors of this shipwreck were in serious danger of going adrift or foundering after the loss of so vigorous a captain. Even so, why wait until now to share this story? It was one thing to commit this to paper in order to purge ourselves of the emptiness and despair as I did at the time. But, much more, it was really important to have a record of this time, and how we managed our lives, no, that's wrong—*she* made us manage our lives—in the face of something so awful. So the manuscript was put away in late 1997.

But, now that time has rounded the sharp edges, our lives have turned around, we want everyone to have the chance to share our brief and unusual life together. Resuscitating the manuscript and putting it into some shape for publication was both difficult and surprising. Difficult, because of course, it brought back, with frightening immediacy, the details of that time, but the details of the good times were there too. It was surprising because I thought, to use a tired literary cliché, that "every detail of that time had been seared into my memory." Not so: I found that my memory had totally reconstructed parts of these events, putting things in the wrong order, attributing events to the wrong people, and so forth. Of course, I would have sworn to my recollection of these events, but it would have been perjury. This book tells the story as it happened. Thinking about publishing it, I came to believe that this is a unique, surprising, and sometimes barely credible tale; it is also an inspiring one. Susan inspired us. Eldar inspired us. One was facing a totally new life at a very difficult time in his own evolution, and in a totally strange country. The other was facing the extinction of her earthly life at the ridiculous age of 35. What is most unbelievable in this whole story is the fact that *everything you read occurred in just about three years!* It was like living in H. G. Wells' Time Machine and the whole process of life became accelerated incredibly. One more element exhorting me to put this experience in print is Mrs. Eunice Petersen of Bellevue, Washington, our landlady who made the inquiries about the sleeping arrangements. She so fell in love with the story and the characters during the brief time she met them that she has, every Christmas, asked me "When?" The answer I hope—"Now."

By now, everyone who has read this far, is asking: "but what happened to *the boy*?" And, "what became of his mother?" Interestingly, the answers to these questions are just as remarkable, perhaps more remarkable, and as much of a roller coaster, as what you have just read. A neat, literary "tying up of loose ends," however, is not for this book. It would not do justice to the people or the events to compress them into a few sentences. It is, as they say, "another story," but I will tell you that never in my wildest predictions of the future would I ever have guessed where our lives would have taken us in this month of...

January 2005.
Bloomington, Indiana.

Father and son at awards ceremony for Eldar

Eldar and Randall

About the Author

Professor Baker has published eleven books, but he recently moved away from the academic obsession with *being published,* to the more challenging one *of being read.* He has always been an academic, claiming it to be marginally more rewarding than being unemployed. He has always been *driven,* creating or helping to create six new University Departments, making dean at 29—you get the picture. Spending time with the Foreign Legion in the desert, with General Idi Amin, or advising kings and sultans, should be enough for anyone—but none of this prepared him for being chosen for parenthood at 48 by a 13-year old he couldn't even speak to, but then, what 13 year old speaks to a parent? His life became *really* interesting at this point.

Printed in the United States
29537LVS00005B/16-30